T0247957

COAL COUNTRY KILLING

A CULTURE,
A UNION,
AND THE MURDERS
THAT CHANGED IT ALL

ROBERT K. TANENBAUM
AND STEVE JACKSON

Post Hill
PRESS

A POST HILL PRESS BOOK
ISBN: 978-1-63758-848-2
ISBN (eBook): 978-1-63758-849-9

Coal Country Killing:
A Culture, A Union, and the Murders That Changed It All
© 2023 by Robert K. Tanenbaum
All Rights Reserved

Cover design by Cody Corcoran

Post Hill Press
New York • Nashville
posthillpress.com

Published in the United States of America
1 2 3 4 5 6 7 8 9 10

TABLE OF CONTENTS

AUTHOR'S NOTE

FROM ROBERT K. TANENBAUM

The entire manuscript of *Coal Country Killing: A Culture, a Union, and the Murders That Changed It All* was written jointly by Steve Jackson and me. This book is the product of more than four years of investigative work.

More than that, however, eclipsing the voluminous trial records and investigative research, my forty-five-year friendship with Dick Sprague was invaluable. To explain it, as above, I have resorted to the first-person pronoun and briefly, here's how it all began:

In October '76, I received a telephone call from Sprague. At the time, I was an assistant district attorney (ADA) in New York County (Manhattan) hired by legendary D.A. Frank S. Hogan. I had been bureau chief of the criminal courts, ran the homicide bureau, and oversaw the legal training of the staff. I had also successfully prosecuted to verdict several hundred cases and never lost a trial wherein a felony was charged.

Sprague informed me that he was appointed chief counsel and staff director of the recently formed congressional committee entitled House Select Committee on Assassinations (HSCA) regarding the assassinations of President John F. Kennedy and the Reverend Dr. Martin Luther King. Dick asked me if I would be interested in leading the subcommittee investigation into the JFK assassination.

Since Sprague and I had never met or ever spoken to one another, I said, "Why me?" He replied that I was recommended to him by several New York State Supreme Court judges who had presided over several high-profile cases that I had prosecuted. Sprague also stated that he had spoken with prominent defense counsel who advised that I was well-prepared and relentless in court but always fair and honest. Moreover, Sprague added that he had checked out my credentials during my ADA tenure.

Shortly thereafter, Sprague and I met on several occasions, which resulted in my appointment as deputy chief counsel in charge of the President Kennedy probe.

From that time, over the years, we worked together on many different and challenging cases. More than just an exceptional professional apolitical colleague, Sprague became a lifelong friend.

Dick asked me several years ago to write this book. After all that had been written, he wanted the true story to be known. He supplied me with the actual ten thousand pages of trial transcripts of the cases' six trials, which I read and outlined and some of which is quoted herein. In addition, he provided me with police reports, autopsy protocols, his contemporaneous notes, witnesses' affidavits, and statements, as well as other investigative material.

Most valuable, however, were his insights and detailed recollections of the events. We spent countless months going over his trial strategies, including how he tactically outmaneuvered the defense and his investigative vision that led inexorably to checkmating "Tough Tony" Boyle, the corrupt assassin and president of the United Mine Workers of America.

Another character, if you will, that is featured in this book is the unique culture of Appalachian coal country, which affected the investigation and prosecution of these cases. Going back to the early eighteenth century and the mass migration of Scots-Irish immigrants to the Appalachian Mountain range, we seek in this book to illustrate how two hundred years later some members of that pious, proud, hardworking people got caught up in a war between their consciences and their loyalty to a union and its leadership that had protected their way of life for generations. Often maligned and misunderstood by the press and the public, it was fortunate that Sprague and his team saw them as an historic people, not foolhardy stereotypes, and only then were they able to get at the truth.

On one level, *Coal Country Killing* speaks volumes about how a committed individual, Dick Sprague, can make a huge impact. A triumphant, uplifting victory delivered by a righteous legendary figure.

Yet this book is much more meaningful. To do justice in our lives, to be civil, tolerant, rational, and forthright, is to enhance the dignity not only of ourselves but of the public office we may occupy, the job we hold, and the culture in which we thrive. Those values are timeless. We need to experience them so that we may always be reminded who we are and from where we came. When faced with cultural coarsening, we seek affirmation of triumph. *Coal Country Killing* satisfies that need.

Throughout all the time Dick Sprague and I spent going over the case's complexities and values that motivated extraordinary characters to ultimately seek justice, Dick's only admonition was that I must always remain objective. My colleague, coauthor Steve Jackson, and I have fiercely sought to disclose the unvarnished truth throughout *Coal Country Killing*. I assure you our souls remain intact and uncompromised.

During the course of the entire case, investigation, and trials, Sprague demonstrated the imperatives of the prosecutors' mission: seek justice with immutable evidence and with painstaking preparation, exonerate the unjustly accused, and prosecute the guilty with firmness tempered with compassion, regardless of his influence and status.

This book is dedicated to the memory of my dear, courageous, special friend, Richard A. Sprague.

THE VISITORS

DECEMBER 18, 1969

The two young men facing Joseph "Jock" Yablonski late that afternoon fidgeted and kept glancing sideways at each other. Shuffling their feet, they hemmed and hawed as if waiting for the other to say, or do, something they'd planned.

Standing in the doorway of his two-hundred-year-old stone farmhouse, Yablonski, a short, heavy-set fifty-nine-year-old with a face as craggy as the surrounding Appalachian hills, scowled. Something wasn't right with these two men—one skinny and pasty-faced who did most of the talking and the other a moon-faced, thuggish-looking fellow with a five-o'clock shadow and thick dark eyebrows.

A few minutes earlier, they'd pulled up in a maroon '65 Chevrolet Caprice in front of Yablonski's house. Yablonski and his family lived in a house in the country, near the tiny hamlet of Clarksville, just fifty miles south of Pittsburgh in southwestern Pennsylvania. They said they were out-of-work coalminers and were hoping to work at a nearby mine. They wanted his help to get a job.

Suspicion knitted Yablonski's own bushy eyebrows that perched above his deep-set eyes and prodigious nose like two hairy caterpillars. Recent events had made him cautious, and their story sounded like bullshit. Neither looked like a miner, and even if they were, any coalminer in the country knew he was in no position to help anyone get work in a union mine anymore.

Less than two weeks earlier, Yablonski had lost a bitterly contested campaign for presidency of the United Mine Workers of America (UMWA). His opponent was the incumbent, William Anthony "Tough Tony" Boyle, who'd run the union as his personal fiefdom after being appointed to the position in 1963 by legendary labor leader John L. Lewis.

Autocratic and short-tempered, Boyle had been under increasing criticism by some of the rank-and-file for what they perceived as his cozying up to the coal mine owners at their expense. While Boyle had his fiercely loyal supporters, especially those who fell under his protective arm, others felt he ignored mine safety and health issues—most notably black lung disease, the scourge of all coalminers—to assuage the owners...and line his own pockets. At least that's what Yablonski, the former president of his district and a national union official until Boyle removed him, campaigned on as a "reform" candidate.

Boyle did not take Yablonski's candidacy well. He considered it a betrayal and a threat.

Even before the election, strange cars started showing up in Clarksville and around Yablonski's home in the country, as well as following him on the campaign trail. The Yablonskis received death threats on the home telephone, and Jock's sons and friends warned him that his life was in danger from the moment he announced his candidacy.

Their concerns seemed even more justified when goons jumped Yablonski at a Springfield, Illinois campaign stop in June 1969. One of them hit him so hard on the back of his neck that they knocked him unconscious for a few minutes and could have killed him if their aim had been slightly different.

The election was held December 9, 1969, and Boyle emerged as the victor by a two-to-one margin. But with the victory came a deluge of allegations of fraud, tampering, intimidation, and ballot box–stuffing.

Yablonski demanded that U.S. Department of Labor Secretary George Shultz look into the allegations. But the Labor Department, which politically didn't want to get involved in union business, said that Yablonski first had to exhaust his "administrative remedies" by taking his grievances to the union hierarchy—a classic case of the fox watching the henhouse. In doing so, Secretary Shultz was permitting Tony Boyle to be the final arbiter of his own trustworthiness and honesty.

However, Yablonski didn't give up. In a fiery speech shortly after the election, he vowed to fight on. Yablonski, the former coalminer-turned-union reformer filed suit in federal court with the help of renowned labor lawyer Joe Rauh. Rauh's involvement in Yablonski's lawsuit meant there would not just be an investigation of the fraudulent election allegations, but possibly an accounting of union finances.

Boyle had reason to fear both. Desperate times called for desperate measures.

The strangers returned, driving around Yablonski's neighborhood and the town of Clarksville. Rumors traveled along the union grapevine that Boyle wanted Yablonski removed...permanently.

Yablonski was tough too, so at first, he dismissed the danger. The election was over; he thought that any other confrontations between him and Boyle would be done in a courtroom.

He balked when his sons suggested putting up floodlights around the remote house where he lived with his wife, Margaret, and twenty-five-year-old daughter Charlotte. Just a few days earlier, Margaret reported seeing a strange car parked across the road with men watching the house. He then put up the lights and told his sons, Kenneth and Chip, who lived on their own, that he was sleeping with a shotgun next to his bed.

Now, these two dimwits at the front door had the audacity to show up with the nonsensical story about being unemployed, West Virginian coalminers. "Don't think I can help you," Yablonski said and tensely waited for their response.

The two young men looked at each other. Then the skinny one shook his head and mumbled something about how they'd try another way. They turned and walked back to their car.

Yablonski knew some dark moment had passed as he watched them get in the Chevy and drive off. He turned and walked back to his study where he picked up the telephone and called an old friend who'd sometimes accompanied him on the campaign trail as a bodyguard, "I think two guys were just here to kill me."

CHAPTER ONE

THE SCOTS IRISH

The foundation for the tragedy that was to follow that fateful meeting on December 18, 1969 was laid, literally, some 330 million years earlier. That's when the first steps towards the formation of coal in what became the Appalachian Mountains began.

Coal is a black sedimentary rock formed from the remnants of organic material, mostly dead plants, that fall into the waters of swamps and bogs and are then submerged. Swamp water is oxygen-poor, and so the organic material decomposes much slower than it would in a more oxygen-rich environment.

Combined with a temperate climate and acidic conditions that further slow decomposition, peat is created. A carbon-rich material, if dug up and dried peat will burn, as humans looking to warm their homes and cook have known for thousands of years.

When the deposits are covered with sediment, the decomposition is slowed even more. Additionally, the pressure of the sediment layers above the deposits squeezes the moisture and methane gases out, increasing the density of the peat and increasing the carbon level.

In large areas that had formerly been swamps, created peat, and finally been covered with sediment, sink, they're called "sedimentary basins." The basins then fill with more sediment causing an even greater amount of pressure on the peat, turning it into "lignite," or brown coal. Add more heat and pressure over millions of years and brown coal turns into first sub-bituminous coal, then bituminous or "soft coal," followed by anthracite "hard coal," and finally graphite, which is pure carbon.

Geographically, the Appalachian Mountains stretch from Belle Island in Canada to Cheaha Mountain in Alabama. However, Appalachia wasn't always in its current location, nor would it have been as coal-rich if it had been. Up until about 330 million years ago, the land was almost on the equator, and it was a huge swampland. It was covered by massive trees and other tropical vegetation that would die and fall into the waters. But then the tectonic plate below the swamp slowly moved north until reaching its present location.

However, the Appalachian tectonic plate area was not mountainous. That didn't happen until about 275 million years ago when another plate, as well as what is now Africa, crashed into the east side of the North American continent, crumpling the land into the Appalachian Mountains with its peaks and valleys. There, one of the largest coal deposits in the world sat for hundreds of millions of years undisturbed beneath an immense forest of conifers and broad-leafed deciduous trees with a thick undergrowth, impassable except by trails created by the abundant wildlife.

About sixteen thousand years ago, humans arrived in the area—hunter-gathers who followed those game trails, hunted the animals, and lived in harmony with their verdant world, hardly changing the landscape even with their villages. Some of these peoples would discover that a certain kind of black rock occasionally found lying on the surface, or discovered in the roots of fallen trees, or exposed by water that rushed down the narrow vales, would burn and give off heat. In some parts of the North American continent, particularly the Southwest, aboriginal people even dug shallow pits for coal to use for cooking and heat, as well as to bake their pottery.

These indigenous people, however, didn't live in harmony with each other. Long before Europeans arrived, the Americas were a bloody place rife with intertribal warfare. Empires rose that slaughtered, absorbed, and subjugated weaker tribes. The Aztec. The Inca. The Mixtec. All ruled in Mexico and Central and South America. In the Appalachian area, the Iroquois Confederacy ("Six Nations"), as well as the Shawnee and the Cherokee, claimed large areas and defended them from incursions by the others.

Violence was a way of life. They fought over hunting grounds, or to prove their manhood; they took slaves and killed non-combatants.

Most of these war parties were small in nature, and the casualties few. But this was not always was case. In January 1921, hunters in Mingo Hollow, one of the richest coal-mining areas in Bell County, Kentucky, chased a fox into a shallow cave. Inside, they found the skeletons of several men with flint battle-axes, arrowheads, and tufts of long dark hair.

Leaf Sixkiller, a Cherokee Indian living in Wauhillau, Oklahoma, saw news reports about the find and connected it to an oral history tradition of the Cherokee that spoke of at least two battles that had been fought between the Cherokee, who had been located south of present-day Cumberland Gap,[1] and tribes living north of the gap. Both battles were said to have occurred just prior to 1700 or very soon thereafter.[2]

"The first legendary battle occurred when a band of Mingo Indians led by Oogolah, the Eagle, invaded the Cherokee territory south of what was known then as Ouasioto Pass, now Cumberland Gap. A raiding party of fifty braves attacked the Cherokee settlements and killed everyone they encountered including women, children, and men—both young and old alike. They took over one hundred scalps before heading back north through the pass.

"The enraged Cherokee upon hearing of the atrocities gathered all possible warriors and started north to avenge their dead. The Mingos were not moving quickly as they had taken plunder from the Cherokee homes and being unfamiliar with the lay of the land. They became concerned that the Cherokee would easily overtake

---

1   The Cumberland Gap is a pass through Cumberland Mountains, which are part of the Appalachian chain. It is located near the junction of Kentucky, Virginia, and Tennessee and was an important route through the lower central Appalachians.

2   *Three Tragic Events in Mingo Hollow*, smithdray1.net. Referencing: *The Magic City: Footnotes to the History of Middlesborough, Kentucky, and the Yellow Creek Valley*, Ann Dudley Matheny, 2003, Bell County Historical Society and *The Cumberland Coal Field and its Creators*. Pictorial history of Middlesboro and the American Association land companies coal mines in Mingo Hollow, compiled by Clyde Mayes, April 2000.

them on the well-worn Warrior's Path and thus they would be easy prey.

"Therefore, they fled west into the marshes of Yellow Creek once they were through the pass. When they got to Stony Fork, they took the left branch with the Cherokee in hot pursuit. They had lost few men at this point, but as they fled up the narrowing hollow, Oogolah realized he had boxed his forces into a very poor position and the Cherokee were fast overtaking them.

"Oogolah turned his men to face the hundreds of enraged Cherokees and raised his death chant. The legend held that no Mingos survived the slaughter." Sixkiller theorized that a few mortally wounded men may have managed to find a cave and hid there to die with their scalp locks intact."[3]

A second legend from Bell County, according to Sixkiller, told of a great confederation of northern Indians invading the southern Cherokee settlements with a force of 1,500 warriors and led by the most noted chiefs of the tribes. "The Cherokee had been warring for years with the tribes of the north and had learned to post scouts at the gap," Sixkiller said.

"When the tribes arrived at the gap, it was near dark, so they camped along Yellow Creek north of the gap intending to make the passage through the gap at dawn of the next day. The Cherokee scouts, realizing that the northern tribes war party did not intend to attempt the gap that night, hurried to the nearest Cherokee town. Runners were then sent out to warn the other Cherokee villages to the south and to organize war parties to meet the coming challenge.

"Every man in the small Cherokee village marched to the Gap determined to take the advantage offered by the narrow gap in the mountains to ambush the northern tribes war party when they attempted to come through the next day. They hoped to at least stall the advance of the enemy long enough to allow the other villages time to prepare.

"That night there came a huge storm with heavy rain in the area of the gap and to the north. Because Yellow Creek drained a large

---

3   Ibid.

basin of land, it quickly rose and burst from its banks covering the northern tribes' war camp. Many of the sleeping invaders were drowned in the flash flood. The remaining warriors ran for their lives to any available higher ground or crevice for shelter. The night was dark, and the rain fell in torrents. They had fled their camp without taking time to gather their weapons.

"When dawn came, the Cherokee found the camp of their invaders essentially washed away and saw the surviving warriors in a state of confusion. The Cherokee took full advantage of the situation and proceeded to kill all the survivors. The legend says they took over 1,000 scalps that day. Few if any of the northern Indians were thought to have escaped the slaughter."[4]

Sixkiller suggested that maybe a few of the braves escaped up Mingo Hollow and perished in the cave from their wounds. He stated that many Cherokee living in Oklahoma still had tufts of hair said to have been taken in that battle on Yellow Creek just north of present-day Cumberland Gap and very near Mingo Hollow.[5]

The inter-tribal warfare between First Americans went on for hundreds of years. Then, beginning in the late seventeenth century, these aboriginal peoples were confronted by a new group of tribal people, a people perhaps even more inured to warfare than they were. A people who, as a popular book would proclaim, were "born fighting."[6]

This new tribe arrived first on the Atlantic Coast in sailing vessels, most disembarking from Londonderry, Ireland and landing in Philadelphia. The came looking for land to farm, religious freedom, and a way to escape the British yoke.

Ethnically Scots, they'd lived for generations in what was called the Ulster Plantation in Northern Ireland and were called Ulstermen or Ulster Scots in England and Catholic Ireland. In the colonies, they became known as the Scots Irish. Hard-working and loyal to a fault, they arrived with a reputation for rugged individualism, a

---

4   Ibid.
5   Ibid.
6   James Webb, *Born Fighting: How the Scots-Irish Shaped America* (New York: Broadway Books, 2004).

willingness to fight for each other and their beliefs, and an innate mistrust of government.

Long before their arrival in the American colonies, their ethnic forefathers, the Scots, had a long history of fighting for independence and resisting authority imposed from the outside whether it was the Romans or the English. Their first allegiance was to their clans, large extended families, and their communities, which were often centered on their churches.

At great cost, the English were able to conquer their unruly neighbors to the north in three different centuries. But the victories were pyrrhic, and the first two times the Scots regained their independence due to their penchant for guerilla warfare and courageous battles.

The most famous and important of the latter during the First War of Scottish Independence was the Battle of Bannockburn in June 1314. The badly outnumbered forces of King of the Scots Robert the Bruce soundly defeated the forces of King Edward II of England. It would take another fourteen years to secure the victory in the Second War of Scottish Independence, but the battle demonstrated the ferocity of Scots in the cause of freedom and was a defining moment in their history.

In the mid-1600s, Scotland was again subdued by Oliver Cromwell and the English army to conclude the third English Civil War. But rather than impose harsh punishments and abject subjugation and risk a fourth war of independence, Cromwell wisely sought inclusion as opposed to occupation. Scotland was brought into a commonwealth with England as an autonomous, self-governing country. They made it official in 1707 and became the United Kingdom.

The Scots-Irish branch came about as a result of warfare as well. In 1603, the Nine Years' War between Catholic Ireland and Protestant England came to an end with Irish earls ceding an area of Northern Ireland known as Ulster to the British crown. The area and its people had been decimated by warfare, so the English Crown's idea was to entice fractious Scots who lived along the border with England to the "Ulster Plantation" in part to get them away from the border, in part to cultivate the land and pay rent, and in part to keep their Irish cousins in line.

Although they came to farm, the immigrants found themselves in a state of continuous guerilla warfare with the native Irish chieftains and their followers who resented the Scots presence. But as tough as the Irish raiders were, they were no match for Scots hardened by a thousand years of fighting Romans, Vikings, or the English.

Eventually, the Ulster Scots beat back the Irish and enjoyed a period of relative peace. However, with the Catholic Irish uprising in 1641 and another all-out war between the Irish and English from 1688 to 1691, the Presbyterian Ulstermen, who found themselves targets of the Irish, joined with the Anglican English. The Irish were defeated and an English government set up in Dublin.

The Presbyterian Ulstermen expected to be viewed favorably as allies and treated with religious tolerance by the Anglican English. Instead, they were regarded by the government in Dublin with the same disdain and religious persecution as the despised Irish Catholics.

The Ulster population had again been decimated by the wars. Needing someone to work their properties, the English landowners enticed another wave of Scots to the plantation by offering more long-term leases on farmland. In the decade leading up to 1700, an estimated fifty thousand new settlers crossed the North Sea to Ulster.

After the turn of the century, the English Crown and Parliament withdrew all pretense of religious tolerance for the Presbyterian Ulster Scots. The Irish Test Act of 1704 required that all crown officials be of the Anglican faith; this regulation eventually included all those in the military, or employed by civil service, municipal corporations, and educational institutions. The Scots-Irish, devoutly Presbyterian, were not only excluded from any sort of power; they couldn't practice their faith; even their clergy was stripped of its authority to perform marriages.[7]

---

7   Katharine Gartska, "The Scots-Irish in The Southern United States: An Overview,"
    Archives.com, written October 16, 2009, https://www.archives.com/experts/garstka-
    katharine/the-scots-irish-in-the-southern-united-states-an-overview.html.

Already chafing under their second-class status, the final straw for the Ulster Scots broke in 1710 as the long-term leases began to expire. The English landlords reacted by doubling and tripling the rents, which forced many off their farms. Rather than submit to the new economic and religious hardships, entire Ulster communities—sometimes as large extended families, or even congregational groups led by their ministers—shipped out for the American colonies.

By the mid-1700s, nearly two hundred thousand of the Scots Irish, as they became known in the Americas, had immigrated to the colonies. They were joined shortly before the American Revolution in 1776 by another thirty thousand. They were the largest contingent of immigrants in the eighteenth century except for the forced "immigration" of African slaves.

The majority initially chose Pennsylvania as a destination because the Quakers in charge there were more tolerant of different faiths than the Puritans in the other colonies.

Some, especially tradesmen, settled in the cities and towns of more populous coast and Piedmont, the plateau between the coastal plain and the Appalachian Mountains to the west. But most made their way south and west into the mountains looking for land to farm, eager to practice their religion free from oppression.

Although some were impoverished, even arriving in the American colonies as indentured servants, by and large they were not penniless. They pooled their resources as extended families and congregational groups and set out in wagons for the mountains south and west of the more populous and English-dominated coastal regions.

Nor were they uneducated and illiterate as their descendants would someday be stereotyped. They were products of the Scottish Enlightenment that had swept through the region beginning in the early 1700s and carrying on through the rest of the century. In that time, Scotland's greatest thinkers in philosophy, engineering, architecture, medicine, botany, agriculture, and law were equal to any in the rest of Europe. Education and literacy were encouraged, and books treasured. As such, the Scots Irish were some of the most literate of all the immigrant waves to the colonies.

The migration of the Scots Irish into the Appalachian Mountains was encouraged by the colonial governments east of the Appalachian Mountains to push back the wilderness and as a bulwark against hostile indigenous tribes. As they had in Ireland, the Scots Irish desired to farm but found themselves in conflict with the natives who resented their intrusion upon the lands they'd dwelt upon for centuries.

The tribes quickly learned that the Scots Irish were no pushovers, having fought in England and Ireland. Tough, iron-willed men who became the archetype of the frontiersman of American folklore learned from the indigenous warriors how to wage guerilla warfare in the wilderness and brought their own brand of ferocity to the fight.

Out beyond the edge of civilization, there was no help from the government. No army was coming to defend them. The frontiersman had to be able to count on his family and neighbors. A man's word was his bond, and loyalty was treasured above material wealth. As it had always been, the Scots Irish had only their toughness, their faith, and each other to fend off a hostile world.

As it had been in the old country, their martial prowess became legendary. During the French and Indian War of 1754, it was the Scots-Irish frontiersmen who beat back the enemy for the English Crown. But their reward was to again be viewed as second-class citizens—uneducated, uncouth, and uncivilized—by the English-dominated colonialists, and treated with disdain by the British military whose bacon they saved.

One of the hallmarks of the humanist-oriented thinking of the Scottish Enlightenment was the importance of reason combined with the rejection of any authority that could not justify its right to rule. Whether a king "appointed by God," a parliament, or colonial governor, government's powers were by the consent of the governed. It was a philosophy that would make its way into the writings and philosophy of the colonists to the East who would one day declare independence from English rule.

When the American Revolution broke out, the Scots Irish of Appalachia lived far away from the authority of the British crown. But they had no great love or loyalty to the revolutionaries to the east.

They would have likely remained British subjects with no more use for the fledgling government in Philadelphia than the English parliament, except for strategic mistakes made by the British military that turned the frontiersmen against them. One particularly egregious mistake by the British was arming the Cherokee and other tribes to wage war against the Appalachian settlers, something the French had done in the previous war. Atrocities would be committed by both sides during the bitter guerilla warfare that ensued, but such a vicious plan was unforgiveable in the eyes of the settlers.

If that wasn't enough, partway through the conflict the British threatened to hang the leaders of the Scots Irish and destroy their settlements if they did not swear fealty to the Crown. If they met any resistance, real or imagined, the British would burn homesteads, arrest clergy, who were often the leaders of their communities, and confiscate crops and livestock without payment. Essentially, the British, who were winning the war at that point, pushed the independent Scots Irish onto the side of the revolutionaries.

As the Irish learned in Ulster, and the indigenous tribes had experienced all along the frontier, there was no tougher, more capable guerilla fighters than the Scots Irish. Expert marksmen who had learned to fight in the forests from the natives, armed with tomahawks and knives as well as long rifles, no British or Hessian regular wanted to hear their war cries.

Sometimes on their own, and sometimes combined with the Continental Army, the mountaineers terrorized their red- and green-coated opponents. At Fort Thicketty in upstate South Carolina, their mere presence caused the British forces to surrender without firing a shot. At Musgrove Mill in Spartanburg County, South Carolina, they combined with the rebel army and routed the British. At Kings Mountain on the North and South Carolina border they joined forces again and destroyed a third of the British Army in the Carolinas.

Then in January 1781, outside of the South Carolina town of Cowpens, they were instrumental in the fighting that helped the

Continental Army obliterate General Cornwallis's army. Not long after the battle, the humiliated general surrendered at Yorktown.

It can be safely said that without the fighting contributions of the Scots Irish from the hills and dales of Appalachia, the United States of America may have never survived its first decade. In some quarters, their contributions were recognized. When the outcome was still in doubt, George Washington was quoted as saying that if the cause was lost everywhere else, he would make a last stand among the Scots Irish in his native Virginia.

Even the enemy recognized their importance to the American cause. Serving in the British Army, Captain Johann Henricks, one of the despised Hessian mercenaries, wrote home in frustration, "Call it not an American rebellion, it is nothing more than an Irish-Scotch Presbyterian rebellion."[8]

After the war was won and the country established, the newly minted Scots-Irish Americans went back to their forested hills, fertile farms, and verdant pastures. They had no use for their fellow citizens and the opposite was true for the time being.

Even their role as a bulwark against the indigenous tribes was diminished. The revolution spelled the beginning of the end for the native peoples in many parts of Appalachia, especially those who sided with the British. Although the guerilla warfare and occasional uprisings would go on for a time, the native people were gradually forced from the lands where they'd once hunted, fished, and fought over for centuries.

Meanwhile, except for the occasional flamboyant politician sent from the hills to the halls of Congress and even the White House, the Appalachian frontiersman faded into myth and folklore, whether as real characters like Daniel Boone of Kentucky and Davey Crockett of Tennessee, or fictional, such as Hawkeye in James Fenimore Cooper's 1826 classic *The Last of the Mohicans*.

They were left alone as the burgeoning population of the East Coast and Piedmont washed up against the wall of the mountains, which was how they liked it. Their communities were like islands

---

8   Ulster Ancestry, www.ulsterancestry.com.

in a river: most settlers who left the East looking for their own bit of land swept around them and kept on going to new frontiers farther west.

As time passed, the Appalachian communities grew increasingly isolated. The wider world passed them by, and they were content that it did. They were living in a real-life Eden, relying on themselves to govern, rather than dictates from back East, and listening to their preachers on Sunday to steer them on the road to righteousness. Cut off from the evolving world, their culture often resembled that of the Old World their predecessors left including their music, their speech patterns, and their cultural identity.

Occasionally, they would come down from their hills, lining up on both sides, such as when the war broke out between the North and South. But after the war, they again retreated to their mountain homes.

Other peoples would eventually move into the area—Germans, Welsh, Polish, Italians—especially when the coal the Scots Irish had been using for heating and small forges became a precious commodity for a nation that was rapidly expanding and industrializing after the Civil War. But wherever the newcomers originated, they found a strong, vibrant culture that was resistant to outside influences.

Rather than be changed by the immigrants, the Scots Irish brought them into their fold. Within a generation the children of newcomers would be talking with the Appalachian dialect of their region and playing "hillbilly music," adding touches, and instruments, from their own cultures.

Other religions would find tolerance, and Presbyterian would give way to Southern Baptist, Methodist, and small, isolated fundamentalist churches, including those in the Holiness movement known for poisonous snake-handling.

However, by and large, the Scots Irish influence on Appalachian culture would run like a river through the population even as different ethnicities settled in the area. The hallmarks of that culture: they were loyal, especially to family and each other, hard-working, honest, violent in defense of their interests, pious, and mistrustful of government.

Two hundred and fifty years after they began arriving in the Americas and settled in what would become coal country, the Scots Irish culture would play a significant role in what happened to Jock Yablonski and his family, as well as Tony Boyle, the president of the United Mine Workers of America, and those caught up in his web.

All of it formed over a black sedimentary rock from the remnants of organic material, mostly dead plants, that fall into the waters of swamps and bogs.

CHAPTER TWO

BLOODY HARLAN

If the Appalachian settlers could have foreseen how a growing nation's rapacious appetite for coal would transform their communities, their way of life, and their idyllic surroundings, they might have fought it as fiercely as they fought the indigenous tribes and the British. But the changes began slowly.

Coal was discovered in eastern North America in 1673, but with plenty of wood available it was seldom used for heating. Commercial coal mining for residential heat and small forges didn't begin until the 1740s.

After the Revolutionary War, miners in northeastern Pennsylvania discovered significant deposits of anthracite coal, which burns hotter and cleaner than bituminous. It was soon the predominant heating source in Philadelphia and other cities in the state. By the 1840s, anthracite was used to heat residences and commercial buildings all along the eastern seaboard.

However, most coal mined, including in the rest of Appalachia, was bituminous, which was much more plentiful. On the eve of the Civil War in 1861, significant, mostly bituminous, coal mining existed in twenty states.

Coal mining was America's first big industry and soon formed a symbiotic relationship with other major industries of the growing nation, especially railroads and steel-making. Coal powered the

Industrial Revolution after the Civil War and drove the steam-engines of commerce and manifest destiny.

However, the burgeoning demand for coal brought with it enormous changes, particularly in Appalachia, where it would forever transform the culture, the way of life, and the natural surroundings. It would also be responsible for the most dangerous occupation in the world that, along with the demand for better wages and living conditions, would give rise to the United Mine Workers of America.

In the early days of coal mining in the United States, the mines tended to be small operations. A miner would hire a few laborers to help him extract coal, most of which lay on or close to the surface and didn't require deep tunnels or large-scale open-pit mines. The shallow diggings were usually located along waterways where the coal could be transported by barges.

However, as the demand for coal grew, so did the need to find ways to get at the coal in less accessible regions, maximize production, and then transport it over greater distances. The need was met by the railroads, especially after the Civil War.

When the coal companies pushed their way into the Appalachian Mountains, they found agrarian communities that had limited contact with the outside world. Nor did these people want contact. The Civil War and the crowded polluted cities of the eastern seaboard and Piedmont had shown them the "benefits of civilization," and other than commodities they could not make themselves, they wanted no part of it.

Nearly a hundred years after the Revolutionary War, the mountaineers remained a proud people—independent and self-sufficient, content to live out their lives among extended families and tightknit communities centered around their churches. They grew and raised most of what they needed, supplementing it with the creatures of the forests and streams. They had their own way of speaking, their own music, and a tradition of looking out for their own. They were loyal and honest to a fault and maintained a strong belief in a God who rewarded the righteous and punished the wicked, and a general mistrust of outside authority.

The early story of coal mining in Appalachia is one of greed and deceit. A story of how the railroad and steel companies, which determined that it was better to own the coal mines on which they depended, as well as private investors, most of them from northern cities, separated a land from its people.

Agents representing the companies and investors bought up large tracts of unused forests. But much of the acquisition was accomplished with "broad form deeds" that the local landowners—most of them simple farmers, herdsmen, and tradesmen—were persuaded to sign in exchange for cash.

The agents told the landowners that the deeds applied only to the mineral rights, in this case coal, that lay beneath the surface of their property. It sounded like a good deal to the locals. They could keep farming the surface, and the mine operators would tunnel underneath for the coal.

What the agents failed to make clear was that the deeds allowed the mine operators to get to the seams of coal by whatever means were necessary. In the mid-1800s, the demand for coal had moved the industry away from small deposits near the surface to mines with deep shafts and tunnels many stories deep to get at the larger deposits.

Soon Appalachia was honeycombed by large subsurface mines. It meant forests were cut down to clear land and provide timber for the shafts. And the once crystal-clear waters were polluted with the byproducts of mining.

However, a lot of the coal in Appalachia lay in large seams starting comparatively close to the surface and then in tiers further down, like icing between layers of cake. The easiest and cheapest way to get at it was the peel back the surface, dig up the first seam and then continue down until it ran out. To create these open pit mines not only were the primordial forests cut down, but farms and pastures and entire mountain tops scraped flat as pancakes.

The impact on the environment, which in turn affected the culture and way of life of the Appalachian people, was enormous. Once crystal-clear waters were polluted, the fish and wildlife decimated. Nor were there any real laws requiring that the mine operators restore the surface of the land after they were done ravaging the land.[9]

Not all the purchased land, or rights acquired through broad form deeds, was mined right away. A generation or more might pass before a farmer learned that his grandfather signed a deed. But there would be nothing the current occupant could do about it except stand by and watch his land decimated. If he protested or tried to fight it, the law and its enforcers were on the side of the mine operators.

These were a people whose self-image and culture were wrapped up in the land they loved. Their ancestors left Northern Ireland for America and then moved west into the mountains looking for land. They'd found an unspoiled utopia and fought to keep it. If they'd changed the land for their home, farms, pastures, and small communities, it had changed them even more. Their heritage was Scots-Irish, but they were Appalachian mountaineers and that was how they saw themselves.

However, what that meant would undergo an enormous change due to coal. For one thing, mining altered the ethnic makeup of Appalachia. The mostly Scots-Irish inhabitants were used to hard work, but they weren't miners. In need of skilled miners, the coal companies brought in immigrants from the coal-mining areas of the world, especially Wales and England, but also countries such as Italy, Ireland, and Poland.

The dominant local culture, which due to its adversity-hardened and homogenous nature, certainly imparted its mainstay qualities to the newcomers. But the immigrants brought their own brand of toughness and a legacy of hardships they'd overcome getting to America. They had their own cultural traits, as well as different denominations of Christianity, including the old enemy, Irish Catholics. However, they tended to assimilate easily into the local population, even after a generation or two adopting the accent of

---

9   There wouldn't be such requirements until 1977, and even up until
     the twenty-first century, the laws are often skirted.

mountaineers, as well as their music, behaviors, and love for their new homeland.

The evolution from farming to coal mining, as well as the influx of immigrant miners, also affected the types of communities. Towns grew, as did the presence of law enforcement, many of whom owed their paychecks, and sometimes more under the table, to the coal mine operators. But the operators took it further.

In part to lure skilled mine workers to the region, the mine owners also built "company towns" near mines that included housing, schools, community buildings, and even churches. They also established company stores where the mining families could purchase everything from clothing to household items. It was all owned and operated by the coal companies, which determined who could live in the housing and often paid their workers in script only good at the company stores.

As the farms and pastures disappeared, even the long-time locals turned to working in the mines and sometimes leaving their homes to live in company towns. The outside world's image of the Appalachian as frontiersman and farmer changed to that of a coalminer, the lines of his face and hands permanently etched in black coal dust.

Even the children were transformed. They went from farm kids, raised in households where literacy was valued, living healthy lifestyles in the sun and fresh air, to dropping out of school to work in the mines, often before puberty. Photographs of their exhausted soot-covered faces, eyes old before their time, would come to symbolize Appalachia.

Those on the outside, with the help of the national press, created a stereotype of the Appalachian people as illiterate and ignorant hillbillies. They poked fun at the way the mountaineers spoke in funny anachronistic accents and entertained themselves with hillbilly music. They shook their heads about church services where poisonous snakes were handled and pastors worked their congregants into seizures and speaking in tongues. Jokes were made about cousins marrying cousins.

Forgotten were the Scots-Irish forebearers' contributions to the formation of the United States, not just in regard to fighting in the Revolutionary War, but in regards to concepts that made their way into the Declaration of Independence, the U.S. Constitution and the Bill of Rights, such as the rights of the individual and the notion that governments existed only by consent of the governed. Without acknowledging where these concepts came from, Americans in general adopted the mountaineers' toughness, self-reliance, and independence as their own.

By the early 1900s, an entire group of people was thought of by their fellow citizens as backwards brutes not good for much of anything, except mining coal. Their tragedies—the coal mine disasters, the destruction of their mountain home—and their struggles, whether with poverty or the coal mine operators and their henchmen, hardly merited any mention in mainstream newspapers.

In order to power, heat, and build a nation, they toiled in abysmal conditions and, far too often, it cost them their lives. When coal mining moved underground, it created two issues for coalminers and eventually for the union that took up their causes.

One, it necessitated advances in technology, such as pumps to cleanse the mine of poisonous gases and bring in fresh air, as well as the machinery to harvest and remove the coal. The machinery meant that more coal could be produced by fewer laborers, a trend that would continue for a hundred years and impact their union's efforts to keep them employed.

The second issue was the use of explosives, especially after the Civil War. Again, dynamite could get at the coal faster than men could dig, and that meant fewer jobs in relation to the amount of coal produced. But it also increased the risk of mining. By the turn of the nineteenth century, thousands of mine workers were dying every year in the United States due to explosions, cave-ins, floods, fires, and gases.

The danger of methane gas and coal dust—both byproducts of coal mining—as fuels for underground explosions were well-known. Every explosion underground produced the fine black dust that would hang in the air. A small spark could ignite either the methane gas or the dust, or sometimes both in combination. Pumps were used to reduce gas and coal dust buildups. Mine operators were supposed to spread rock dust—generally pulverized limestone—to mix with coal dust and diffuse its explosive capabilities, but these requirements were often ignored by the operators and government inspectors.

As bad as the fatalities from mine accidents were, they didn't take into account a more insidious danger: the air the miners breathed. Anyone associated with underground coal mining was aware that even young men would develop deep coughs, hacking up viscous blue-black phlegm. Many died old before their time, gasping for breath.

Autopsies revealed lungs stained black. But the first recorded connection between coal dust and miners was described in 1831 by Dr. James Craufurd Gregory. After chemical analysis of the lungs of a former coalminer who'd essentially suffocated, he was the first to consider "black lung disease" to be an occupational disease related to coal dust.

Gregory even alerted other physicians to watch for the disease in miners, but the industry did almost nothing to protect miners. Initially respirators were developed for emergency use only, such as escaping a detected gas buildup. It wouldn't be until the mid-twentieth century that respirators would be commonly worn while working in a coal mine.

Showers to rinse the coal dust off when miners emerged from the shafts weren't provided. So, they took the dust home with them—homes that usually didn't have running water for bathing or washing clothes. A fine layer of black dust covered everything, exposing other family members to its effects on their lungs.

For most of the nineteenth century, the mine operators pretty much operated as they wanted. Mine workers had to accept what the operators were willing to pay, the poor working conditions, and the lack of mine safety, or they could look for a job elsewhere. The company towns didn't just ensure that the operators had enough workers, but also was a way to control them. Complain, or try to organize a union, and a miner would find himself and his family on the streets without a job.

In the early days of U.S. coal mining, "management" was generally working alongside the help, and that made labor relations pretty simple and straight forward. Everybody was in it together. Although there were attempts to organize mine workers in the 1840s and 1850s, they didn't have much influence and generally folded soon after they were formed.

In 1875, the largest and most organized miner's union of that time was formed by the Knights of Labor. It was called the National Federation of Miners and Mine Laborers of the United States.

Initially, the Federation's goals weren't higher wages—that wouldn't come until the 1890s. Instead, the union's stated objectives were an eight-hour workday and better working conditions.

However, the federation was poorly organized and had more of a philosophical bent about the plight of the working man than a practical one to improve his life. Faced with rapidly dwindling numbers, the Federation joined with the National Progressive Miners of America and on January 25, 1890, created the United Mine Workers of America (UMWA).

Recognizing the challenge to their profits and authority, the coal mine operators were determined to destroy the union. It was no accident that the birth of the UMWA coincided with the start of a violent period of labor unrest in the coal fields of America known as the "Coal Wars." Fought off and on in the years between 1890 and into the 1930s, the conflicts were waged predominantly in Appalachia, though deadly confrontations would also break out in Colorado and Illinois.

Sometimes wages were the main focal point of UMWA demands. However, the union's main emphasis was on combating the exploitation of mine workers, especially in company towns, and improving mine safety and working conditions. The main tactic was to call a strike to shut down production until demands were met.

However, meeting those demands would cost the mine operators money and control. They responded by firing workers and turning them and their families out of company-owned homes, sometimes for as little as attending UMWA informational meetings. But they also hired "gun thugs" and employed "detective agencies"—especially the Pinkerton and Baldwin-Felt agencies—to confront the organizers and the striking miners. Their money also bought local sheriffs and politicians, who could be counted on to protect the interests of the owners, even if it meant calling in the state or national guards to deal with strikers.

Created to better the lives of coal workers, the UMWA found itself fighting a war. The union was only a little more than a year old when on April 3, 1891, deputized members of the 10th Regiment of the National Guard fired on a crowd of mostly immigrant strikers in Morewood, Pennsylvania. Ten strikers were killed and dozens more were wounded.

On September 10, 1897, nineteen miners were killed in Lattimer, Pennsylvania during a march in support of the union. Between those two dates in Morewood and then Lattimer, there were many more instances of individuals being assaulted, killed, or blacklisted and chased out of town.

In the early days, the effectiveness of the UMWA was hit and miss. Four years after it was formed, the union called for its first nationwide strike. Known as the "Bituminous Coal Miners' Strike of 1897," the union was reacting to the mine owners slashing workers' salaries up to 30 percent due to a downturn in the economy and a related drop in demand for coal.

The National Guard was called up in several states to keep the strikers and their replacements apart. But soldiers sided against the UMWA.

In the end, the strike fizzled because the owners were willing to wait it out and because the strike was disorganized: some heeded the call to strike, but others didn't. After three weeks, when the UMWA leadership wanted the strike to end, some strikers stayed out.

Nothing much was accomplished by the strike. However, it did show that the UMWA was capable of coordinating a nationwide strike, even if it also demonstrated that the union leadership could not control all of its members.

The growing influence of the UMWA became clear during the Coal Strike of 1902. Led by the UMWA and centered in eastern Pennsylvania, the strike only ended after President Theodore Roosevelt stepped in as a neutral arbitrator by which the union won some concessions regarding mine safety and wages.

However, violence was more often the result than arbitration and negotiation. In October 1903, the UMWA called for a strike in Colorado. Mine operators responded by paying the Pinkerton Agency to infiltrate the union and then went after the union officers and organizers.

Beginning in 1910, fifteen thousand coalminers went on strike in Westmoreland, Pennsylvania led largely by immigrant Slovak union miners. Sixteen people were killed during the strike, most of them miners and their family members.

In April 1912, union mine workers in Kanawha County, West Virginia went on strike. This time mine operators hired the Baldwin-Felts Detective Agency for the violent repression of the miners. Before it was over, fifty people, mostly miners, had died violent deaths; another fifty miners died of starvation and malnutrition, making it the worst conflict in terms of casualties in American labor history.

One of the most infamous, however, was the Ludlow Massacre during the Colorado Coalfield War of 1913–1914, during which the Colorado Fuel and Iron Company, owned by John D. Rockefeller Jr., was pit against mineworkers in Ludlow.

On April 20, 1914, armed police officers, Baldwin-Felts detectives, hired gun thugs, and the Colorado National Guard attacked a tent city of miners and their families. The miners had been kicked out of their company-owned housing for complaining about the unfair practices of the company stores and for attending UMWA meetings. An estimated twenty inhabitants of the camp, including women and children, were killed.

UMWA members were not above initiating the killing. During the Hartford coal mine riot of July 1914, two non-union miners were murdered by union miners. The mine owners, and their political, media, and law enforcement lackeys, worked to sway public opinion by portraying striking miners as illiterate, violent brutes who murdered innocent men trying to make a living.

When four hundred thousand members of the UMWA went on strike on November 1918, during the height of World War I, the federal government intervened on behalf of the mine owners. U.S. Attorney General A. Mitchell Palmer invoked the Lever Act, a new law criminalizing interference with the production of wartime necessities, such as coal. The courts agreed with the government and issued an injunction ordering the miners back to work.

At the same time, the mine operators used the strike to evoke the bogeyman of the Russian revolution and communism. With the help of a friendly press, they put the word out that the UMWA was in the pay of Lenin.

The court of public opinion outside of coal country was not on the side of mine workers. The Coal Wars reinforced the Appalachian mountaineers' long-held belief that they were on their own against a hostile outside world that didn't care about them, their struggles, or their lives. They couldn't count on the law. Or the government. Or even their fellow Americans. But they had each other and, though there were still going to be growing pains, they had their union.

The year 1920 was pivotal in UMWA history. One reason was the introduction to the world of one of the most dynamic and controversial labor leaders of the twentieth century.

Prior to 1920, the UMWA had eight presidents of varying degrees of effectiveness. But none like John L. Lewis, a beetle-browed, leonine-headed, charismatic force of nature. He was loud, fearless, aggressive, and confrontational and would at the beginning of a career in which he would become a revered, nearly mythological, icon among the union membership. However, before he became a legend, the man and his union nearly became a mere footnote in the history of American labor.

In early 1920, Lewis decided that the union needed to organize Mingo County in southern West Virginia. Most of the state's coal fields had been brought into the UMWA fold, but they were having trouble bringing the counties in the south part of the state into the fold.

One of those counties, Logan, was controlled by the vehemently anti-union Sheriff Don Chafin, who had deputized an army of gun thugs to enforce the will of the mine operators. But Mingo, the next county over, was leaning pro-union, including Cabell Testerman, the mayor of Matewan, the county seat. Testerman had appointed twenty-seven-year-old Sid Hatfield, who'd worked in the mines as a teenager, as the town police chief, and he was decidedly, and violently, pro-union.

Under Lewis's direction, the union quickly made inroads in recruiting miners in Mingo. The operators responded by firing union sympathizers, blacklisting them, and having Baldwin-Felts detectives evict them from company housing.

The UMWA countered by setting up a tent colony for the homeless miners and their families. By early May, three thousand out of the four thousand miners in Mingo County had joined the union.

The back and forth could have only led to escalation. That escalation arrived on May 19 when eleven Baldwin-Felts detectives, including two of the founder's brothers, were leaving Matewan after serving eviction notices. They walked into a trap set by Hatfield. By the time the smoke from the gunfight cleared, seven of the Baldwin-Felts men, including the two brothers, as well as Mayor Testerman, were dead.

The miners won the initial fight and spirits were high after beating the hated Baldwin-Felts detectives. But it was just the beginning of a period of guerilla warfare. Men died on both sides, including Hatfield and a friend; they were unarmed and murdered in cold blood by Baldwin-Felts detectives.

The fight over southern West Virginia culminated in 1921 with the Battle of Blair Mountain in Logan County. Seven thousand lightly armed miners took on three thousand heavily armed deputies and Baldwin-Felts detectives led by Sheriff Chafin.

The miners held their own until U.S. President Warren G. Harding authorized the use of the West Virginia National Guard to attack the miners' positions on the mountain. National Guard planes were deployed and dropped bombs, including poisonous gas bombs.

The running gunbattles lasted several days and resulted in the deaths of approximately one hundred miners and fifty of Chafin's men. Nearly a thousand miners, many of them army veterans of World War I, who had refused to fire on National Guard troops and surrendered, were tried for murder. Some were acquitted by sympathetic juries, but others spent decades in prison.

The Battle of Blair Mountain was the largest labor uprising in United States history. It was also a watershed event for the UMWA. It crushed the union in West Virginia, which prohibited union organizing until the 1930s, and demoralized union organizers elsewhere in coal country.

During the rest of the decade, as the post-war economy tanked and, with it, coal prices, the mine owners and operators essentially chased the union from Pennsylvania, Ohio, Indiana, and the West. The UMWA had never had much luck organizing the southern Appalachian coal fields and lost ground there, too.

Nationally, union membership shrank from nearly four hundred thousand in 1920 to less than one hundred thousand by 1929, most of them in Illinois. Some of the losses were attributable to increased mechanization used to extract coal, which meant fewer jobs. But after the debacle in West Virginia, there was a perception that John Lewis and the UMWA were ineffective and powerless against the anti-union forces arrayed against them.

By the end of the 1920s, the United Mine Workers of America was broke, on the run, and losing ground in coal country. However, although it wasn't at first evident, the tide was about to turn.

The line in the sand was Harlan County, a mountainous coal-mining region of eastern Kentucky that would earn a reputation as "Bloody Harlan." The Harlan County War was a vicious nearly ten-year conflict between the union and miners on one side and coal firms, their gun thugs and corrupt law enforcement on the other.

Fought mostly in Harlan County, as well as neighboring Bell County, the Depression-era struggle would be the longest, most vicious labor dispute in U.S. history. It didn't, however, begin on a high note for the UMWA.

As the nation entered the Great Depression, the coal industry, which had always been known for its boom-and-bust cycles, was in a slump. Overproduction and competition from home heating fuels, and a nation that was turning to oil and gas to meet its transportation and industrial needs, contributed to lost jobs and lower wages in coal country.

By 1931, four thousand Harlan County miners, nearly a third of the workforce, were unemployed. Those who did still have jobs made less than eighty cents an hour and only worked a few days a week. Many had been evicted from their company homes and lived on the edge of starvation with their families.

The UMWA was of no help. During the 1920s, the union had made headway into the Central Appalachian coal fields. However, when miners in Bell and Harlan Counties went out on strike in 1931, the union withdrew its promised support. Historians would later blame the perfidy on Lewis, who was worried that broad-based strikes would deplete union relief funds.[10]

The UMWA's abdication of its place in the fight left the door open for the National Miners Union (NMU), which had been formed by the American Communist Party. The NMU started by setting up soup kitchens at which they recruited miners.

The coal operators responded by having gun thugs dynamite the soup kitchen in Evarts. Miners who tried to guard other NMU kitchens were arrested on flimsy charges by deputies who worked for corrupt Sheriff J.H. Blair. Anyone thought to be a union organizer or sympathizer was beat and expelled from the county.

On August 30, 1931, two miners were shot and killed by gun thugs at the soup kitchen in Clovertown, a company-town in Harlan County. One of the men responsible for killing the two miners was tried for murder. But the jury, regaled by the prosecution and sheriff about the communist sympathies of the victim, determined that the killer had acted in "self-defense" when he shot the unarmed miner. The gun thug was acquitted. If it wasn't clear before, the murders

---

10   Members of the National Committee for the Defense, *Harlan Miners Speak*: *Report on Terrorism in the Kentucky Coal Fields* (New York: Harcourt, Brace and Company, 1932).

were proof that miners couldn't depend on the justice system to protect them.

Judge D.C. Jones, who presided over the trial, said afterwards, "No one belonging to a 'Red' organization has any right to look to this court, or to any other court in the country, for justice."[11]

Sheriff Blair made it clear whose side he was on. "I did all in my power to aid the operators," he later told a pro-union journalist. "There was no compromise when labor troubles swept the county and the 'Reds' came to Harlan County."[12]

Tensions continued to escalate with miners, unable to feed or shelter their families, growing increasingly angry. On the other side, the operators hired strikebreakers and armed guards to protect them.

The inevitable boiled over in May 1931 when heavily armed detectives and gun thugs protecting supplies on their way to strikebreakers were confronted by armed miners on a road near Evarts. Shooting started and by the end of the violence, three deputies and one miner were dead.

Over the next few days, federal troops were called in by governor, ostensibly to separate the two groups, but they sided with the mine operators and helped break the strike. Union leaders were banned from mines in the county, and forty-four miners were made to stand trial; many of them were convicted and sentenced to jail.

In January 1932, the NMU called for another strike, but very few minors participated. With that, the NMU was done in Harlan County, and the miner workers were left on their own. Literally starving to death and watching their families suffer, they were branded as communists in the eyes of the outside public and national press, even though most couldn't have said what communism even meant.

While at first it didn't help with the public perception, the mine workers' cause was picked up by members of the National Committee for the Defense of Political Prisoners, a group of openly socialist writers such as Pulitzer Prize–finalist Theodore Dreiser

11   Ibid.
12   Ibid.

and novelists John Dos Passos and Sherwood Anderson. Dreiser and Anderson traveled to Harlan County where they interviewed miners until they were arrested and escorted out of the county by Blair's men.

The Dreiser Committee report was subsequently published as *Harlan Miners Speak: Report on Terrorism in the Kentucky Coal Fields.* The report described the plight of the miners, as well as the treatment of journalists trying to cover the story. It caught the attention of the mainstream press who followed up with their own reports.

A reporter for the *New York Times* wrote, "Terror continues to flourish in Harlan County in the comfortable obscurity furnished by a virtual censorship on news." He described not only the treatment of miners and their families by coal operators and law enforcement, but also "the shooting and intimidation of reporters."

Thirty years later, firebrand civil rights activists and anti-war protest songs would rock the nation's establishment. But it can be argued that the icons of the 1960s movements got their role models in the 1930s coal fields of Appalachia.

Irish-born labor activist Mother Jones, who already had a national reputation as a vocal champion of working men, showed up in Harlan County to help organize mine workers despite death threats and promises of law enforcement action. Folk singers who penned songs about struggles of the working man, especially Appalachian coalminers, made the radio airwaves and began to change the public's perception, long before Bob Dylan penned "Blowin' in the Wind."

Florence Reece's song "Which Side Are You On?" about the plight of Harlan County mineworkers became one of the most popular songs on the radio and at organizational meetings.

> My daddy was a miner, and I'm a miner's son,
> And I'll stick with the union, 'til every battle's won.
> They say in Harlan County there are no neutrals there.
> You'll either be a union man or a thug for J. H. Blair.
> Oh, workers can you stand it? Oh, tell me how you can?
> Will you be a lousy scab or will you be a man?

> Don't scab for the bosses, don't listen to their lies.
> Us poor folks haven't got a chance unless we organize.

Another popular tune with significant national airplay was "The Ballad of Harry Simms" by Aunt Molly Jackson and Jim Garland. It told the story of the murder of Harry Simms, a nineteen-year-old NMU organizer from Springfield, Massachusetts, and the lack of justice for his killer in Harlan County.

On February 10, 1932, Simms and a friend were walking along a railroad track in Knox County when a deputy, who also worked as a mine guard, approached and, without provocation, shot the young man in the stomach. The deputy and his partner took the wounded young man to Barbourville where they left him sitting on a rock outside of the hospital.

The hospital refused to admit Simms unless someone would guarantee payment. Simms waited for hours until someone finally had mercy and agreed to pay his bills. He died the next day. No one in law enforcement did anything about the murder.

But the days of the miners taking the abuse without responding in kind were now over. A few months after the murder of Harry Simms, the deputy who killed him was ambushed himself and shot to death.

Guerilla warfare between the miners and the mine operators' hired guns ensued. Both sides engaged in beatings, assassinations, bombings, and destruction of property, including sabotaging of mines and mining equipment.

However, the forces on the side of the mine operators were much better financed, more heavily armed, paid, and better organized. Plus, they had the justice system, law enforcement, the local press, most politicians, and even state and National Guard units on their side.

There was a glimmer of hope for the miners in 1934 even as the UMWA was trying to claw its way back into the county. That fall, "reform candidate" Theodore Roosevelt Middleton defeated J.H. Blair for sheriff of Harlan County.

To get the miners' votes, Middleton ran on a platform promising to rid the office of bias and corruption, as well as provide equal protection for union miners and their representatives. However, after the election, Middleton acquired five coal mines, allied himself with an anti-union judge and, if anything, was even more brutal and oppressive towards miners and the union than his predecessor.

The tyranny didn't go unnoticed outside of Harlan County. In 1935, a state commission looked into the treatment of miners in the county and wrote the following report: "There exists a virtual reign of terror, financed in general by a group of coal mine operators in collusion with certain public officials: the victims of this reign of terror are the coalminers and their families...a monster-like reign of oppression whose tentacles reached into the very foundation of the social structure and even into the Church of God.

"The homes of union miners and organizers were dynamited and fired into. It appears that the principal cause of existing conditions is the desire of the mine owners to amass for themselves fortunes through the oppression of their laborers, which they do through the sheriff's office."

Still, despite the studies and reports, there was little change in Harlan County, as well as coal country in general. The mine operators, particularly in Harlan and Bell Counties, remained in complete control.

However, events in 1935 would begin to change that, though it had nothing to do with anything Lewis or the UMWA did. As part of President Roosevelt's plan to drag the country out of the Great Depression, the pro-organized labor Wagner Act was passed. The act established the National Labor Relations Board, which among other things included the right of workers to organize into unions and enter into collective bargaining agreements. The new law particularly affected the anti-union practices of coal operators by banning blacklists, which prohibited fired miners from finding work elsewhere, and making it illegal to discriminate against union members.

Almost overnight the national ranks of the United Mine Workers of America skyrocketed as coal operators, tired of the constant work interruptions and financial drain of lawsuits and hiring gun thugs and paying off law enforcement, decided to abide by the provisions in the law. Everywhere, that is, except Harlan County.

Instead, coal operators in Bloody Harlan ignored the law. Sheriff Middleton and his deputies, as well as gun thugs hired by individual mines, ramped up their brutality.

Nor was the federal government any help to the miners. In fact, the Harlan operators called in the National Guard three times after the Wagner Act was passed to put down mine strikes.

Then on February 9, 1937, Middleton's deputies made a tragic miscalculation. They shot into the home of Minister Marshall Musick, a union organizer, killing his fifteen-year-old son, Bennett, who was doing his homework. When word of the brutal act got out in the national media, even the federal government couldn't ignore the public outcry.

Wisconsin Senator Robert M. La Follette Jr., head of a U.S. Senate subcommittee on education and labor, launched an investigation into the practices of the coal mine operators in Harlan County. As a result, the U.S. Department of Justice prosecuted sixty-nine Harlan County operators and law enforcement officers for "criminally conspiring to violate the Wagner Act."

The brand new Federal Bureau of Investigation got into the act when U.S. Attorney General Robert H. Jackson asked Director J. Edgar Hoover to send special agents to investigate. After a month-long investigation, the Justice Department criminally indicted twenty-two companies, twenty-four operators, Middleton and twenty-two of his deputies.

Although most of the subsequent trials ended in hung juries, and charges against Middleton were dismissed by Governor A.B. "Happy" Chandler, the action by federal law enforcement spooked many of the Harlan and Bell Counties' mine operators. They signed union contracts, and UMWA membership soared to nine thousand, 65 percent of the county's miners, by August 1937.

However, the decade's violence in Bloody Harlan didn't stop; this time perpetuated by the union miners. In April 1939, the UMWA, which had been steadily gaining members since 1935, called for a nationwide strike. Not all miners in Harlan County went out on strike, and they were attacked by union miners who resorted to some of the same violent tactics as their former antagonists.

Beatings, bombings, murder and coercion did not disappear from Harlan County, only the enemy changed. Union men like Albert Pass, William J. Prater, and Silous Huddleston, who would all figure into what happened to Jock Yablonski and his family in Clarksville, Pennsylvania in late December 1969, cut their teeth on the front lines of the Harlan County War—first against the mine owners and their gun thugs, then, after that battle was won, against non-union miners and the mine owners who hired them.

UMWA District 19, which encompassed eastern Kentucky and Tennessee and with Harlan County as its heart, earned its reputation as the most fanatically loyal and violent district in the union, so when Lewis's hand-chosen successor, Tony Boyle, decided to eliminate his rival, Jock Yablonski, he knew where to turn.

"District 19," Boyle was assured, "will get it done!"

CHAPTER THREE

BITTER RIVALS

John L. Lewis retired as the president of the United Mine Workers in early 1960. After forty years as the union president, his tenure was a mixed bag. Through sheer strength of will, fiery oratory, a rough charisma, and violence if persuasion didn't work, Lewis had built the UMWA into one of the most powerful unions ever in the United States. Especially in the early days of the union when he'd fought for better wages and safety measures. He'd negotiated with the owners to create the Welfare and Retirement Fund based on tons of coal shipped. Originally the fund collected five cents per ton, but over the years, it had been raised to forty cents a ton.

During his tenure, the grip mine owners and operators had over union mine workers and their families that bordered on slavery had greatly diminished. The existence of company towns all but disappeared. Violence instigated by the thugs and corrupt law enforcement would be met, and even surpassed, by the violence from men like Albert Pass and Silous Huddleston. At a word from Lewis, mines could be shut down and owners forced to the bargaining table.

The victories of the union even improved conditions for non-union mine workers who could use the threat of organizing to lobby for their own financial compensation and working conditions. It didn't mean violence between the union and non-union forces stopped, but the union was more likely to make gains by sending in disciples to preach the gospel of unionism than blowing up someone's house. Not that it and other acts of brutality were completely a thing of the past.

Lewis also had made the union a force to be reckoned with in Washington, D.C. Presidential candidates, as well as those running for the House, Senate, and state races in coal country, sought his blessing and support.

However, he'd made mistakes that had hurt the union, too. He'd opposed U.S. involvement in World War II and supported Nazi Germany when FDR was preparing for the inevitable war. Then Lewis called for strikes during World War II when the rest of America was pulling together and making sacrifices on behalf of the country. Those stances and the strikes cost him and the union the goodwill of the patriotic American public at a time when new threats from automation cost union jobs and the growing influence of oil and gas companies was threatening coal's clout.

Faced with the threats to mining jobs and the loss of influence, there'd been times when he looked the other way—or even backed—the mine owners and operators when they'd balked at safety and health concerns. He called it "convenient memory lapses" when the owners failed to rectify safety issues noted by federal mine inspectors—sometimes with fatal results, such as the 1954 Farmington mine explosion that caused sixteen deaths.

Nor had he done anything to combat the scourge of coalminers—*pneumoconiosis*, better known as black lung disease—because of the added costs for owners. In fact, he'd fought against it being declared a compensatory ailment, as well as balked at preventative measures like showers to rinse the coal dust after work.

Some of these decisions could be rationalized as Lewis's attempts to protect jobs and stave off the impact of the gas and oil industry. If the cost of labor grew to be too much, the coal mine owners might shut down mines. If that happened, the miners wouldn't just be underpaid, they'd be out of work. Of course, out-of-work miners couldn't pay union dues either, so it was in the union leadership's best interests to keep them employed.

He'd done it all with an iron fist. Under Lewis, there'd been no democracy. He appointed the presidents of the districts and locals, as well as officials with the national offices and boards. The UMWA's policy-making International Executive Board (IEB) had granted Lewis the power to revoke the charters of districts and appoint individuals to oversee union affairs at the district level. He could dismiss union members who fomented dissent or opposition to his policies.[13]

Lewis alone negotiated contracts with coal operators. Nepotism and cronyism were rampant. The only position up for grabs was the national union presidency, and he kept a tight grip on that by stuffing ballot boxes; rewarding loyal supporters; and intimidating dissenters, including at polling stations. He had plenty of money at his disposal to pay for it all.

The union kept its money at the National Bank in Washington, D.C. with an account worth more than $180 million. He also created a side account of $67 million whose purpose was for his personal investment on behalf of the coalminers. Since it was non-interest-bearing, it lost $3 million a year that rightfully belonged to the union.

Lewis made sure that "the union," meaning himself, controlled the bank, even its investment portfolio, by buying up 52 percent of its stock and sitting on the board. As a result, no one questioned the existence of the non-interest-bearing account.

The union's resources in money and potential voters meant politicians and bureaucrats tended to look the other way. The union was often, and blatantly, in violation of the Landrum-Griffin Act of 1959, which had been passed due to corruption, racketeering, and other misconduct by the labor movement, including the UMWA. Among other issues, the act was designed to protect the rights of union members from unfair practices of their unions, including the right to elect union officials, which Lewis ignored.

---

13   Kenneth Wolensky, "Living for Reform," *Pennsylvania Heritage* 27, Winter 2001, 14–23.

The Landrum-Griffin Act was supposed to be enforced by the U.S. Department of Labor, but during Lewis's tenure there had never been an investigation of UMWA practices.

When Lewis retired, he appointed his vice president, seventy-three-year-old Thomas Kennedy, as his successor. However, he kept his seat on the three-member Welfare and Retirement Fund Board, which meant he still controlled the purse strings. But there was also another appointment he made that would have enormous and tragic ramifications.

At the same time that he named Kennedy as his successor, Lewis also installed William A. "Tough Tony" Boyle as vice president of the union. He would have liked to appoint Boyle as the union president, but Kennedy was better known and liked by the membership than his younger subordinate.

However, he knew it was only a matter of time before his preferred choice would ascend to the top. Kennedy was in failing health, and from the beginning of his tenure, Boyle all but ran the union.

Born on December 1, 1904 in a gold mining camp in Bald Butte, Montana, Boyle was the son of a miner. In fact, several generations of Boyles had been miners in England and Scotland before immigrating to the United States.

Boyle dropped out of high school in the ninth grade and went to work in the mines at age fifteen with his father, who died soon after from tuberculosis. In 1928, he married Ethel Williams, and they had a daughter, Antoinette. He might have remained an unknown miner in Montana if it had not been for the UMWA.

Joining the union shortly after he started working in the mines, Boyle quickly earned a reputation as a union organizer and enforcer. Although short in stature, he was a pugnacious and quick-tempered bully who earned the nickname "Tough Tony." And his willingness to do anything for the union soon got him noticed by leadership at the national level.

In 1940, with Lewis's blessing, he was "elected" president of District 27, which covered Montana, and served on several governmental wartime production boards. Then in 1948, Lewis called Boyle to Washington, D.C. as his special assistant. There he acted as

Lewis's main trouble-shooter and chief administrator of the union. Lewis also made him president of District 50 and regional director of the Congress of Industrial Organizations (CIO) for four western states.

By November 1962, Kennedy was too ill to continue his duties, and Boyle was named acting president. A month later, Kennedy died, and Boyle was elected president. At the time, the UMWA had 125,000 active members and 40,000 retired pensioners with 1,300 locals spread over twenty-three states and four Canadian provinces.

After "winning" the election, with the usual allegations of fraud and corruption, there was significant opposition to Boyle from rank-and-file members of the union and even some of the leadership in the locals. Miners not in Boyle's camp agitated for greater democracy, including being able to elect their own local presidents, and more autonomy for their locals.

The feeling that had begun to grow under Lewis's last years—the feeling that union leadership was protecting the owners' interests above those of the members—was exacerbated under Boyle's leadership. For instance, grievances filed by union members against mine owners or operators, including health and pay issues, often took months, even years, to be resolved, especially if they ran contrary to the interests of the owners.

Lewis's iron grip on union activities began to slip under Boyle, who lacked his predecessor's cachet as well as charisma. It loosened further when in 1963, Boyle secretly negotiated a new contract with the Bituminous Coal Operators Association for the UMWA's 125,000 active miners. The miners had not received a raise since 1958 but all Boyle secured was a two-dollar-a-day wage increase and a hike of twenty-five dollars in vacation pay. It wasn't much, and Boyle also gave in to the owners on what the rank and file believed was a key demand for sick pay.

Still, Boyle emerged from the negotiations declaring that the deal was the "best ever." But the rank and file were not impressed. Pennsylvania's soft-coalminers were particularly infuriated, ridiculing Boyle as "Two Dollar Tony." Ensuing wildcat strikes shut down dozens of mines in western Pennsylvania's District 5.

Enraged, Boyle demanded that the District 5 president, Joseph A. "Jock" Yablonski, get the men in his district back to work. Yablonski did as he was told, but he sympathized with the miners.

Born March 3, 1910, Yablonski was also a son of a miner. He quit school after the eighth grade and went into the Pennsylvania coalmines with his father, an immigrant from Poland, but Stephen Yablonski was killed in a mining accident several years later. His death propelled his son, Jock, who vowed to improve working conditions and pay for coalminers, to the front lines of the UMWA coal wars of the 1930s.

Favored with a powerful voice, charisma, and an appeal to miners as one of their own—something Boyle lacked despite his own beginnings—Yablonski, again with Lewis's support, was elected president of UMWA Local 1787 in District 5. In 1940, he also was voted to the prestigious position of District 5's representative to the IEB.

In spite of his lack of a formal education, Yablonski was something of a renaissance man in the UMWA. He was in demand as a guest-lecturer at colleges, giving speeches about labor's goals and philosophy. He also became a force in Pennsylvania politics and, beginning in 1952, participated every four years as a delegate to the Democratic National Convention.

Yablonski didn't forget his vow to improve the lives of miners. In 1954, he created Centerville Clinics Inc., which provided health care for Pennsylvania miners and their families who could not otherwise afford it. He also served as chairman of the board of the new Brownsville General Hospital, near his home outside of Clarksville.[14]

He was all about the union, even at his second wedding. After a first marriage that had produced one son, Kenneth, and a bitter divorce, he was wed in 1939 to Margaret Wasicek by western Pennsylvania's "labor priest," the Reverend Charles Owen Rice.[15]

---

14 Paul Guggenheimer, "50 years later, wounds remain from Yablonski family killings," TribLIVE, December 28, 2019, https://triblive.com/local/regional/50-years-later-wounds-remain-after-yablonski-family-killings/.
15 Kenneth Wolensky, "Living for Reform."

The labor leader took great pride in being a self-taught man and voracious reader of books, newspapers, and magazines. Much of his intellectual pursuits could be credited to Margaret's influence. She was an avid reader herself, and a prolific writer who'd penned screenplays, theatre productions, short stories, and magazine articles. Several of her articles were published in *Esquire*, but because the magazine didn't accept work from female writers at the time, the stories had been submitted and published under her husband's name.[16]

Yablonski was a man's man whose life revolved around the union and his family. He was known to enjoy a well-made cigar and had an affinity for good scotch. In order to house his growing family, which included a second son, Joseph "Chip" Yablonski, Jr., and daughter, Charlotte, he purchased a large, three-story, century-old farmhouse and a small farm just outside of the borough of Clarksville, fifty miles south of Pittsburgh. In doing so, he dismissed stories of the house being "cursed"—in the nineteenth-century, the owner hung himself from the basement rafters, and in the 1930s, a Pennsylvania state police officer was shot to death inside the house while responding to a domestic dispute.[17]

These were happy years in the Yablonski household. When he wasn't involved in his union duties and political interests, he worked the farm with his children—bringing in the hay, planting, raising cattle, and birthing calves.

In 1958, Yablonski's career took another step up when Lewis combined the positions of District 5 president and IEB representative and then scheduled an election to fill the post. Of course, Lewis's man, Yablonski, won overwhelmingly.

Lewis relied on Yablonski's oratory skills and often dispatched him to coal fields around the country to spread the union gospel and bring wildcat strikers into line, as well as convert non-union miners. The old union president even told Jock that he would be good candidate to lead the union someday.

16   Paul Guggenheimer, "50 years later, wounds remain from Yablonski family killings."
17   Kenneth Wolensky, "Living for Reform."

So it was a disappointment that when Lewis retired, he appointed Boyle as the vice president and then, after Kennedy died, backed "Tough Tony" as his choice for president. The relationship between Boyle, who, like Lewis. demanded absolute loyalty from his subordinates, and Yablonski, who sometimes strayed from that fealty, had its ups and downs since their early days as Lewis's favorites. But Boyle's ascension to UMWA president marked the beginning of the end for any amicable relationship between the two men.

The wildcat strikes in 1963 that so angered Boyle did nothing to improve the relationship, even when Yablonski persuaded the wildcatters to go back to work. A year later, the issues of member dissatisfaction with UMWA administration continued to deteriorate, as did the relationship between Boyle and Yablonski.

In 1964, U.S. President Lyndon Johnson declared the "war on poverty." Mostly remembered as an effort to help African Americans living in urban areas, but it was also intended to assist the most impoverished and forgotten people in the United States: the people of the coal-mining towns of Appalachia. In fact, several of the most iconic photographs from the federal effort were of Johnson's visit to Appalachia, where as much as 60 percent of the population fell below the poverty line. Photographs of the president shaking hands with grimy, tattered locals made all of the national newspapers and television broadcasts.

Some residents of Appalachia complained that the publicity surrounding the program, and Johnson's visit, further stereotyped the population as poor, uneducated hillbillies in the minds of the media and their fellow citizens. However, it did bring some relief with federal programs like Medicaid, food stamps, and Head Start programs for children.

Activists pointed out that the people of Appalachia were poor because they'd been unfairly robbed of their natural resources from coal mining and timber harvesting without being adequately compensated. These activists found increasingly sympathetic ears with miners who did not believe that they were being well-represented by the UMWA with Lewis gone. This weakened the power of the union and increased calls among members for change.

It came to a head in 1964 when miner Steve "Cadillac" Kochis announced he was challenging Boyle for the presidency. Faced with the opposition to his authority, Boyle let it be known that he expected district officials and others who owed him for their jobs to campaign relentlessly for his reelection.

This loyalty test was particularly aimed at Yablonski. And Boyle was hedging his bets there. Out of the blue, he sent the District 5 president a check for $10,000 to be used for the campaign expenses.

Yablonski was suspicious of the sudden largesse from his rival. He made sure his campaign staffers were extra careful to record every transaction and make sure the funds were spent only on legitimate expenses.

In September 1964, the UMWA national convention in Bal Harbor, Florida, roiled with controversy. Only delegates who supported Boyle had their expenses paid for the eleven days; everyone else was on their own dime. Rumors swirled that Boyle spent tens of thousands on bands, food, and liquor for his supporters.

Derided in some quarters of coal country for his tastes in expensive suits and driving new Cadillacs, Boyle didn't settle for just rewarding his delegates, he did his best to intimidate dissenters. His supporters from District 19, which encompassed Kentucky and parts of Tennessee, ringed the convention hall wearing white helmets that proclaimed, "Loyal to Boyle." They were led by the district's notorious secretary-treasurer, Albert Pass. Nicknamed "Little Hitler," he was Boyle's right-hand man and enforcer.[18] He was rumored to have had union "enemies," including an uncooperative mine owner, assaulted and murdered, and was feared by members in and out of his district.

At one point during the convention, three of the white-helmeted District 19 "security team" beat a union officer from District 5 who protested the presence of a U.S. Steel company official who had come at Boyle's invitation. Yablonski demanded that Boyle call off the goon squads or he was going to pull the District 5 delegates

---

18   Ibid.

out of the convention. Such a move would have threatened the legitimacy of the convention, so Boyle acquiesced. But in his mind, it was more proof of Yablonski's lack of loyalty.

In the December 1964 elections, Boyle defeated Kochis by an overwhelming seventy-seven thousand votes. But instead of reveling in the victory, Boyle was incensed that the margin wasn't greater because Yablonski had refused to stuff the ballot boxes in District 5.

In 1965, Yablonski again broke ranks with Boyle. The General Assembly of Pennsylvania was in the process of amending the Commonwealth's 1939 Occupational Disease Act to establish a coal operator-financed fund to compensate anthracite (hard coal) mineworkers afflicted with black lung. It was a measure supported by Boyle as it would not have been as much of a financial burden on coal operators.

However, Yablonski successfully lobbied the legislators to broaden the legislation to include bituminous (soft coal) miners, who were far more numerous. When Gov. William Scranton signed the measure into law, Boyle was livid. Outwardly, he tried to claim credit for the expanded coverage, though he also praised those who'd opposed it. But privately, he vented that Yablonski had stabbed him in the back; retribution came swiftly.

In June 1966, Boyle accused Yablonski of financial improprieties during the 1964 campaign and launched an audit. Now it became clear what the purpose of the $10,000 check was for: he'd hoped that his rival had misused the funds and could be charged with maladministration and removed from his position. Yablonski feared that Boyle would place District 5 in receivership, declare it insolvent, and appoint all new officers.

Fortunately, Yablonski could account for every cent being spent on legitimate costs. But that didn't stop Boyle from continuing his threats to destroy Yablonski and end his UMWA tenure.

Yablonski could have fought the accusation of mismanagement, but he knew that Boyle would find another way to ruin his reputation and remove him. So he resigned as president. Boyle immediately replaced him with a loyalist as the president of District 5 though Yablonski kept his seat on the IEB.[19]

In spite of all of this, and for reasons that would remain unclear, by 1968 the two men had patched up their differences. At the April 1968 convention in West Virginia, Yablonski walked to the podium and spoke glowingly about Boyle, defending him from complaints by disgruntled miners that the president wasn't looking out for their interests.

"No other labor leader has done so much in so short a time," he told the assembled delegates as Boyle grinned and soaked in the praise.

Two days later, Boyle appointed Yablonski as the acting director of Labor's Non-Partisan League, the lobbying arm of the UMWA in Washington, D.C. It was a lucrative and powerful position within the union. Loyalty had its rewards.

Then in September 1968, at the union convention held in Denver, Colorado, Yablonski was even more effusive as he spoke in favor of a resolution asking Boyle to accept "lifetime tenure" as the union president, as well as a $50,000 raise.

"I lack the words which would enable me to describe the love, the devotion, and the respect I have for our distinguished president, W.A. 'Tony' Boyle," Yablonski gushed.

The resolution didn't pass, however. Not everyone was as thrilled with Boyle's leadership. One of the topics on the minds of rank-and-file miners at the convention was black lung disease. With a bank account worth $180 million, they wondered why more resources weren't being devoted to fighting the insidious disease, as well as making it compensable so that those afflicted and those who couldn't work could receive benefits to help them get by. However, Boyle had remained adamant that he was opposed to any black lung legislation so as not to ruffle the feathers of the mine owners and operators who would have to bear the financial brunt.

After the convention, some miners from West Virginia contacted Dr. Donald L. Rasmussen, a lung specialist who worked for

---

19   Auditors later found no mismanagement of District 5 finances during Yablonski's tenure.

Appalachian Regional Hospital in Beckley, as well as Drs. Isador Duff and Harley Wells, who specialized in treating black lung disease. The doctors encouraged the miners to form the Black Lung Association to lobby for legislation requiring compensation and medical benefits on a national scale.

Boyle did not take it well. He made sure that the West Virginia miners were told by their district officials that they might be expelled from the UMWA for "dual unionism." It took real courage for the miners to buck the union president. Not only might they be kicked out of the union, but they could also lose their jobs, as well as their pension and health benefits. It was a frightening prospect, but some took the risk anyway.

The issue did catch the attention of Congressman Ken Hechler of West Virginia who strongly criticized the UMWA for being MIA regarding legislation to deal with black lung. Hechler then introduced federal legislation called the Coal Mine Health and Safety Act that proposed to reduce the amount of coal dust permitted in mines, imposed more mine safety requirements, and guaranteed operator-funded compensation to mineworkers diagnosed with black lung.

Conscious of the cost of more safety measures and the compensation to mine owners, Boyle testified against the bill before Congress. He said that the bill was backed only by "self-proclaimed do-gooders," like Ralph Nader, as well as "outside agitators" and "overnight experts" who were misleading mineworkers and politicians.

Strangely silent through this was Yablonski. He'd fought to make black lung a compensatory illness for all coalminers in Pennsylvania, but now he didn't challenge Boyle or support the legislation.

However, a disaster loomed on the horizon after which his silence was no longer an option.

CHAPTER FOUR

"AN UNFORTUNATE ACCIDENT"

5:30 A.M.
NOVEMBER 20, 1968

Most of the six hundred people in the coal-mining town of Farmington, West Virginia were asleep when the dragon woke beneath the mountain. What began as a deep rumble below the surface quickly grew louder until the beast burst into the open with a roar, spouting flames and billowing clouds of thick, black smoke from mine entrances.

Word quickly spread as residents crawled out of bed or stopped their chores and went outside, their faces turned north. There'd been an immense explosion in Mountaineer Coal Company's No. 9 mine located two miles from town. The blast was so powerful that it launched the steel cage that took miners up and down the 576-foot-deep Llewelyn Run shaft through the roof of the portal housing building like a child's toy missile.

A motel clerk working twelve miles away in the burg of Fairmont later reported feeling the earth shake beneath her feet. Miners, knowing what the sound meant, grabbed their gear and headed for the mine to rescue their kinfolk and friends. This was not the first time the dragon had stirred, but it would be the worst.

Nestled in the central Appalachians just south of the border with Pennsylvania, Farmington got its name in the early 1800s from the obvious fact that most of the settlers were farmers. Self-sufficient. Healthy lifestyles. They grew crops and hunted and fished in what was a veritable Garden of Eden. It wasn't easy. The work was hard, the winters long. They fought with Indians, and when the Civil War broke out, the men marched away—not necessarily to the same side—and not all came back. But those who did return to the green valleys and wooded hills took up their old lifestyle again.

Everything changed, however, when a large seam of bituminous, or "soft," coal was discovered in the late 1800s. After that, everything from employment to the size of the population of the town was tied to coal.

The first U.S. Census to include Farmington in 1870 recorded 89 total residents. In 1909, the population jumped to more than 500 when Jamison Coal and Coke Company opened the Jamison No. 9 mine. The population continued to climb to 700 by 1920 and 819 by 1930. During that time, the mine produced more than 100,000 tons of coal every year—except in 1922 when production dipped with the economy and only 3,000 tons were extracted and at the beginning of the Great Depression in 1930 when the price of coal dropped and production was cut to just 4,000 tons.

The mine closed that year, throwing men out of work and families further into abject poverty. Nor did the mine reopen for three long years. Then, in spite of the still flagging economy, the mine opened again in 1934. The pay was low, especially after the UMWA took its cut, but it was better than nothing. A job of any sort in those days was good for a man's morale, and these in particular were a people who took pride in their mountaineer toughness and "earn my keep" work ethic.

The population peaked in 1940 at eight hundred and eighty and held steady through the war years with the mine producing more than a million tons of coal every year. But by 1950, both the number of residents and coal production had peaked and were on their way down. In 1954, the Pittsburgh Consolidation Coal Company, the parent company of Mountaineer Coal, purchased the mine from Jamison, and seven hundred people lived in and near the town.

When disaster struck twelve years later, the population was about six hundred—more than half of them employed at the mine. Most of everybody else in town was related to someone who worked there or owed their livelihood to miners' income. So when something bad happened at the mine, it effected the entire town.

The miners and their families knew the risks. But thanks in part to the union, their pay and benefits were better than at many other mines. An experienced mineworker at the No. 9 could make thirty-plus dollars a day, which were good wages in 1968. The days when most lived in clapboard houses with tar paper roofs were gone, giving way to modest brick homes that wouldn't have been out of place in any middle-class neighborhood. The danger, however, was so much greater than what most of middle America faced when going to work.

About half an hour after the initial blast, twenty-one men working the "cat-eye," midnight to eight, shift made it out of the eight-mile long mine just as another gigantic explosion tore through the tunnels, damaging the Mod's Run portal. They reported that the initial blast had raised so much coal dust that they couldn't see in front of their faces and had to find each other by calling out. But these twenty-eight men were the last to emerge; seventy-eight others were either already dead or trapped beneath the surface.

A pillar of fire rose from the Llewelyn shaft while smoke continued to pour from it and the Mod's Run shaft, which were nearly two miles apart. Seven highly trained mine rescue crews from other mines in the area had arrived by 9 a.m., but all they could do was wait and try to keep the Farmington miners' spirits up.

Fed by the same black rock the men risked their lives to get, the inferno burned so hot, coupled with ongoing explosions, that rescue attempts were out of the question. Everyone knew what fire meant in a mine. Fires create extreme heat and release deadly smoke and noxious fumes—particularly black damp, which is a mix of carbon dioxide and nitrogen that contains no oxygen, and white damp, which is carbon monoxide. But fires also need oxygen and in an enclosed area like the tunnels of a mine, they'll greedily suck it out of the air even at a distance. Plenty of miners have suffocated during underground fires without having felt heat, seen a flame, or been exposed to fumes.

With the flames and smoke pouring unabated out of No. 9, terrified family members, many of them women with frightened children in tow, wandered from place to place trying to get information. Others gathered at a church to pray and wait for news. Meanwhile, local mine officials were having difficulty determining who was working that shift because the records were kept in an office in the Llewelyn Run portal office, which had been destroyed by the blast and subsequent fire.

One thing was clear: this was a disaster for the entire town. Seventy-eight men was more than a tenth of the town's total population at the time and represented 44 percent of the mine's workforce. Most were breadwinners or contributed to their family's income as sons. If they didn't make it out alive, there were going to be a lot of mouths to feed and no money coming in to buy groceries. It was lost on no one that it was a month before Christmas and a long Appalachian winter loomed.

The Red Cross arrived and set up shop to distribute coffee and food. Ministers tended to those who needed their words of hope. Meanwhile, smaller explosions continued throughout the day. Each a cause for cries of anguish among those waiting.

Governor Hulett C. Smith showed up, as did executives from Consolidation Coal and ranking officials of the West Virginia Department of Mines, the U. S. Bureau of Mines, and the UMWA. The media swooped in with them—several of them were caught trying to sneak into the disaster area disguised as miners. They also started asking uncomfortable questions about how the disaster had happened and whether anyone was at fault.

James R. McCartney, the director of personnel and public relations for Consolidation Coal, set up press headquarters in a local store and presided at a series of briefings held throughout the day. One such briefing was attended by Governor Smith; John

Corcoran, the president of Consolidation Coal; Cecil J. Urbaniak, the president of UMWA District 31; Lewis Evans, safety director for the UMWA; and Elmer C. Workman, the director of the U. S. Bureau of Mines.

"I would like to explain that this is an accident," the governor told the assembled media, as the others looked on. "I have confidence that the mining industry is seeing the most improved safety measures are being taken. We have experienced tragedy here many times before. Mining is a hazardous profession."

Smith said he'd been in contact with former Texas governor Price Daniels, who President Lyndon Johnson had named director of the Office of Emergency Preparation. Daniels had offered his office's assistance. However, Smith said he told him they didn't need any additional help and that Consolidation Coal, as well as federal and state mines departments and the UMWA, were handling the disaster effectively.

"First, we are going to try to rescue the trapped men and then, if necessary, offer assistance to their families," Smith announced to the press. "The cooperation here has been wonderful, and we have received many offers of help from every part of the country."

However, in a later afternoon press conference, William Poundstone, Consolidation Coal's executive vice president for operations, said that although "the best and most skilled mine rescue teams in the business" were available, they were on standby. "Rescue operations are still impossible because of the intensity of the fire. We expect no further developments until the flames die down."

"Some changes in ventilation" had been made to "calm" the fire, Poundstone said. He didn't offer details, but miners and the waiting families knew what it meant. The company was sealing the return air shaft at Mod's Run where the huge fan had been blown out of the shaft by a second explosion fifteen minutes after the first. Sealing it would cut down on the oxygen available to the fire, but it would also deprive the trapped men.

Poundstone admitted that there had been no communications with the trapped miners and there was no way to know if any still survived. But, he said, the company had not given up hope—

that, perhaps, some of the men had enough warning to barricade themselves against the explosion and subsequent fire.

However, away from the official briefings, experienced miners told reporters that the explosions occurred in the area where the men were known to be working and it was unlikely that they would have had a chance to flee such a sudden and horrific blast. Even if they'd survived the explosion, they would have been contending with the tremendous heat, deadly fumes, and the oxygen-stealing flames.

The news didn't get any better as the day wore on. It wasn't until nearly 10 p.m. that a list of the entombed miners was made available by coal company officials. Other records had to be searched and then a personal check made on each miner carried on the rolls of the midnight shift. Nothing changed. Seventy-eight men were still missing.

A little later, another massive explosion ripped the seal from the Mod's Run ventilating shaft and sent it flying across a road as more smoke billowed out with renewed vigor. Over at the Llewelyn shaft, flames shot 150 feet into the air. The fire department from nearby Mannington was called in to wet down the cars left in the mine's parking lot. Covered with ash and debris, the vehicles were painful reminders that their owners had not returned for them, but the heat and smoke made it impossible to remove them.

Rescue planning went on throughout the night though everyone involved knew there'd be no attempt until the fire burning between the Llewellyn and Mod's portals could be brought under control. But it was apparent that wouldn't happen anytime soon. The world's largest coal furnace was burning so hot it could be felt on the surface through hundreds of feet of rock.

The media kept questioning what caused the explosion. During his press conference the previous afternoon, Poundstone said that answer wouldn't be known until the recovery work was completed and the mine had been inspected. But he noted that methane was probably involved and that the mine was "moderately gassy."

There are two main types of coalmine explosions: methane gas and coal dust. Methane is a byproduct of coal formation and is found in or around the coal. It's released as the coal is mined, or it migrates from sources above or below the coal seam through fractures created when coal is extracted. Methane explosions occur when a buildup of methane gas, sometimes due to a change in barometric pressure, contacts a heat source. Similarly, fine particles of coal dust, in the right concentration, in contact with a source of heat can also be explosive.

Hybrid explosions consisting of a combination of methane and coal dust also occur. Because methane is more easily ignited than coal dust, it will sometimes combust first, creating the scenario for an even larger coal dust explosion by blowing fine particles into the air and then igniting them. Once the dust is ignited, a chain reaction can occur, and the fire can spread over long distances in the mine and gobbles up fuel and oxygen.

Coal operations counter the danger of a methane explosion by using large ventilation fans to keep methane from building up to combustible levels. They also use water to cool mining equipment where it contacts the rock and might cause a spark.

Meanwhile, coal dust is mitigated by spreading limestone powder, known as rock dust, throughout the mine on a regular basis. The powder helps prevent the dust from lifting into the air, and if a methane explosion does occur, the rock dust absorbs heat and can stop the chain reaction of the coal dust igniting, too, or at least reduce the intensity of the explosion.

Both ventilation and rock-dusting require constant vigilance. The air has to be monitored frequently for methane. And even a thin layer of additional coal dust deposited on a previously rock-dusted area can restore the explosive conditions.

It was no secret that No. 9 had a lot of methane and could be dangerous. In 1909 when the mine first opened, a Jamison official noted that the "gasses are liberating" from the coal in the mine. As a result, mineworkers were required to use locked safety lamps so that no open flame came into contact with the gas.

Then on November 13, 1954, disaster struck for the first time when a Saturday maintenance crew of sixteen men was killed in a blast. James Hyslop, the vice president of Pittsburgh Consolidation Coal Company, which had recently acquired the corporate stock of Jamison, surmised that the blast was caused by the ignition of methane gas. But, he noted, the atmosphere in the mine had been tested and declared clear just thirty minutes before the blast.

"Something suddenly happened to release a considerable portion of methane," Hyslop told a local newspaper.

Cecil J. Urbaniak, the president of the local UMWA District 31, said he'd never expected to hear of an explosion at the No. 9. "They had the best housekeeping here of almost any mine I know of," he said, "and there is just no answer [to] how such a thing can happen when conditions were as favorable as they were here."

One of the last trips to coal country John L. Lewis made before his retirement in 1960 was to Farmington to commemorate the men killed in the 1954 explosion. He'd visited the town immediately after the explosion, and then again six years later when he lauded the steps taken by the coal company to improve safety.

After the 1954 disaster, the men returned to the mine—most because it was all they knew. They'd followed their fathers into the mine and expected their sons would follow them. There was a certain pride working one of the most dangerous jobs in the world, and some even enjoyed the work underground despite the dangers. Yes, if the mine didn't get them outright, many would die young of black lung. But the union, they were told, was looking out for them.

However, the No. 9 wasn't done killing. On April 30, 1965, four more men died in a shaft explosion when the Llewellyn portal was under construction, and on November 20, 1968, the dragon woke up.

At his press conference, Poundstone insisted that the No. 9 workings were heavily rock-dusted. He said that probably accounted for the "lack of fire and violence" at the front of the shaft from which the twenty-one men escaped.

Yet, another story was starting to emerge. Some of the men who'd escaped reported that there'd been a fire earlier that night and, while a crew had put it out, it was large enough that the mine should have been evacuated until it could be determined to be safe.

The miners who made it out claimed that there was something wrong with the ventilation system and crews had been working on it during their shift. Even more damning, they contended that contrary to Poundstone's assertion, the mine had not been properly rock-dusted.

What neither the miners who worked in the No. 9 nor the press knew was that the Mountaineer Coal Company had been cited by state and federal mine inspectors numerous times. Since 1963, Federal Bureau of Mine inspectors had visited No. 9 on sixteen occasions and every time had cited mine officials for ignoring rock-dusting regulations. In the two years prior to the explosion, inspectors had cited mine officials for twenty-five other safety violations. But nothing was done about it—not by the company, not by the government mine inspectors, and not by the union whose leadership should have insisted. Instead, every time the company was cited again for the same problem, they would claim "forgetfulness" and the problem would remain unresolved.

Boyle arrived in Farmington the day after the explosion. He called it "an unfortunate accident." Then, like his predecessor Lewis had on nearly the same spot, he went on to praise the company for its safety precautions and efforts to rescue the trapped miners. He then quickly left town and returned to Washington, D.C.

There would be no saving the seventy-eight miners inside the No. 9. For ten days, smoke continued to belch from the portals as fires burned and explosions rumbled underground. Two rescue teams tried to enter the mine but were ordered back out when they ran into high levels of methane gas.

In a meeting among government, company, and union officials, a decision was reached. There was no way the trapped miners could have survived the conditions in the mine, even if they'd lived through the initial explosions. The fires had to be extinguished and the only way to do that would be to seal the airways into the mine and cutoff the oxygen. There would be no more rescue attempts.

As the news was announced in Farmington, the wives, children, fathers, mothers, siblings, and friends were forced to accept the inevitable. They'd kept up their vigils at home and at the churches, comforting each other, praying for miracles, and telling each other to "not give up hope." They allowed their spirits to rise when rumors swept through town—like there'd been some communication from someone in the mine or that someone had emerged from the mine—only to sink further into misery when each rumor proved false.

Now, there would be no more rumors, no more hope. Some hung their heads and wept; others wailed in despair; and a few begged for just a little more time. A mine was no place to bury a man. But until the fires went out and recovery teams could enter the No. 9, it was to be a giant crypt for seventy-eight men. *An unfortunate accident.*

CHAPTER FIVE

A FAILED LEADERSHIP

MAY 29, 1969

Standing at the podium in front of an audience of coalminers and the media at the Mayflower Hotel in Washington, D.C, Jock Yablonski paused for a moment before taking an irrevocable step towards the tragic events that would transpire in seven months. But there was no turning back now.

Looking out from under his bushy eyebrows with his intense brown eyes, his stentorian voice boomed as he announced that he was challenging William "Tough Tony" Boyle for the UMWA presidency. "I have been part of a failed leadership."

Yablonski's sudden opposition to Boyle's authority caught many both in the union and without by surprise. Some would question what caused Yablonski to choose that moment and method to defy the union president.

Granted, Yablonski had at times bucked Boyle, including refusing to stuff ballot boxes, then there was the goon squad flap at the Bal Harbor convention and, most infuriating to the union president, Yablonski's support for the Pennsylvania black lung legislation. But Yablonski had always found his way back into the union president's good graces. Just in the past year he had twice been more than a little ebullient praising Boyle, "*I lack the words to describe the love, devotion and respect I have for our distinguished president...*"

Some speculated that Yablonski hoped to be named by Boyle as his successor when the latter retired. But then he'd finally realized that in spite of his kowtowing, his rival did not trust him and would never pass the mantle on to him willingly.

Some would later argue that Yablonski had looked the other way when it came to Boyle because of his love for the UMWA, which was like a religion to him. He'd joined the union after his father was killed. He'd been on the front lines facing off against the hired gun thugs and police working for the owners during the coal wars, and he'd been Lewis's front man in the coal fields due to his oratory skills. For twenty-six years, he'd been part of the union hierarchy, a member of the governing council of the IEB, the director of the union's political Non-Partisan League, and the president of District 5.

As an admirer of the autocratic Lewis, Yablonski believed that a challenge to the leadership was a challenge to the union as a whole. Left unchecked, its enemies could then come in and destroy it, then everything he'd worked for would be for nothing. The industry was already fighting a battle with the gas and oil companies; if it lost, the men he'd known and worked with all of his life would be thrown out of work, their families put out on the streets. An entire culture and way of life that had been in existence for a hundred years was threatened. Where would they go? How would they survive?

Still, he was troubled that the union had often failed to protect its members. Lewis had resisted efforts to deal with black lung disease and Boyle had been no better. Both presidents had too often come down on the side of the owners on other safety issues as well, often looking the other way when operators ignored, or conveniently forgot, citations from federal mine-inspectors.

Was it the Farmington mine disaster that was the straw that broke the camel's back for Yablonski? His own father had died in a mine accident, and Boyle's Farmington response had been to praise the efforts of the operators despite the numerous coal dust violations.

The union president had even refused to meet with the widows of the disaster. "What should I say to them?" he asked his aides.[20]

Perhaps, Yablonski could no longer tolerate his own complicity in the union's questionable practices. Or maybe he just noted the growing dissension with Boyle's rule among the rank-and-file and thought that there was never going to be a better time to challenge him for the presidency.

In early 1969, mine safety legislation was being pressed on national and state levels, including by a group of women recently widowed by the Farmington disaster who appeared before Congress in support of Hechler's bill. But not everyone was supportive. Union vice president George Titler, who'd been selected by Boyle over the more popular Yablonski in 1963, scolded the congressman.

"You remind me of the newborn calf who follows the father rather than his mother and doesn't realize the mistake until feeding time. Stop playing dog in the manger," he sneered at one hearing.

At the same time, an article in the *UMW Journal* quoted Boyle as saying the Black Lung Association members were "arrogant troublemakers" and "agent provocateurs." The union was doing its job, according to the article, "and only finks say otherwise."

However, the Black Lung Association was gaining strength in West Virginia, including with a bill in the state legislature making miners with the disease eligible for compensation. When the UMWA again threatened expulsion, forty-two thousand out of forty-four thousand active miners went on strike.

Boyle labeled the strikers as "black tongued loudmouths" and ordered them to get back to work. But they ignored him and instead, on February 25, 1969, they marched on Charleston in support of the legislation and held a rally at the civic center. Among those from outside the union who attended in January 1969 was Representative Ken Hechler.

The West Virginia congressman criticized Boyle as being "insensitive and inactive" when it came to the health and safety of mine

---

20   Trevor Armbrister, *Act of Vengeance: The Ablonski Murders and Their Solution*
      (New York: Saturday Review Press, 1975).

conditions. He noted that Boyle had a "mine safety division" that consisted of only one full-time employee.

Speaking to the miners present, Hechler waved a twelve-pound bologna sausage in the air. "This," he said, "is the answer to the UMWA's attitude towards coal mine health and safety."

In the wake of the Farmington disaster, his words appealed to the men who'd been dismayed by Boyle's opposition to Hechler's legislation.

In February, Hechler, joined by Pennsylvania Representatives Daniel Flood and John Dent, drafted a new version of his legislation to increase its chances of passage. The proposed law was intended to reduce the amount of coal dust permitted in mines, which had led to the Farmington disaster, as well as several other mine safety regulations. But its main thrust was to guarantee owner-provided compensation for black lung disease.

Boyle saw the legislation as a personal criticism of his leadership regarding mine safety issues. He testified before Congress that the bill was supported only by "self-proclaimed do-gooders" like activist Ralph Nader and that "outside agitators and overnight experts" were misleading mineworkers and politicians."

The union president's distaste for Nader had been growing ever since the latter had started openly criticizing the UMWA for not complying with the 1959 Landrum-Griffin Act that required unions to permit districts to elect their own officers, instead of the union president appointing them.

Boyle was not about to let go of his grip on the throne. Nothing, but nothing, happened in the union without his permission and that was accomplished by having his own people in the important positions.

Until Yablonski declared his candidacy Boyle faced little opposition. The federal government wasn't willing to intercede. After the passage of the Landrum-Griffin Act, the U.S. Department of Labor under Secretary George Shultz had sought "voluntary compliance." When compliance was not forthcoming, the department had then waited five years before filing suit. Another four years passed without any movement regarding the lawsuit on the part of federal prosecutors. Nobody wanted to mess with "Tough Tony" Boyle.

Except Nader. Known for his activism in consumer protection, environmentalism and government reform, he was also looking into the activities of the National Bank of Washington, where Boyle sat on the board of directors. He was particularly interested in the large cash reserves being kept in the non-interest-bearing accounts.

On March 8, 1969, the West Virginia legislature passed its bill. No sooner was passage announced than the UMWA flip-flopped and tried to take credit for the new law. The *UMW Journal* even lauded Boyle for supporting the bill, while at the same time praising the two legislators who voted against it.

However, Boyle made no real attempt to separate himself or the union from the interests of the mine owners. On March 11, he was reelected to a third term as chairman of the National Coal Policy Conference, a joint coal industry labor lobby. Testifying before the Senate Labor Subcommittee, he stated, "The UMWA will not abridge the rights of the miner operators in running the mines. We follow the judgment of the coal operators, right or wrong."

The back and forth continued through March and April. On April 7, Hechler called for a congressional examination of the UMWA funds at the National Bank.

Nader followed that up on April 26, by writing a letter to Senator Ralph Yarborough who was chairman of the Committee on Labor and Public Welfare. "The UMWA is the control center of an authoritarian private government that affects the livelihood, safety and welfare of thousands of miners and their families," the activist wrote. He went on to allege that the UMWA had "milked the Welfare & Retirement Fund in order to expand the operations and profits of the National Bank of Washington" of which the union owned 52 percent of the stock.[21]

The leadership was corrupt, Nader said, and engaged in nepotism "of the most pristine variety." Among the abuses the activist listed were examples of nepotism including Boyle's daughter, Antoinette,

---

21   Ibid.

who was paid $43,000 annually as the union lawyer, and his brother, Richard, who he'd appointed president of District 27 at a salary of $36,000 a year.

Also, Nader noted, Richard Boyle had been paid $17,000 in 1967 for "organizing expenses." But in the union's annual financial statement, which it was required to file under the Landrum-Griffin Act, District 27 had listed no organizers or salaried employees.

During this time, Jock Yablonski had remained on the sidelines. But unknown to Boyle, Yablonski was being courted by Nader to run for the union presidency with an election slated for December 9 of that year.

On May 9, Yablonski met at his nephew's law office in Washington, D.C. where Nader first broached the subject. But he left the meeting without committing.

On May 17, they met again. This time, Yablonski's son, Chip, was present. Still, Yablonski was undecided. He knew that running against Boyle would be the end of his days in the union if he lost. But he was also worried that his adversary would react with violence and harm his family.

After yet another indecisive meeting with Yablonski on May 22, Nader wrote a letter to Lewis. Although the legendary labor leader was eighty-nine-years old and not in the best of health, he was still chairman of the powerful three-member Welfare and Retirement Fund board and held considerable sway among the rank-and-file.

Noting the corruption of Boyle, Nader asked Lewis for his support in ousting the union president in the December 9 election. He suggested that he throw his weight behind Yablonski. But Lewis didn't respond.

On May 24, a Saturday morning, the men met again at the law office. Yablonski was still worried that his life, and possibly that of his family, would be in danger the moment he announced his candidacy. Why risk it? He had a good life with a devoted wife who had her own successful writing career. His two sons were both attorneys; Chip practiced in Washington, D.C. and Kenneth had hung his shingle in the city of Washington near Clarksville.

Charlotte was doing well, too, She'd received her master's degree in sociology in 1967 from West Virginia University and started working at Mercy Hospital in Pittsburgh. There she worked with alcoholics, drug addicts, and people at risk of committing suicide.

Yablonski could have walked away from Nader's entreaties, toed the line with Boyle, and lived out his life comfortably. But instead, he talked it over with Margaret and decided the time had come to act. "I'm going to do it!" he announced to everyone in the room.

With that settled, Nader and Yablonski got down to business. Boyle was going to go ballistic when he heard, and they had to be prepared. Yablonski warned his sons and inner circle of supporters that Boyle was ruthless and would not take this betrayal well. He told them that if there was violence, it would originate with Boyle but be carried out by District 19 in Middlesboro, Kentucky and led by its ruthless secretary-treasurer, Albert Pass.[22]

Four days after Yablonski agreed to run for the UMWA presidency, Nader brought on well renowned labor lawyer Joseph Rauh. Highly skilled and fearless, Rauh had established his legal chops clerking for U.S. Supreme Court justices Benjamin Cardozo and Felix Frankfurter. He'd also served on the staff of General Douglas MacArthur during World II. Since then, he'd made a name for himself as a labor activist and general counsel to the United Auto Workers.

The next day, Yablonski held his press conference in the Mayflower Hotel. After admitting that he'd been part of the "failed leadership" of the union, he promised reform and to fight for member issues, including black lung, better wages, improved mine health and safety conditions, and increased retiree benefits.

When a member of the press asked why he was now challenging Boyle after remaining silent for so long, Yablonski replied by quoting the seventeenth-century poet George Herbert, "When ye be an anvil, hold ye still. When ye be a hammer, strike with all your fill."

---

22   Ibid.

CHAPTER SIX

A PLOT IS HATCHED

On June 11, 1969, labor giant John L. Lewis died at age eighty-nine. After passing the torch to Kennedy, he'd retired to his family home in Alexandria, Virginia. In 1964, he'd been awarded the Presidential Medal of Freedom by President Lyndon B. Johnson.

While he had many admirers and was a hero of godlike stature to many UMWA mineworkers, Lewis also had made a lot of enemies. However, after his passing even many of them praised him. "He was my personal friend," wrote Reuben Soderstrom, the president of the Illinois AFL-CIO who had once labeled Lewis as an "imaginative windbag."

Lewis, said Soderstrom, would be remembered for "making almost a half million poorly paid and poorly protected coalminers the best paid and best protected miners in all of the world."[23]

Whatever his public legacy, Lewis did worry about one thing he'd done. Shortly before his death, he confided that paving the way for Boyle's appointment to the union's top post was among the worst decisions he'd made.[24] Still, he'd never responded to Nader's request to back Yablonski's candidacy.

Boyle made sure to use Lewis's death for political purposes. In a special tribute issue, the *United Mine Workers Journal* made much

---

23   Carl W. Soderstrom, Robert W. Soderstrom, Chris M. Stevens, Andrew W. Burt, *Forty Gavels: The Life of Reuben Soderstrom and the Illinois AFL-CIO* (Illinois: CWS Publishing, 2018).

24   Kenneth Wolensky, "Living for Reform."

of Boyle being the old man's hand picked protégé. There were also more photos of Boyle in the "memorial edition" as there were of the late union boss, including one of him on his knees praying at Lewis's grave.

As expected, Tony Boyle had been outraged by Yablonski's "betrayal." But not just because losing the presidency would end his authoritarian rule and all the perks that came with it for him and his cronies.

Supplied with the inside information by Yablonski about some of the union's dirty secrets, Rauh filed five lawsuits against the UMWA alleging corrupt election practices and misappropriation of union funds, some in violation of federal criminal statutes. Boyle was afraid of his legal jeopardy and that a court would agree with Nader and Rauh and order an audit of the National Bank in Washington, D.C.

Boyle retaliated. On June 23, less than two weeks after Lewis died, the IEB met to replace the old man on the three-member Welfare and Retirement Fund board. But Boyle was the only candidate and the IEB rubber-stamped his appointment. He was consolidating his power, in control of the union's vast wealth, and making sure that anything and everything to do with the union passed by him first.

Getting on the Welfare and Retirement Fund Board wasn't Boyle's only goal at the IEB meeting. At his direction, IEB board officers created a commission to oppose Yablonski's presidency. He also proposed a resolution to fire his rival from his position as Director of the Non-Partisan League because "he opposes union policies" and wanted to kick pensioners out of the union.

Yablonski was the only member to oppose the resolution, saying it was only due to his candidacy. He and Boyle exchanged angry accusations back and forth. That was followed by three other IEB members accusing Yablonski of treason.

Scowling menacingly, Albert Pass rose to his feet and, glaring at Yablonski, roared, "Anybody that gets in the kick that they are going to destroy my dad's pension has got something else to think about!

"We have got a great union and we are going to keep our union. President Boyle we are not going to leave you and the other officers sitting out in that field and these damned fellows behind the bushes shooting at you by yourself. By God, we will run them out from behind those bushes, we are going to back you!"

Boyle's resolution was quickly passed and Yablonski was removed from the Non-Partisan League. The commission then directed that a petition demanding Yablonski's recall in his home district be initiated. They also said they planned to audit his expenses for fraud and theft.

Even with that victory, Boyle wasn't done with his intentions to destroy his rival. Early in the afternoon of June 23, he met up with William Turnblazer, the president of District 19, and Albert Pass in the hallway outside the meeting room. Ardent Boyle loyalists, they were talking about the events of the day when the union president stalked up to them.

The little man was boiling over. "We are in a fight," he snarled. Yablonski, he said, needed to be "done away with."

Ever the good soldier, Pass immediately responded that "if no one else will do it, District 19 will get it done."

After Boyle stomped off, Turnblazer looked at Pass. "He wants us to have him killed!"

Pass scowled. "Nah," he said, shaking his head, "I don't think so. I think he just wants him out of the race."

Turnblazer disagreed and said he believed that their leader had just stated that he wanted his rival dead. But for the time being, the men dropped the subject.

In the meantime, Boyle had another trick up his sleeve. He cornered Welfare and Retirement Fund trustee George Judy, who represented mine operators, and told him he wanted to raise the monthly allotment for each of the UMWA's forty thousand voting pensioners by $35—from $115 to $150. "That will get me votes," he said.

Judy pointed out that such a move had to be approved by all three fund board members, but the third, Josephine Roche, who was the neutral board member, was in the hospital. No problem, Boyle said, he'd spoken to Roche, and she'd given him her proxy. They could move forward with the raise.

It was a lie. Boyle never talked to Roche. But Judy believed him and voted for the increase.

Following the IEB meeting, Rauh countered Boyle's resolution to remove Yablonski from the Non-Partisan League. He filed a motion in federal district court arguing that the removal was an illegal reprisal for running against Boyle. He demanded that Jock be reinstated. The judge took it under advisement.

Stewing over Rauh's motion, Boyle wasn't content trying to buy the loyalty of miners and pensioners with the increase to the monthly pensions. He turned to violence and intimidation.

On June 27, Yablonski flew to Springfield, Illinois to speak at a meeting set up for him at the statehouse by George Morrison, a miner from Benton, Illinois. Nearly ten thousand miners worked the coal fields of southern Illinois, and it seemed a likely spot to campaign.

However, local union leaders loyal to Boyle put out the word that attendance would be greatly frowned upon. Only fifteen miners attended.

Yablonski spoke anyway. But as he was leaving the room, he felt a tug on his sleeve and then a massive blow to the back of his neck. He crumpled to the ground unconscious and remained that way for several minutes. When he did wake up, he'd lost all sensation in his hands.

Feeling gradually returned to his hands. But X-rays revealed that the blow, described by some who witnessed the attack as a "karate chop," nearly killed him. He'd been "lucky" enough to have gotten off with injuries to his third and fourth cervical vertebrae.

Apparently, no one was able to identify the attackers!

After the attack, Rauh demanded a meeting with the Secretary of the U.S. Department of Labor, George Shultz. He'd hoped that the lawsuits he'd filed in June would spur the Labor Department and the U.S. Department of Justice, headed by Attorney General John Mitchell, to investigate Boyle and the union. But there'd been no movement; they made excuses, and it was evident that they just didn't want to get involved.

Now Rauh beseeched Shultz to get involved before someone was killed. "This is going to be on your conscience, not on mine," he warned Shultz. "If you don't investigate this union now, there will be violence and more violence."[25]

Shultz's response was that whatever was going on was an internal matter in the union. The federal government, through his office, was not going to act prior to the union election.

With Yablonski back on his feet, Boyle suffered a setback when on July 15, Federal District Judge Howard Corcoran agreed with Rauh and ruled that Boyle's dismissal of Yablonski as director of the Non-Partisan League was an "illegal reprisal" in violation of the Landrum-Griffin Act. He ordered Boyle to reinstate Yablonski.

Once again, Boyle was incensed. It was a blow to his absolute authority to be told what he could and could not do regarding his union. Also, it gave Yablonski a position with the national union and an office at the headquarters in Washington, D.C. Boyle ignored the reinstatement order and tried a different tact to get Yablonski out of the race. To get on the ballot, it took fifty nominations from locals, so he pressured district officers to make sure the union locals didn't nominate Yablonski.

However, Yablonski's home district, which was loyal to him, had more than fifty locals. He easily received enough nominations.

Boyle went through the roof. Nothing was working — not the physical assault, and not the shenanigans. Shortly after Judge Corcoran's reinstatement order, Boyle called Pass and insisted that he come to his office in Washington, D.C.

Behind closed doors, the union president was fit to be tied. "That god-damned Yablonski," he shouted at his loyal henchman. "That damned dumb Polack son of a bitch, he's not satisfied with what I've done for him."

Even as he raged, however, Boyle knew that he needed to persuade Pass on the necessity of what he was going to ask. And the best way to do that was to appeal to the man's absolute loyalty to

---

25   Arthur H. Lewis, *Murder by Contract: The People V. 'Tough Tony'*
     Boyle (New York: MacMillan Publishers, 1975).

the union by invoking the bogeyman of the oil companies. He intimated that Yablonski was in bed with them.

"The oil companies are trying to take control of the union," he told Pass, "and if Yablonski is elected president of this union, it will be destroyed."

Boyle said that the oil companies would use Yablonski to show that money was illegally spent by the union into Labor's Non-Partisan League during the 1968 U.S. elections to support Hubert Humphrey's presidential bid, as well as other senators and congressmen known to be friends of the union. With Yablonski feeding inside information to the oil companies, "we would all go to jail."

Letting that sink in for a moment, Boyle looked hard at Pass. "He is going to have to be taken care of."

This time there was no mistaking what Boyle meant. "You mean you want Yablonski killed?" the enforcer asked to be sure.

"That's exactly what I mean."

Pass thought about it. He'd known Yablonski since 1942 and had no personal animosity towards him. But he was fanatically loyal to Boyle and if the union's president said that Yablonski was going to collude with the oil companies to destroy the union, then he needed to be stopped. Permanently. But how?

"I don't know anyone I could get to kill Yablonski," Pass advised.

"What about Bill Prater?" Boyle shot back.

Pass thought about it. Prater, a fifty-year-old field representative and fervent union organizer who lived in LaFollette, Tennessee, had already engaged in violence against those who allegedly opposed the union.

"It's going to take money to get this done," Pass noted.

Boyle said he'd get the money and put it into a District 19 relief fund. "But be sure you tell Prater that I don't know anything about a plan to kill Yablonski," he warned Pass.

After meeting with Boyle, Pass returned to Tennessee where he called Turnblazer. "You were right. Tony wants Yablonski killed," he said, "and he expects District 19 to get it done."

CHAPTER SEVEN

BLOOD MONEY

On July 18, Boyle flew into the Knoxville, Tennessee airport to meet with Pass. He asked "Little Hitler" about the status of the murder plot. Pass assured him that he'd talked to William Prater who was working on finding the men who would do the job. Boyle told him to hurry up and ended the conversation.

A few days later, Prater told Pass that he'd been arranging for the killers through long-time union enforcer Silous Huddleston, who thanks to Tony Boyle had been appointed president of Local 3228 in LaFollette, Tennessee, which was part of District 19. Although now afflicted with black lung, Huddleston had gone into the mines as a boy and was a fervent union man.

In defense of Union activity and aggressive against those who were antagonistic to it, he was suspected of all sorts of violence and mayhem. He'd been arrested only once, which was more of a nod to the influence of the union and its ability to intimidate witnesses and victims than his innocence. In 1946, he'd been convicted of grand larceny in Tennessee and was sentenced to three years in the penitentiary.

To justify the murder, Prater told Huddleston that Yablonski needed to die because he was in league with Consolidated Oil Company. The company was anti-union and intent on replacing coal with oil and gas in the homes and factories and railways of the United States. It was all the old miner needed to hear.

Pass let Boyle know about Huddleston. But he kept it to himself that a growing number of people had been told that the union president was behind the plot. Turnblazer was the only one who was supposed to know, but Prater had figured it out, and it had to be assumed that Huddleston did too.

Towards the end of September 1969, Boyle again ordered Pass to come see him in Washington, D.C. This time it was to lay out the plan he'd come up with to get the blood money for the killers that at the same time would be untraceable to Boyle.

First, Pass, Turnblazer, and Prater were to ask trusted field representatives to select twenty-three retired coalminers who were loyal to the union—and especially to Boyle—and would do as told, as well as keep their mouths shut. These twenty-three pensioners would comprise the "Research and Information Committee," or R&I, whose alleged purpose was to recruit non-union miners working for independent mines in District 19 territory.

Boyle directed Pass to write a direct request to him for $20,000 from the UMWA account at the National Bank. Ostensibly, the money would be used to pay "expenses" that the twenty-three R&I members allegedly incurred during their recruitment efforts. But in reality, they would be given checks, which they were to cash and then return the money to Pass through Prater. The money would then be used to pay the killers.

The field representatives and pensioners were not to know the real purpose of the money. They would be told that it was going to be funneled to help the political campaigns of politicians who were considered friends of the union. It was illegal to use union funds that way too, but the field representatives and pensioners wouldn't care about something that would support the union.

The request for the money was to come from Pass in two separate letters, Boyle told him, each asking for $10,000. Pass was to explain in his letters that District 19 had fallen behind in paying these expenses and needed help from the national office.

Returning home to Tennessee, Pass directed Edith Roark, an over twenty-year veteran secretary and bookkeeper for District 19, to write up the letters—the first dated September 24 and the second dated September 30. Writing the letters directly to Boyle was odd to Roark. In the past, any such request was always sent to John Owens, the secretary-treasurer of the UMWA, and never to Boyle. But she did as she was told.

When Boyle received the letters, he directed his office assistant Suzanne Richards, an attorney who began working for the union as an assistant to John Owens in 1947, to draft memos to her former boss requesting the money be transferred to the District 19 bank in Middlesboro, Kentucky as soon as possible. She, too, thought it odd that the request for the funds had gone to Boyle, but like Roark, she completed the task.

When Pass explained the plan to Turnblazer, the district president and a lawyer, Turnblazer told him he didn't like the idea. "It will stand out like a sore thumb," he warned. "There's no way to cover up this type of embezzlement."

Pass, however, insisted that the plan was set in stone. It was then that Turnblazer realized that it was Boyle's idea and therefore would be carried out, like it or not.

The field representatives were called to attend a meeting at the District 19 headquarters in Middlesboro. Pass had contacted some of them; Turnblazer got in touch with the others.

Pass did most of the talking at the meeting. The field representatives were told that some money had been given to the district from the national office to be used for political activities in Bell and Harlan Counties, Kentucky. Some of the money, he said, might be used for the reelection campaign of Tony Boyle.

The field representatives were asked to supply a list of retired union men they knew and trusted. These men would be issued checks that were to be cashed. Then, they would hand the cash over to their field representatives who would give it to Prater and Pass. "They're to tell no one that they gave us back the money," he warned.

The field representatives got their list of names back to Pass a few days later. He then instructed Roark to issue the first of twenty-three checks payable to the men suggested by the field representatives. The checks were then given to the pensioners.

About a week later, twenty-three more checks were issued to the same men; the total amount of the forty-six checks was about $20,000. Not long after that, Pass told Turnblazer that he'd received all of the money back.

The pensioners were honest, God-fearing, family men who'd worked in the mines since childhood, married the daughters of mining families, and raised sons who followed them into the mines. So, why'd they do it?

They were tough, hard men—many of them suffering from black lung disease, or other mining ailments—and they were old enough to remember that all that stood between coalminers and the "gun thugs," corrupt cops, politicians, and mine owners was the union. Their loyalty to the UMWA and its leaders was absolute.

They were also aware that their pensions and medical care depended on their good standing. Without it, they would be destitute, desperately ill, and alone in the world.

At first, Pass didn't tell Turnblazer how Yablonski was to be killed, only that "I'll handle it." The district president did note that Pass was spending a lot of time in closed-door meetings at the district office with William Prater. However, sometime that fall, Pass told him that he was talking to Prater and Silous Huddleston about arranging the murder. But he didn't say who would do it or how much money would be spent to have it done.

Apparently, Turnblazer's misgivings about how the blood money was obtained got back to Boyle, who decided to remind him of what was at stake. Boyle and UMWA vice president George Titler flew into Middlesboro, Kentucky, ostensibly for a local union meeting. But first Pass was told to bring them to Turnblazer's home.

The president of District 19 and his wife were in their driveway when the union officials drove up. They all exchanged pleasantries until Turnblazer's wife excused herself to go back into the house. The conversation then turned to the murder plot with a common-sense warning.

"You got a real nice place here," Boyle noted. "You don't want to let Jock Yablonski take it away from you."

The threat was clear to Turnblazer. But it wasn't Yablonski he had to fear.

CHAPTER EIGHT

A PHOTO IN THE MAIL

Even as the blood money scheme was hatched, Silous Huddleston was arranging for the killers. The odd thing was that after all the efforts to keep the murder plot a secret among staunch union men and Boyle loyalists, he inexplicably took a different tact to find someone willing to murder for money.

Huddleston went to see his daughter, Annette Gilly, who lived in Cleveland with her husband, Paul. The old man took a Greyhound bus so that no one would see his car and there would be no record of his visit. He asked his daughter if she could find someone.

Tall, pretty, and with a reputation for liking to have a "good time," Annette was, in the parlance of the era, a "tough cookie." She'd had a rough start to life growing up in Oneida, a poverty-stricken coal town in the backwoods of Kentucky. Her mother died young and her father, Silous, walked out and left her with an aunt to be raised in poverty. She was just fourteen years old when she got pregnant and ran away to get married.

Divorcing that husband, Annette moved to the "big city" of Cleveland to get away from the squalor and dead-end dirt roads of her youth. There she met and, after a whirlwind romance, married Paul Gilly, a thirty-six-year-old housepainter with a third-grade education who also owned a restaurant called The Cozy Corner, a dump known as a place burglars hung out to fence their ill-gotten loot.

Annette took her father's question seriously. She knew his violent reputation as an enforcer for the union and that he had no qualms about arranging for murder. She'd found a letter that summer from a cousin, Harvey Huddleston—who lived in Zanesville, Ohio—to Silous. Her dad had apparently asked Harvey to kill someone, but her cousin said he couldn't do it.

Later, when she questioned her dad about the letter, he told her that he'd also asked his step-grandson, Roy Rogers of Columbus, to murder a man in Tennessee. But he refused because if he got caught "it would kill my mother."

Then, in July 1968, he told her, he'd offered $10,000 to Robert G. Tanner "to kill somebody." Tanner might have taken the job, but he was shot by a suburban housewife who caught him burglarizing her home in Cleveland.

Apparently, he was now out of options for contract killers. Because he asked Annette to find someone and sensing a payday, she suggested that she ask her husband.

In addition to house-painting, Paul Gilly was also a small-time criminal who pulled off the occasional burglary, sometimes with Annette waiting in the car. But he mostly bought and sold items his friends stole, especially guns, running this business out of the basement of his restaurant.

Annette knew she could persuade her husband to do it. They'd married three months after they met, but the relationship was on the rocks. She often went out alone to bars, and he was convinced that she was sleeping around, but he also was desperate not to lose her. She played on that when she asked him to "do a favor" for her father.

As she expected, Paul agreed to talk to Huddleston. Over the next few days, the two men spoke privately several times. When his father-in-law left after a week, Paul confided to his wife that Huddleston wanted a "small-time" UMWA official named Joseph Yablonski killed. He was paying $5,000 for the hit. Paul said he'd agreed to do it and get a couple of his criminal friends to help.[26]

---

26   From the affidavit of Annette Gilly given to FBI Agent William Curtis.

Gilly started by telling Claude Vealey, an oafish-looking thug with a perpetual five-o'clock shadow, that he'd been offered a $4,200 contract to kill a small-time union official "who got out of line."

"Some guy named Tony has a grudge against him," he said. He asked Vealey if he wanted to participate for a cut of the money.

Twenty-six-years old and not the brightest bulb in the room, Vealey had dropped out of school after the ninth grade. He enlisted in the Navy when he was seventeen and got out two years later. He almost immediately started a new career as a burglar working with his friends James "Charles" Phillips and, more recently, twenty-three-year-old Aubran Wayne "Buddy" Martin.

Gilly didn't know Martin well, but he told Vealey to recruit Phillips, a barrel-chested twenty-one-year-old thug with multiple convictions for burglary. Vealey asked Phillips if he wanted to help kill a man. "It's easy money," he promised, and Phillips was sold.

With his team assembled, Gilly told his father-in-law that they were ready to spring into action. Huddleston then contacted Prater, who told Pass.

When Pass asked Prater about the identities of the hitmen, his friend said he couldn't tell him because that was part of the agreement for them to do the job. "But they're professionals," Prater assured him.

Nothing important happened in the UMWA without Boyle's blessing, so Pass made sure he told the union boss that the killers were onboard and ready to proceed.

However, the whole scheme started with a change of plans. Instead of Yablonski, Gilly was suddenly informed that there was a new target, Ted Wilson, an attorney for the rival Southern Labor Union. Wilson lived in Winfield, Tennessee, where they were to kill him in his home and take whatever was of value—rumored to be a rare stamp collection, guns, and cash—to make it look like a burglary gone awry.

Yet, before they could kill Wilson, Gilly was told by Huddleston that their mission had switched back again to Yablonski. Gilly, Vealey, and Buddy Martin—a baby-faced, diminutive, tough-talking newcomer to the group—decided to go through with the burglary part anyway.

Martin was a different level of criminal than the others. Gilly didn't have a record, and Vealey and Phillips had nothing more than burglaries on theirs. But in addition to burglary, Martin had a rap sheet that included resisting arrest, assault, and obstructing a police officer.

The burglary of Ted Wilson's house was a flop. They didn't find a rare stamp collection or even much cash, and only came away from it with a few rifles and handguns.

With the plot to kill Yablonski back on track, Gilly decided he wanted to meet someone higher up in the UMWA than Huddleston and Prater. So, it was arranged for him to meet Pass, who was introduced to him as the secretary-treasurer of District 19 and the right-hand man of union president Tony Boyle.

Annette Gilly had asked her father and husband if she could go to the meeting with Pass. But they told her no. "He doesn't trust women to keep a secret," her father said.

At the meeting, Gilly was told that the contract to kill Yablonski had been doubled to $10,000. When he got back to Cleveland, he didn't tell his accomplices about the increase but did assure them that the hit was condoned at the highest levels of the UMWA.

On that note, Gilly and the others spent the middle part of October just trying to catch up to their target. But Yablonski was busy campaigning for the presidency throughout coal country in the east and Midwest, and while they put a lot of miles on the Caprice, the trio couldn't seem to cross his path.

After one of their disappointing forays, Gilly told Huddleston and Prater that his guys were losing their motivation. He wondered if they could show him a little of the money that he could tell the others about as a carrot to dangle in front of them.

Prater said that he wasn't authorized to do so. "Pass is the boss over that," he explained. "The money's at his house." He passed on the request to Pass who said he'd get back to him.

A few days later, Huddleston called Annette and told her that he needed to see Paul in La Follette right away even though it would be late at night before they could get there driving. "It's very important," the old man said. "Call me when you get here."

When the couple reached LaFollette, they called Silous who told them to drive past the house, turn around, and park by the front walk with the lights off. No sooner had the car stopped then Huddleston left his house and got in the front seat of their car on the passenger side.

"Let's go," he growled. He explained that his wife's family was visiting, and he didn't want them to know about the meeting.

They drove for several hours before stopping at a restaurant in Kentucky for breakfast. There he finally told them the purpose of the meeting. "I got five thousand dollars in my pocket," he said.

Returning to the car, Huddleston handed them an envelope which contained the cash in a variety of denominations from hundreds to fives.

"Where'd you get the money?" Annette asked.

"Two dollars here and two dollars there," he said with a shrug. "All from a collection taken up in District 19. The bills have been wiped clean of fingerprints."[27]

Huddleston didn't say what the money was for; he didn't have to. They knew. All three returned to the Gillys' home in Cleveland where Paul put the money in a safe. The old man then stayed with them for a few days before his son-in-law drove him back to Tennessee.

So far, the assassination team had accomplished little. Then another wrench got thrown into the works when Vealey and Phillips were both arrested for burglary in Youngstown, Ohio.

Paul and Annette drove to Youngstown where they posted a $750 bond for Vealey, while Phillips took care of his own.

While all of this was happening, a letter arrived in the mail for Paul Gilly. The envelope contained a page from the *UMW Journal* depicting a photograph of three men standing together and smiling for the camera. Someone had drawn an arrow on the photograph pointing to Joseph Yablonski.

27   Ibid.

Gilly didn't know it, but Pass had drawn the arrow and given the photograph to Huddleston during a meeting that Prater also attended. Huddleston then mailed it to his son-in-law. The message was clear: *This is the guy you're supposed to kill!*

The day after Vealey was released from the jail, Paul told his wife that he was going to Washington, D.C. He was all dressed up and said it was for a business trip, but she knew he was going to look for Yablonski.

What he didn't say was that Pass had suggested to Prater, who passed it on to Gilly, that Gilly and his two accomplices should go to D.C. and kill Yablonski there. Even then the city was known for its high crime rate, and the thinking was that nobody would look into one more murder.

While on the road, Paul called his wife to tell her he was having trouble with the Caprice. The brakes were going, among other things, and he was having trouble finding parts.

The next day, Paul called her again. He said that now he was trying to find the UMWA building, but he'd forgotten which street it was on. He instructed her to look at a map of Washington, D.C., he'd left in a kitchen drawer on which there was a line indicating the location of the UMWA building.

Gilly had been told that they might be able to intercept Yablonski in a small park near the headquarters building that he would pass on his way. Or they could wait for him at a restaurant where Yablonski was known to eat breakfast.

They chose to wait at the restaurant. But Yablonski never showed.

Having struck out yet again, the hapless assassins spent a cold night trying to get some sleep in the car. Gilly called his wife from a pay phone and told her what had happened. She told him to wait, and she'd get back to him with another plan. When she called back, she gave him an address in Bethesda, Maryland that she said was the home of Yablonski's son Chip and where he was known to stay when in D.C.

Arriving at the home about 8 a.m., Gilly dropped off Vealey and Phillips. He'd said he'd park down the block and be ready to roll after they shot Yablonski. He'd shown them the *UMW Journal* photograph on the drive so that they'd know who to shoot.

However, this plan also went south when a middle-aged woman answered the door. The two scruffy-looking triggermen fumbled around before asking for Joseph Yablonski. They said they were out-of-work miners and were hoping he might help them get a job.

The woman, Chip's wife Shirley Yablonski, called for her husband to come to the door. When Chip arrived, the pair repeated their story about needing work and again requested to speak with Joseph Yablonski.

Chip looked narrowly at the two. They seemed like a couple of lowlifes. Neither looked like he'd done a day of hard labor in his life, much less worked in a coal mine.

Although he knew that his father was upstairs in the house, Chip sensed there was something wrong about these jokers. The campaign had grown increasingly bitter with both candidates accusing the other of corruption. The virulence had ratcheted up the day before when his father organized a protest outside the UMWA headquarters in D.C. Jock had even engaged in a shouting match in front of the building with John P. Owens, the secretary-treasurer of the union.

Even before that Yablonski's sons had grown increasingly worried about the possibility of violence initiated by Boyle and his henchmen. The two goons at Chip's door made him wonder if that possibility was about to become a reality. "Sorry, he's in Scranton, PA," he lied before shutting the door in their disappointed faces.

Deflated, Vealey and Phillips walked back to where Gilly sat in his car and explained what happened. Phillips thought they should firebomb the house. But Gilly wouldn't go for it.

Instead, they decided to drive to Scranton and see if they could find Joseph Yablonski there. But once again they were out of luck. He wasn't in Scranton, and so they headed back to Cleveland.

On the drive, Gilly called his wife and complained that the union should help more with locating Yablonski. She talked to her father and then got back to her husband with: "He lives outside of Clarksville, Pennsylvania. Go find him there."

CHAPTER NINE

HAM AND CHEESE SANDWICHES

OCTOBER 31, 1969

The murderous, but not particularly bright, trio drove to Clarksville and located the Yablonski home. However, they appeared to be in no hurry to complete their heinous act. Instead, they spent a couple days "reconnoitering" the neighborhood and watching the comings and goings at the house from a vantage point on a hill behind the house.

In doing so, they'd been putting a lot of miles on Gilly's run-down Chevrolet Caprice and getting on each other's nerves. Gilly complained in telephone calls to his wife that Vealey's personal hygiene was lacking and that he "smells bad." Both for financial reasons and to avoid leaving a trail, they slept in the car instead of a motel, which was getting more uncomfortable as the temperatures dropped at night.

When asked by Annette why they still hadn't gone through with the job, Gilly explained that there always seemed to be someone in the house in addition to their target. The hitman business was turning out to be a lot more difficult than he'd thought.

However, on Halloween day they decided to take their scouting a step further. They pulled up to the Yablonski house and stopped the car. Gilly had called the home from a phone booth in Clarksville using a phone number he'd been given, and no one had answered. They were pretty sure no one was home and that was fine with them. They'd decided to first break into the two-story house to get an idea of the layout. Then they'd return at some other time to murder Yablonski.

Still, just in case, they were armed with a snub nose .32 caliber revolver and a pair of .28 caliber semi-automatic handguns that Huddleston had purchased and given to his son-in-law. If their target came home while they were there, they'd be ready to shoot him.

"You guys go in," Gilly said, nodding towards the house. "I'll keep a lookout and be ready to roll."

It seemed like a good idea so while Gilly waited, Vealey and Phillips broke into the house. They quickly discovered that they were not alone: a small white dog greeted them happily and followed them around as they checked out the premises.

Experienced burglars, the pair first went through Yablonski's study on the ground floor looking for a coin collection and a large amount of cash he was rumored to have. They didn't find anything worth stealing, so they climbed the circular staircase to the bedrooms on the second floor. They looked around there, too, but other than some loose change and a couple of foreign coins, their luck was no better.

Returning to the ground floor, the burglars decided that they were hungry and went to the kitchen. They found a ham and some cheese in the refrigerator and made themselves sandwiches. Fed and feeling relaxed, they then left the house to jump in the car with Gilly.

Except he wasn't there. Nor was there any sign of him.

Angry and sticking out like sore thumbs in that neighborhood of widely spaced homes and farms scattered among the thickly wooded hillsides, the pair started walking down the road back to town. A few cars passed them and they tried to hitchhike, but no one was willing to pick them up; the murders of actress Sharon Tate and four others by the Manson Family in Los Angeles were still fresh in everybody's mind. No one was taking a chance on a couple of disheveled vagrants.

Vealey and Phillips had walked about a mile when Gilly came roaring up. With a few choice words directed at him, they demanded an explanation. Sheepishly, he told them that they took so long in the house that he got spooked and took off.

Phillips wasn't having it, and with good reason. This was the second time in the last few months that his "getaway driver" left him stranded at a house he and Vealey were burgling, the last one being in Kentucky. That time the getaway driver had been their pal, Buddy Martin, who also got spooked and took off, but Phillips had had enough.

"I quit," he declared, and no amount of cajoling by Gilly and Vealey on the way back to Cleveland could convince him to change his mind.

Down to just the two of them, Gilly and Vealey made several more trips to Clarksville over the next few weeks, enough that people in the neighborhood and surrounding area started commenting about the car and its passengers.

At times, the aspiring assassins seemed oblivious to being seen. Yet at other times, they exercised caution as befitted "professional" killers. For instance, before every trip to find and kill Yablonski, Gilly would sit at the dining room table next to his gun cabinet and wipe each bullet he was taking clean of fingerprints. They continued sleeping in the car rather than checking into motels, too.

On Thanksgiving, November 27, they returned again to the Yablonski neighborhood and prowled around. Huddleston had suggested that they catch Yablonski on the road and shoot him in his car. He might even crash, the old man said, so that the cause of death wouldn't be immediately discovered.

Intent on their plan, the two friends didn't notice the two young girls sitting behind a large picture window in one of the homes they passed. Thirteen-year-old Kathy Jo Rygle and her twelve-year-old cousin Patty Barwiolek were playing a game. As cars drove past, they wrote a description of the vehicle and jotted down the state and license plate information in a notebook that Kathy kept.

The fifth car they recorded that day was a "maroon with dark top Chevrolet Caprice" with Ohio plates. Kathy carefully wrote down the details, including the license plate number: CX457. The girls then eagerly awaited the next car.

None of it may have ever mattered if what happened next had put an end to the murder-for-hire plot. On November 29, Huddleston called Gilly, who had just returned from Pennsylvania, and told him the contract had been canceled, at least temporarily.

Gilly wasn't told why. But on Thanksgiving, Boyle, who was set to speak at a UMWA conference in Madisonville, Kentucky on November 30, had his administrative assistant, Suzanne Richards, call Pass and tell him to meet him with Prater at the Knoxville airport the day prior because "something important has come up."

On the drive from the airport to Madisonville, Boyle told the other men that he was going to win the election easily and had decided to hold up on the assassination plan at least for the time being. He had everything going for him, much of it nefarious.

The union newspaper, the *UMW Journal*, was a pro-Boyle, anti-Yablonski propaganda machine; during the campaign, its newspaper articles mentioned Boyle 166 times and Yablonski not once. The magazine's editorial board's opinion page often quoted Boyle warning the readers that a Yablonski presidency would destroy the union—and with it pensions and hospitalization benefits. One of Boyle's constant warnings was that Yablonski wanted to deny pensioners the right to vote in union elections.

In addition to his over-the-top, incendiary speeches and virulent attacks in the journal, Boyle had an additional one hundred thousand ballots printed to stuff the ballot boxes. With those efforts, as well as buying votes and intimidating Yablonski supporters, he'd decided there was no way he was going to lose.

However, he was concerned that if Yablonski was murdered before the election, it would look suspicious. With guys like Rauh, as well as Yablonski's supporters around to stir things up, the last thing he wanted was to draw attention to himself. He decided he'd figure out what to do with his archenemy after the December 9 election.

The next day, November 30, at the convention in Madisonville, Boyle went all out with his attacks on his rival. "Joseph Yablonski lies through his teeth," he roared from the podium. "He is a hypocrite, defames the memory and accomplishments of John L. Lewis; he talks with two tongues about democracy—on one hand, he is claiming it doesn't exist within the UMWA and on the other, running to the courts in a vicious attempt to stop the UMWA election and denying eighty thousand UMWA members the right to vote!

"Joseph Yablonski is guilty of a serious conflict of interest affecting the welfare of UMWA members. He is guilty of a cruel hoax that seeks to turn UMWA members against UMWA members. He has associated himself with outsiders to try to take over the United Mine Workers. He has dragged the good name of your union through the dust by filing expensive lawsuits against the UMWA. He has tried to use the courts as a forum and substitute the judgment of the courts for that of the UMWA membership because he is guilty of lies, defamation of John L. Lewis, conflict of interests and anti-union acts. Joseph Yablonski is unfit to be president of the United Mine Workers. He will be rejected by the membership as a power-hungry opportunist and hypocrite!"[28]

As a demagogue, Boyle knew how to arouse his audience. During the campaign he'd done his usual railing against communists and "dual unionists," which always appealed to the membership. But he saved his most damning attacks for Yablonski by invoking the hallowed name of John L. Lewis, alleging disloyalty to the sacred union, and accusing his rival of consorting with "outsiders" and using the courts to destroy the UMWA and kick pensioners out of the union, which Yablonski had never suggested.

Obviously, one purpose of his hyperbole was to get a leg up in the election. The other was more despicable: If the union members saw Yablonski as a traitor and a threat to their livelihoods and way of life, well, if something bad was to happen to him, he would have had it coming.

---

28   *Commonwealth of Pennsylvania v. William Prater.* Introduced by Richard A. Sprague at trial.

CHAPTER TEN

THIEVES
AND ENEMIES

As the union boss knew he would, Boyle easily "won" another term as president of the United Mine Workers of America by a nearly 2–1 margin.

Election Day had been marred by reports of fights breaking out at polling places between Boyle- and Yablonski-supporters involving fists, lead pipes, and bats. Reports poured into the Yablonski campaign headquarters about voting irregularities, such as ballot stuffing and Yablonski supporters being given wrong polling locations.

None of that mattered. The next day the incumbent union boss declared that the union membership had spoken.

That might have been the end of the assassination plot except for one thing: Yablonski wasn't ceding. The reform candidate immediately fired off a telegram to Labor Secretary Shultz complaining that the election was rigged and the department needed to investigate.

Yablonski then gave a fiery speech to campaign workers, supporters, and the media in Pittsburgh. "Working coalminers in this country aren't going to take this lying down," he declared. "We have contacted the Department of Labor, asking them to do certain things. Yesterday, the undersecretary of labor called me to read a letter saying there will be a conference to discuss the contents of our telegram of complaint that the election was rigged."

Noting that he fairly won the vote of more than fifty thousand union members, he said he intended to speak for them. "I am not interested in bringing about a division in the United Mine Workers of America. I know the only way this union can go forward is to go united. So, this fight is going to go on! I say to you, let's stick together. We know all the thieves and the enemies.

"All of those thieves and all of the enemies know how to get in touch with me.... Your candidate is not giving up. The fight is going to go on to bring about a union that's responsible to its members."

Yablonski's complaint was doomed from the beginning. The Labor Department had a long history of overlooking UMWA shenanigans and labor violations, and Shultz had no desire to take on the most powerful union in the country and its irascible president, "Tough Tony" Boyle.

Shultz said that before the Labor Department could intercede, Yablonski had to go through the union's own grievance procedures first. As the UMWA grievances were heard by the IEB that Boyle controlled, Shultz's abdication of responsibility meant that the union boss was the final arbiter of Yablonski's complaints. The attempt to get the federal government to intervene, which might have impacted the tragedy that followed, was shut down by Shultz before it even got started.

With no help coming from the Labor Department, Rauh immediately filed five lawsuits in federal courts asking the court to overturn the election. Yablonski and Nader had a falling out over the summer. But Rauh had remained a loyal friend and political advisor in addition to his legal salvos.

In the lawsuits, Rauh said Yablonski was alleging that: Boyle and the UMWA had denied him the use of the union's mailing list as was required by law; he'd been removed from his position as acting director of Labor's Non-Partisan League in retaliation for his candidacy, and despite a judge's ruling, Boyle had refused to reinstate him; the *UMW Journal* was improperly used by Boyle as a campaign and propaganda mouthpiece; in violation of the Landrum-Griffin Act, the union had no rules for fair elections; more than fifty thousand illegal ballots had been printed and counted for Boyle and should now be destroyed; and the union had violated its fiduciary duties by spending union money to support Boyle's reelection.

Rauh had already warned Shultz that unless the Labor Department investigated there would be "violence and more violence." Now he and others, such as Yablonski's family, worried the lawsuits would light a fuse, but Jock insisted they be filed.

The tragedy that would shortly unfold was, perhaps, destined from the moment Yablonski announced his candidacy and intended to "be a hammer and strike." But there were a number of other points that could have been the tipping point for Boyle, such as the June 23 IEB meeting where the two rivals publicly traded insults and accusations. Or when the judge ordered that he reinstate Yablonski to the Non-Partisan League. Or when Yablonski picketed union headquarters on October 27. Or maybe even as far back as Yablonski's perceived betrayals by supporting the black lung legislation and threatening to pull District 5 delegates at the Bal Harbor Convention.

However, his fate was sealed when Yablonski gave his post-election speech promising to fight on, followed by Rauh filing the lawsuits. Shultz's refusal to get involved also all but greenlit the plot in Boyle's mind. This was a union issue, and the union would settle it.

As much as he hated Yablonski and wanted him dead for personal reasons, Boyle feared what would come of the lawsuits. The union's internal affairs, including its finances, might be exposed to examination by the opposition's lawyers and investigators. And he, and other union officials, would likely be deposed under oath, and even have to testify in court.

Boyle was also concerned about the potential for federal charges for illegal union contributions from the Non-Partisan League to the presidential campaign of Hubert Humphrey and other politicians. He called Pass on December 16 and, referring to his rival as "that goddamned Yablonski," who now that he got beat in the election was going to stir up "serious trouble" over the contributions.

Boyle decided that Yablonski had to go. If he was dead, the lawsuits would be dismissed. The union president believed that he had created a foolproof scheme to pay the killers that would never be

traced back to him, that the killers and most of the other conspirators didn't know he was the instigator, and that he could count on
the loyalty of all involved. He told Pass to call Prater and "get the
job done."

Pass relayed the message to Prater who told Huddleston, who
informed his son-in-law. "But it has to be done before the first of
the year," he warned Gilly.

CHAPTER ELEVEN

OHIO LICENSE PLATE CX457

DECEMBER 18, 1969

Paul Gilly and Claude Vealey had it all worked out when they pulled up to the Yablonski house. They would walk up to the door, ring the bell, and when their target appeared, Vealey would shoot him on a signal from Gilly.

Simple as that. Then they'd drive back to Cleveland, divvy up the blood money, and live large. They didn't know why they'd been told the hit was back on; they didn't care. They just wanted the money.

Once the assassination team got the word to move forward, they at first started thinking about other ways to kill Yablonski instead of shooting him, which didn't seem to be working out. Huddleston talked to a former miner and his son about using dynamite and offered to pay $2,400. They even got as far as discussing how sticks of dynamite could be attached to a long pole that they would lean against the house outside of Yablonski's bedroom window. But after a few days of discussions, the former miner and his son declined to get involved.

Someone floated the idea of kidnapping Charlotte Yablonski and then killing her father when he came to the rescue. That idea was shot down, as was a suggestion to firebomb the house.

Another idea was to dip a cigar in arsenic and deliver it to Yablonski, a known cigar aficionado. But that idea hit a dead-end when Annette, who called around trying to find the poison, was told she'd need a prescription. She and her father bought rat poison instead, but it made the cigar too soggy and the cigar fell apart.

The conclusion was that there was only one way to get the job done. Gilly and Vealey needed to shoot him.

The pair drove back to Clarksville and, after a couple of days of trying to work up their courage, drove up to the house and rang the bell. Yablonski answered the door. It was time to act, but still they hesitated.

Later each man would blame the other for failing to act. Vealey said his partner never gave him the signal to pull his gun and shoot. Gilly said he gave the signal, but Vealey didn't act.

Instead, Gilly came up with a lame story about being out-of-work miners and hoped Yablonski might help them find a job. The older man's eyes narrowed beneath his bushy eyebrows. "Don't think I can help you," he said and stood there waiting for their response as if he knew what they were thinking.

The pair of wannabe killers just looked at each other. Then Gilly shook his head and they'd turned and walked away, mumbling under their breath to each other.

As Yablonski watched the pair get in the maroon Chevrolet Caprice and drive away, he was pretty sure that he'd literally just dodged a bullet. It didn't take anyone smarter than those two dimwits to know that neither one of them had ever worked a day in a coal mine. Nor that finding a job wasn't the reason they rang his doorbell.

He'd heard the comments about strange men who'd been prowling around the neighborhood and Clarksville since that fall. Clearly worried, Margaret told him about the car parked across the road and the two men watching the house. He'd put up the floodlights his sons suggested and leaned a shotgun next to the headboard of his bed. But he still hadn't bought into the idea that Boyle would still want to do him harm.

Until this latest intrusion. It had him. He'd actually looked in the eyes of two young men, strangers he had no beef with, and knew they were there to kill him.

After the Caprice pulled out of the driveway, he walked back into the house and into his study. He didn't want to alarm Margaret and Charlotte, so he said nothing about the visitors. Instead, he called one of his oldest friends and volunteer bodyguard, Karl Kafton, a big, rough-hewn, former coalminer from West Virginia who came right over.

The two men were still in the study talking shortly before 6 p.m. when Kenneth Yablonski walked into the room. An attorney like his brother, he'd also taken up his father's cause and represented coalminers in several legal cases. This included winning a precedent-setting case in 1964 regarding a mine explosion on December 8, 1962 that killed thirty-seven miners in Greene County, Pennsylvania. His lawsuit forced the local coroner to perform an inquest into the disaster that helped the families of the deceased win expanded benefits from the Pennsylvania Workmen's Compensation Board.

On December 18, Kenneth had just gotten off work in the city of Washington some forty miles away and was stopping by to check on his parents and sister. The women, who were in the kitchen, told him that his father was unusually quiet and seemed troubled.

"What's going on?" the younger Yablonski asked when he walked in and saw his dad and Kafton talking quietly in the study.

"There were two men at the house today to kill me," his father replied tersely.

Kenneth froze in shock. It was one thing to think it was a possibility that his father was in danger, but to hear him just put it out there like that was frightening. "What do you mean? What's this all about?"

Jock Yablonski told him about the visitors and his suspicions they'd been there to murder him. He had no idea why they hadn't acted; whether they'd decided to wait on a better time or had simply lost their nerve. But he was sure that's what they'd come to do.

The three men decided to drive to Clarksville to see if the visitors were still around. They'd just crossed a bridge going into town when Jock pointed. "That's the car."

Looking where he indicated, the other two saw a maroon Chevrolet Caprice with a dark top parked on the side of the road near the Koremooth Tavern. Kafton made a U-turn so they could come up behind the vehicle.

In the glare of the headlights, they could see that one or more people were sitting in the car. They could also see the Ohio license plate clearly, and both Kafton and Kenneth Yablonski wrote the number down on pieces of paper.

When they went back to the house, Kafton wrote it down again on a yellow legal pad lying on Jock's desk. Just five symbols, a random combination of letters and numbers—CX457.

Kafton picked up the telephone and called a number he had for a Pennsylvania state trooper. He asked his friend to run the license plate for him. He soon had an answer: the car was registered to Annette Gilly, a resident of Cleveland, Ohio. His friend gave him a telephone number associated with the vehicle registration.

He called the number, and a woman answered. He told her he was a Pennsylvania state trooper and that he was trying to locate her husband. "He may have been a witness to an accident," he said.

The woman identified herself as Annette, Paul's wife. "Is he all right?" she asked.

"Yes," Kafton replied. "Do you know if he was in Pennsylvania looking for work?"

"No," the woman answered. "He's a painter here."

Kafton thanked the woman and hung up before turning to the Yablonski men. "Well, we know who one of them is: Paul Gilly."

CHAPTER TWELVE

NO ONE LEFT ALIVE

DECEMBER 30, 1969

On a bitterly cold winter's night in Pennsylvania, three young men sat in a borrowed car at a wide spot on a mountain road as they watched the back of the Yablonski home a hundred yards lower than their vantage point and a quarter mile away. They were determined that this night would be the night that their efforts would come to a fatal conclusion and were drinking beers and whiskey to gin up the courage.

There would be no more following Jock Yablonski around, hoping to catch him on a deserted road to gun him down in his car. No more going up to the house on the pretense of asking for a job, only to lose their nerve. No more trips back and forth to Cleveland, Scranton, or Washington, D.C. looking for an opportunity. No more crazy plans to poison, firebomb, or blow him up with dynamite.

Tonight, they'd finish what they started with the .38 caliber, chrome-plated, pearl-handled revolver and the M1 carbine they'd brought for the job. Then they'd get their blood money and be high rollers.

A week after meeting Yablonski at the door of his house, Paul Gilly and Claude Vealey had returned one more time to the area to do the deed themselves. They'd splurged for once and spent the night of December 26 in the West Brownsville Hotel about twelve miles from Clarksville. But while they'd watched the house the next day, waiting for an opportunity, there were too many holiday comings and goings at the Yablonski house.

Jock was never alone, they told Huddleston and Annette when they returned. Huddleston replied that the people with the money were growing impatient.

Pass had inquired as to what was taking so long. He told Prater to up the payment to $15,000 if they'd get it done before January 1. But if Huddleston's guys couldn't get it done, District 19 would find another way, he told Prater, who passed it down to Huddleston. "We've never let the union down yet."

Huddleston asked Prater what the hitmen were to do if they couldn't catch Yablonski without his wife and daughter. "Kill them all," Prater snarled. "I don't care if they kill the whole family or the whole town as long as it gets done. Run him down with an airplane if that's what it takes."

So, they'd returned on December 30 and parked on the hill where they could see the Yablonski house. But there was one significant change.

Vealey had been making remarks about not being sure he could go through with the murder, and Gilly was concerned that his partner was losing his nerve. He decided to find someone more "cold-blooded," someone he could count on to pull the trigger and kill a man in his house, possibly even other members of the family.

So just the night before, Gilly had met with Aubran Wayne "Buddy" Martin at the Family Tavern, a beer and wine bar in Cleveland, to recruit him. He didn't know him as well as Vealey and Phillips, but he knew he was a different level of criminal.

Of the three, Martin looked the least like a cold-blooded killer. He was small, more pretty than handsome, and wore his long blond hair in what was called a "duck's ass," a little outdated for 1969 but still popular with the rebel-without-a-cause set. But the look was just a thin veneer for a stone-cold sociopath who liked to boast that he didn't "take no shit from nobody."

Asked by Gilly to help kill a man and get paid for it, Martin grinned and said he was in. Vealey only learned that Martin was joining them when he walked into the tavern to meet up with Gilly and saw the two of them at a table. He'd known Martin for about six months, and they'd pulled a few home burglaries together, but he was still surprised to see him.

After Gilly informed Vealey that Martin had agreed to be the third member of the team, Gilly then turned to the newest accomplice and told him who was being targeted: Jock Yablonski *"and anybody else in the house."* He then said that the three of them would be splitting $5,250, though Vealey would only receive $1,000 after Gilly subtracted the $750 he'd posted for his bond a month earlier.

Gilly "forgot" to mention that the contract money had now been increased to $15,000. He'd also been told that Boyle had agreed to give a pension to his dad, a former mine worker who had not worked in a union mine, after the murder was accomplished.

Martin asked why Yablonski was supposed to be killed. Gilly replied that the victim was a "small-time" union operator and "some guy named Tony" wanted him dead. Telling them to be ready to go with him the next day to Clarksville, Gilly then left the bar.

The following afternoon when Gilly drove to Vealey's house to pick him up, he was in a blue 1966 Chevrolet sedan. He'd explained to Annette that he didn't want to use his Chevrolet Caprice because the license plate was known. So, he asked her to borrow a car from his brother Billy Gilly under the pretext of going to visit her sister in Akron.

After Annette returned with the car, Paul and Vealey picked up Martin. However, they didn't immediately leave for Clarksville. Instead, they drove to a house that Gilly had recently purchased. He thought it was a good idea to familiarize themselves with the weapons first. They went to the basement, where they took turns shooting a piece of wood. Only then did they leave for their rendezvous with murder.

Along the way they stopped for a six-pack of beer and a bottle of whiskey for liquid courage. Then they'd made their way to the spot on the hill where they could see the back of the Yablonski house and the driveway to observe any comings and goings.

As they waited, they finished off the six-pack, tossing the empties into a snow-covered ravine. But the thought of murder was thirsty business, so when they finished the first six beers, they drove back to Clarksville where they bought another six-pack. Returning to their vigil, they passed the time polishing off the booze, eating potato chips, smoking cigarettes, and occasionally relieving themselves on the snow.

Finally, the last of the lights went out in the big house. Sure that there were only three people in the house, Yablonski, his wife and the daughter, they agreed that all of them had to die. "No witnesses!"

At approximately 1 a.m. on December 31, 1969, the young men decided the occupants had enough time to fall asleep and drove down the hill. Pulling into the driveway, they got out of the car and distributed the weapons; Martin got the carbine, Vealey the revolver. Those two walked up to the front of the house and peered in the windows, but no one was stirring that they could see.

Vealey snipped the telephone lines with a pair of wire-cutters he'd brought. They then walked over to Yablonski's car and deflated the tires before lifting the hood and removing the coil from the carburetor so it wouldn't start. Then they slashed the tires on Charlotte's blue Mustang and disabled the carburetor. They wanted to make sure that no one could escape and go for help.

In the meantime, Gilly had been following another line that he thought might be a second telephone. When he returned, they approached the back door.

Their burglary experience was useful as Martin used a screwdriver to remove the stripping so that the storm door could be removed noiselessly. They entered the kitchen, where they encountered the small white dog that Vealey and Phillips had met on Halloween. But the friendly terrier neither barked nor growled as they petted him and removed their shoes.

Thanks to the newly installed floodlights there was plenty of light in the house as the men quickly searched the downstairs rooms to make sure they missed no one. They then made their way to the bottom of the circular staircase.

There Martin said he wanted to trade weapons with Vealey; he took the revolver and handed his cohort the rifle. "I'll take care of the girl," Martin said. "You kill the other two."

With that, the three began to quietly climb the stairs to the bedrooms.

CHAPTER THIRTEEN

SOMETHING WORSE

JANUARY 5, 1970

It was the dog that left no doubt. However, if he'd been honest with himself, Kenneth Yablonski knew without knowing that something terrible had happened when he tried to call his parents that morning and there was no answer. He even told his friend, Bill Stewart, who offered to accompany him, that he was worried that "maybe an accident or something worse" had befallen them.

Still, he'd hoped that the knot in his gut that caused him to ignore the speed limit on the forty-mile drive from his law office in Washington, Pennsylvania to the farmhouse was just a lot of worry over nothing.

When they pulled up in the driveway, Kenneth saw his dad's car, but he didn't see his sister Charlotte's. It was a relief. He reasoned that she and their parents must have just stepped out for the day.

Even a week's worth of newspapers and full milk bottles piled up at the back door didn't mean his worst fears were realized. After all, when he last saw them on December 29, 1969, they were fine. They could have just gone to visit someone and forgot to cancel the deliveries, or let him know, he reasoned.

Then again if that was true, they'd also failed to inform his younger brother, Chip, of their plans, too. Chip had called him that morning asking if he'd heard from them.

"I thought they might be with you," Kenneth told him.

However, all the wishful thinking fell to pieces when he unlocked the backdoor, entered the kitchen, and saw Rascal, his mother's small Bedlington terrier: Rascal was hungry, thirsty, wagging his tail, and alone. They would have never left the dog, and that's when he knew.

Kenneth left the kitchen and walked towards the dining room. It was winter outside and snow covered the ground, but inside it was hot, the temperature in the eighties. Then he was assailed by an odor so terrible that he was nearly overwhelmed.

"You smell something?" he asked Stewart.

His friend nodded though the look on his face already said he had. "Yes."

As they walked through the dining room and into the living room, Kenneth saw that the place was in disarray. Papers were scattered and lying on the floor.

They moved on to the circular staircase and looked up. That was where the smell was coming from.

Kenneth Yablonski ran up the stairs. Stewart, who remained below, heard his friend moving from room to room, crying out as he made his terrible discoveries. Kenneth then appeared at the top of the stairs, his face contorted with fear and grief, and shouted, "Where's my dad? Where is he? What did they do to him?" He disappeared again.

A few minutes later, Kenneth staggered down the stairs. "We need to call the police," he said and picked up the phone to dial. "The line's dead." They were going to have to drive to a neighbor's to call. Kenneth Yablonski's worst fears had been realized.

Something worse was first reported on the radio and then was all over the evening newscasts and evening newspapers. The *Pittsburgh Press* reported the killings under the blaring headline "YABLONSKIS BELIEVED 'EXECUTED'" and subhead "Killings Baffle Police."

CLARKSVILLE: The brutal slayings of Joseph "Jock" Yablonski, a top United Mineworkers official, his wife and daughter remain a mystery today under tight police security.

However, it was revealed that Mr Yablonski may have tried to fight or scare off the slayers by reaching for either a shotgun or a rifle when he was gunned down.

The newspaper article revealed that police investigators believed that: more than one killer was involved; that the murders were "precisely planned;" at least nine bullets were used; and that the murders "probably occurred New Year's Day."

The article noted that the carburetor coil for Jock Yablonski's car had been removed, and the two front tires had been deflated. Margaret's blue Mustang[29] had also been disabled and the tires slashed.

The Washington County coroner's office described the slayings as "an execution," adding: "They did it. They did nothing else and then left." According to the article, robbery had been ruled out because money "left out in the open was untouched by the slayers."

State Police Captain Joseph Snyder said his men had come up with "no possible motive, no leads..." When asked if he thought the killings were the work of "professionals," he replied, "I don't know."

---

29   The car was parked behind a barn at the rear of the house which
     is why Kenneth Yablonski did not initially see it.

CHAPTER FOURTEEN

THE CHURCH HAS BEEN PAINTED

JANUARY 5, 1970

No one knew quite what to say that morning as Albert Pass sat at his desk across from William J. Prater and Silous Huddleston. It had been a nerve-wracking week waiting to hear whether the hired hitmen had killed Yablonski on schedule, and still no one was sure.

Two days after Christmas, Prater told Pass that the message about the increased blood money had been delivered and that everything was going forward. But this particular group of erstwhile killers had proved to be inept for two months, and there was no reason to be confident that had changed.

However, there was cause for hope. Huddleston said he'd received a cryptic phone call a couple days after the new year from his son-in-law who spoke in some sort of code. "He said 'the church has been painted,'" the old man told the others. "That was it. Then he hung up."

Huddleston said he took it to mean that, maybe, the job had been done and Yablonski was dead. But he couldn't be sure and, paranoid that his phone was tapped, he didn't call back to find out.

Whatever Gilly meant by painting the church, there'd been nothing on the news about Yablonski. "I don't know what to do," Huddleston said.

Pass thought about it before shrugging. "Well, just let it alone for thirty days, and we'll see what happens."

They didn't have to wait that long. That afternoon, after the other two were gone, Pass was listening to the radio when he heard the news that Jock Yablonski, his wife, and their daughter had been murdered. Paul Gilly's message was suddenly crystal clear.

Later that evening he was watching a television newscast about the murders a little after 6 p.m. when Prater called. "You watching the news?" his friend asked.

"Yeah," Pass replied.

"Is it okay to go ahead and pay the money?"

There was no need to ask what money. "Yeah."

In Washington, D.C., Tony Boyle had also been on pins and needles waiting to hear back. He'd been told by Pass that the assassination would take place by the end of the year. But January 1 had come and gone with no word—not from the assassins, who seemed to have a hard time finding their target much less pulling the trigger, and not from the media. The wait was especially tough because he didn't want to take any chances by calling Pass for an update.

Yablonski, his wife, and their daughter had been shot and killed while sleeping sometime prior to the New Year. The initial reports were that while the police believed that several killers were involved, they had no suspects.

In the days that followed, Boyle himself was all over the news expressing how shocked he was about the killings. In spite of their rivalry and the sometimes heated rhetoric of the campaign, he told every reporter who would listen that he and Yablonski had been friends since 1942. And what sort of dastardly killer would shoot Margaret and Charlotte Yablonski?

However, his reactions away from the media was decidedly different. Boyle's administrative assistant, Suzanne Richards, suggested that the union should offer a $100,000 reward for information leading to the arrest and conviction of the killer or killers. At first, he balked entirely, but when she insisted that it was the right thing to do, he said he'd think about it.

Boyle considered Richards's suggestion and decided she was right, but how much? Too little and some might wonder how interested he really was in finding the killers, but too much might encourage the wrong person to talk. It was more than he wanted, but he finally agreed to a $50,000 reward, confident that no one would ever claim it.

He also announced to the press that he was setting up a special UMWA committee in Pittsburgh to assist with the murder investigation. The union would pay for attorneys, stenographers, and whatever else it took and act as a sort of clearinghouse for anyone who wanted to offer information.

The public relations stunt was upended, however, when Yablonski's sons complained publicly that the committee would be interfering with the FBI investigation. Chip and Kenneth Yablonski had not been shy about telling the press, and apparently the cops, that they thought Boyle was responsible for the murders. He, of course, had vehemently denied the accusation, but the clearinghouse idea was dropped with little fanfare.

In general, he was not faring well in the court of public opinion. Shortly after the murders were discovered, thousands of miners in western Pennsylvania and West Virginia walked off the job, an obvious statement about who they thought was responsible.

Then on January 9—a frigid, windy day in western Pennsylvania— hundreds of coalminers and their families gathered at the Washington Cemetery for the funerals of Jock, Margaret, and Charlotte Yablonski. The national media had been on hand to report on the outpouring of grief, horror, and anger.

Before the bodies were laid to rest, Kenneth Yablonski gave an impassioned statement to the press about how the funeral would proceed. "We loved and admired our father," he said. "We respected him, and my brother and I would like to carry him to his final resting place. But we deem it proper to do otherwise.

"My brother Joseph, with our cousins from my mother's family, will carry our mother, and I, with our cousins from my father's family, will carry our sister Charlotte. We entrust our father to the coalminers, whom he loved so much."[30]

At the memorial service, the Monsignor Charles Owen Rice, the "labor priest" who had married Jock and Margaret, compared the slaying of Jock to the assassination of the Kennedys and Martin Luther King, Jr. Then later that afternoon, Joseph Rauh, speaking at a meeting with miners in the church refectory, urged those gathered to continue to fight for the reforms championed by Yablonski.

Boyle complained to his inner circle that Yablonski was being made into some sort of martyr. He insisted, as if he was still on the campaign trail, that his rival was a corrupt liar who was trying to destroy the union.

The fallout from the murders wasn't all just talk and news reports either. The day before the funeral, Rauh publicly demanded that the U.S. Department of Labor launch an immediate investigation of the 1969 election. Up to that point, Labor Secretary George Shultz had done nothing about Yablonski's earlier complaints except to say that he had to exhaust his remedies through the union first. It was a response that had pleased Boyle.

However, now Shultz gave in to Rauh's plea and assigned 230 investigators to look into the allegations of corruption and voting irregularities and, by inference, the murders of the Yablonskis. Not only that, but the Department of Justice under U.S. Attorney General John Mitchell had assigned federal prosecutors to the investigation, and Mitchell had persuaded FBI director J. Edgar Hoover, who initially balked and wanted "the locals" to handle it, to get his agents involved.

On January 9, the same day as the funerals for the Yablonskis, the FBI showed up at UMWA headquarters. Agency auditors demanded access to union books. Special agents also interviewed Boyle in his office.

The agents asked him about the Yablonski brothers' allegations, which he again denied, and then asked if he had any ideas on who might want to harm his rival and the two women. He acted surprised,

---

30   Yablonski Cause Cited By Eulogist, Ben. A Franklin, *New York Times*, January 1970.

as if the idea had never occurred to him. Then he said that while he didn't believe any union member was involved, he knew that pensioners were upset that Yablonski had filed a lawsuit to do away with the pension fund, the only money most of them had to live on.

After the agents thanked him for his time and left, Boyle got word to Pass to meet with the District 19 field reps involved in the R&I Committee. He was confident his man would know what to tell them.

Pass did. He and Prater met with the six field reps at the District 19 office in Middlesboro. The district secretary-treasurer told them to contact the twenty-three pensioners. If the FBI came sniffing around, they were to stick to the story: the money they received was reimbursement for expenses incurred while recruiting for the union. They were to say they spent it.

The first indication the conspiracy might be unraveling was that about the same time Boyle was talking to the FBI agents, other agents showed up at Paul Gilly's house in Cleveland. The agents sat Huddleston's son-in-law down and asked him if he'd had any legitimate business in Clarksville on December 18. In particular, they wanted to know if he'd had a reason to be driving in the area of the Yablonski house.

Apparently, Pass had been told by Prater, who got it from Huddleston, that Gilly fed the agents a wild story. Gilly had told the agents he'd met a country-western singer named Jeanne at Ray's Bar in Cleveland. She'd persuaded him to drive to West Virginia where she was performing at a concert, but somehow, he got lost and ended up in Pennsylvania.

"And I might have driven past the house," he said.

It wasn't much of a story, but Gilly later told his father-in-law that he thought the agents bought it. They'd thanked him for his time and left.

In Washington, Boyle still thought he was safe. He believed that only Pass and Turnblazer knew that he was behind the murder plot. The R&I Committeemen had been told that the money was for political campaigns. They had no reason to believe anything else, and they were all staunch union men from a district known for its loyalty to Boyle.

As long as everybody stuck to the story, he thought, he'd get away with murder.

CHAPTER FIFTEEN

SOME GUY NAMED TONY

Initially, the murders baffled the first investigators on the scene. It took almost a week for the bodies to be discovered, and no one had reported anything out of the ordinary.

In fact, the Yablonski house seemed to have been a magnet for teenagers looking for a place for privacy that week. State police investigators talked to four male high school seniors who came forward and said they'd been returning from a New Year's Eve party when they parked on the front lawn to drink a six-pack of beer. The teens also said they'd seen another classmate's car parked around back where he and his girlfriend "were up to something." The boys noticed that the Mustang's tires were flat but thought nothing of it, or the fact that no one seemed to be home in the big house.

Another teen couple contacted the police and confessed to using the grounds for their romantic trysts on the nights of January 2, 3, and 4. But they, too, didn't notice anything out of the ordinary. The young woman, when told by the police investigator what had happened in the house, promptly fainted.[31]

Investigators were also at a loss for a motive on why someone would murder not only Jock Yablonski, but his wife and twenty-

---

31   Lewis, *Murder by Contract.*

five-year-old daughter in their sleep. Could it have been a burglary that went south when Jock woke up and went for his shotgun, which was not even loaded? The study downstairs had been ransacked and papers strewn about, but it didn't seem like the killers had taken anything.

Or might it have been tied to Yablonski's activities with the United Mine Workers of America? Maybe a grudge carried by a non-union mineworker, or someone connected to another rival union. Violence was a part of the culture in coal country, though the sort that carried over to include a man's family went beyond the pale.

It was also no secret that the campaign for union presidency had been a bitter one between Yablonski and the incumbent W.A. "Tough Tony" Boyle. Yablonski's sons, Kenneth and Chip, had immediately voiced their opinion that the killers had been sent by Boyle. But they had no proof.

Boyle also had a lot of supporters who could have resented some of the accusations Yablonski made about their leader during the campaign and acted without any guidance from the top. Or maybe they'd reacted on their own to Boyle's fiery accusations that Yablonski was in league with oil and gas companies and trying to destroy the union.

When FBI agents showed up at the UMWA headquarters in Washington, D.C. on January 9 and talked to Boyle, he told them that some members were upset with a Yablonski lawsuit to get pensioners out of the union. The agents had since learned from Rauh that there'd been no such lawsuit. The only pension Yablonski had questioned during the campaign was the overly generous pension Boyle would get if and when he retired. So why had Boyle said that?

Still, none of the possibilities proved anything. FBI special agents who lived and worked in coal country knew that even if Boyle was involved, getting to him was going to be problematic. The UMWA was sacrosanct to a large percentage of its members; the pronouncements of its leadership since the days of John L. Lewis were gospel. They relied on the union to make a living and protect their interests, including their pensions and medical benefits.

It was also part of the cultural identity they inherited from their Scots-Irish predecessors of "mountain folks against the world." It was, and had always been, the coal-mining community against outsiders who looked down on them and their way of life, stereotyping them as dumb, in-bred, ignorant hillbillies.

No one else had ever looked out after them except themselves until the UMWA. Not in the days two hundred years earlier when they were left to fend for themselves in a violent wilderness. Not when the British burned their farms and hanged their leaders. And later, after coal became king, not against the owners and operators with their gun thugs and corrupt cops or the politicians who sicced state and federal troops on them.

Only the UMWA and its two-fisted leadership epitomized by John L. Lewis had made them a force to be reckoned with against the outsiders, owners, cops, and Pinkerton men. Only the union had and given them pride as a people.

Yet things were changing in coal country. The old guard who still remembered the bad days before the union and the subsequent time when the UMWA was fighting for its existence were dying off and retiring. They were being replaced by a younger generation, many of them college-educated and influenced by the youth culture of the '60s that emphasized resisting authority, and the rights of the individual as opposed to a member of a group.

Most of Boyle's support in the election had come from the old guard, though some of them had grown tired of his authoritarian style, flashy lifestyle, and his cozying up to the owners at a cost to their safety and swung to Yablonski. But the younger men and, in recent years, women, who had been recruited as coal made a comeback and old-school mining was replaced by mechanization and engineering, were all in on the "reform" candidate.

If the murders were part of a plot by union officials out to get Yablonski, there wasn't much to indicate in the early days of the investigation how far up the union chain of command the plot went. Local level? District? National? But several events soon changed that.

The first big break came about as a result of Ohio license plate CX457.

Kenneth Yablonski told investigators about an incident that occurred eleven days before the murders. According to Kenneth, on December 18, two young men had shown up at the house pretending they were looking for work in a mine. At the time, his father said he suspected that they intended to kill him but had backed out at the last minute.

Later that afternoon, his dad told him and a friend, Karl Kafton, about the suspicious visit. Together they'd gone to Clarksville looking for a maroon Chevrolet Caprice with a dark top that the young men had been driving. They'd found it, too, and took down the license plate number, CX457, which Kafton had written on a yellow notepad.

Kafton then asked a friend with the Pennsylvania State Police to run the license plate and it had come back as registered to Annette Gilly, the wife of Paul Gilly. Kafton called a number provided by his friend and reached Annette. He pretended to be a state police trooper investigating a traffic accident involving her husband. She'd asked if Paul was hurt in the accident, but otherwise didn't know why he would be looking for work in Pennsylvania. He was just a painter in Cleveland, she said.

The yellow legal pad on which Kafton had written the license number from the Ohio plates—CX457—was still lying on Jock's desk when the murders were discovered. State Trooper Elmer Schifko remembered the pad and located it with the rest of the evidence taken from the Yablonski house to process at a warehouse that had been commandeered as an investigation command center.

Following up on that lead, agents also had talked to the bartender at the Koremooth Tavern where the car had been parked. He recalled two scruffy-looking guys who had come into his bar on that date. He said he thought they were casing the place for a robbery, so he sent a patron outside to check out their car. The patron had written down the license plate: Ohio CX457.

So, on January 9, when Special Agents Grover Twiner and John Sullivan from the Cleveland office went to speak to Paul Gilly at the request of Pennsylvania State Patrol investigators, they already knew that his story about the country-western singer was nonsense.

But they thanked him for his time and left. They were still in the evidence-gathering mode and not ready to make an arrest that might send others running for cover. Let him think he was in the clear.

The next break in the case had more to do with the stupidity of one of the suspects, an associate of Gilly's, than luck. An informant in Cleveland told police that a drunk, moon-faced, itinerant burglar named Claude Vealey shot his mouth off while playing pool at the Family Tavern with another lowlife named James Phillips, who went by his middle name of Charles. According to the informant, Vealey boasted for all to hear that he was spending blood money. The alleged killer claimed that he, Gilly, and another friend named Buddy Martin killed the Yablonski family and had been paid for it.

It didn't take long for the FBI agents to learn that Vealey and Phillips had been arrested for a burglary in the fall of 1969 and that Gilly had posted the bond for Vealey, connecting the three. They also corroborated that Aubran Wayne "Buddy" Martin was a known associate of Vealey and Phillips.

Combining Gilly and the license plate, Vealey's boasts, and the links proving an association between the four young men, the FBI agents and their police counterparts in Cleveland and Pennsylvania focused the investigation. A search of criminal records revealed that Gilly was the only one without a record. Vealey and Phillips had burglary arrests and convictions. Martin, however, in addition to his current resisting arrest conviction, had a history for assault as well as burglary. The federal investigators also learned from the Cleveland police that Martin was a suspect in the firebombing of a house in which a child had died.

They located the whereabouts of Vealey, Phillips, and Martin, which wasn't hard because he was in jail serving a sixty-five-day sentence for resisting arrest in another matter. But the investigators kept their cards close to the vest until they were ready to move.

Then on January 17, Phillips was picked up and brought in for questioning by FBI agents Twiner and Thomas Bader. The same informant who told them about Vealey's boasts said that Phillips knew details about the murders.

At first, Phillips denied knowing Vealey or Gilly. But confronted with the evidence from the burglary arrest and bail records that past fall, he quickly realized that the smart move was to cooperate. He admitted participating in the initial plot to kill Yablonski, including the home invasion on October 31 when he and Vealey stopped long enough to make sandwiches. He said he'd quit after Gilly, who'd been the lookout and was supposed to be waiting in the car, took off and left himself and Vealey stranded.

Phillips also connected the murders to the UMWA and its leadership. On the way to kill Yablonski in Washington, D.C., he said, Gilly told him and Vealey that their target was a "minor" union official who got on the wrong side of someone higher up in the organization named "Tony."

Phillips said he was also present when Annette Gilly talked to her father, Silous Huddleston, the president of a UMWA local in Tennessee, about the murder plot. He said he once met Huddleston in LaFollette. "I think he worked for some guy named Tony."

If true, the statements made by Phillips confirmed that one way or the other, the union was involved in the murder plot. The agents assumed that "some guy named Tony" had to have been a reference to the union president. But even if it was more than a rumor, they were a long way from proving it.

After interrogating Phillips, Agent Bader sent a teletype to his boss in Pittsburgh. The case, he wrote, was now centered on "Paul Gilly et al." The FBI was ready to act.

On January 19, agents served the Gillys with a search warrant. In a kitchen drawer they found a roadmap with Clarksville underlined in red ink and a map of Washington D.C with the location of the UMWA building underlined. The G-men also located a large number of weapons in the basement and concluded that Gilly was not just a house painter. They did not, however, arrest him.

The next day, Claude Vealey was brought in for questioning by Agents Joseph Masterson and Burke. At first, he denied any association with Gilly, Phillips, or Martin, as well as any complicity in the Yablonski murders.

However, after being confronted with what the agents already knew from Phillips, as well as Vealey's drunk boasting at the Family Tavern, he too saw the writing on the wall. Every criminal accused of a crime with accomplices knows that the first one to talk—especially in what could be a death penalty case—was the most likely to get a deal for cooperating. After sleeping on it in a jail cell, he was ready to talk. He gave a full, detailed confession implicating himself and his two murderous companions.

Some of Vealey's statements were important for corroborating other evidence tending to connect the killers with the crime. One of the most damning was his recounting the events of December 18, the day he and Gilly met Yablonski at his home. It matched Kenneth Yablonski's recollection and connected the license plate number found on the yellow pad in the Yablonski home, as well as the statement of the Koremooth Tavern bartender. Corroborating evidence was vital because confessions such as Vealey's can't legally be used in court without it.

Vealey also revealed some details about the killers' actions before, during, and after the murders that matched the evidence that only the killers would know and hadn't been revealed to the public. Unfortunately, the initial press coverage had reported a number of facts, such as that the telephone lines had been cut and the cars disabled. The initial reports also quoted the coroner, Jackson Farrell, regarding the disposition of the bodies and the wounds.

However, Vealey's gruesome step-by-step account of the murders matched, as well as added to, what was known. He also remembered the presence of the small white dog and the reason Yablonski's study was in disarray with papers strewn around.

The killer described the hours he and his co-conspirators spent drinking and working their courage up as they waited on the hill overlooking the back of the house. He said they'd left their empties lying around where they'd parked.

Also, apparently oblivious to the idea of ever getting caught, the three killers made no attempt to disguise themselves. Whether buying beer and whiskey, flirting with a waitress in Clarksville, or filling their car with gas at a local Sunoco, they'd shown their faces at a variety of places, all of which could be checked out.

In addition to leaving more breadcrumbs than Hansel and Gretel in the forest, the killers had gone home to Cleveland and started spending their blood money on used cars and partying, including really tying one on that New Year's Eve.

Vealey said that after they got back to Cleveland, Gilly had given them each an envelope containing money—their share of the murder contract. They'd been promised $1,500 each, but Vealey still owed Gilly $750 for bailing him out of jail, so Vealey was supposed to receive only half. But Gilly had mixed up the envelopes, which meant Martin got shorted. The mistake had been quickly sorted out after Martin angrily complained.

The money confirmed that the Yablonski massacre was a contract murder, not some burglary gone wrong, or some lone wolf union member settling a grudge. However, who knew how many layers—such as Annette Gilly and Silous Huddleston—there might be between the gunmen and whoever ordered the hit. And if it was Boyle, there was a big difference between suspicion and proving a murder case in court.

After confessing, Vealey was placed under arrest for the murder of Jock Yablonski, Margaret Yablonski, and Charlotte Yablonski. Later that day Paul Gilly was arrested for the same crimes. Martin was in jail when he was told that he was now a triple-murder suspect and placed under arrest.

Over the next few days, the agents attempted to wring confessions from Martin and Gilly. The lawmen thought at first that they might get Martin to talk based on his physical appearance. Just five foot six and baby-faced, he looked like a kid. But he'd adopted a smirking tough-guy posture and denied knowing anybody named Paul or Claude.

Acting tough didn't make him smart. A slip of paper with the names "Paul" and "Claude" and two telephone numbers written on it was found in his wallet. Then a search of his home located a gray ledger, the "Personal Telephone Directory of Aubran Wayne Martin," that also contained the names of his accomplices and their telephone numbers. Confronted with those facts, Martin shrugged and continued to deny having anything to do with murders or that he'd ever been to Pennsylvania in December.

Paul Gilly also seemed like a good candidate for different reasons. Thin, pasty-faced, and obviously scared to death after a few nights in jail, he was the only one without a criminal record. But Gilly also was the suspect with the closest ties to the UMWA. He was related by marriage to a president of a union local in Tennessee who by all accounts had been a union enforcer in his day. And Gilly's wife, Annette, herself seemed up to her eyeballs in the plot. He was bound to be under a lot of pressure, and threats, to keep him from talking to law enforcement.

After reading Phillips's and Vealey's statements, seasoned FBI agents and police officers could not imagine a more inept trio of assassins. They'd blundered their way from Cleveland to Washington D.C. to Clarksville trying to catch up to their target and then left a trail of evidence a blind man could have followed all the way back to Ohio.

They had ultimately been successful in their heinous task. But that only went to show that it didn't take a genius to commit murder, just to get away with it.

CHAPTER SIXTEEN

THE CHINK
IN THE ARMOR

JANUARY 21, 1970

Albert Pass walked into Boyle's office at the UMWA headquarters in Washington, D.C. and settled his thick frame into the chair across the desk from the man he'd come to see. "Well, it is all done now," he said.

Boyle nodded. "Yes, it is all over with." Concerned about the heat coming down from the FBI and worried about wiretaps, he had not been able to talk much to Pass after the Yablonskis' bodies were discovered. But Pass was in D.C. for the meeting of the International Executive Board (IEB) scheduled for the next day and it gave them a chance to catchup.

"The U.S. Department of Labor has been down to my office in Middlesboro checking on records for the district and the locals," Pass said.

"Are the records in order?" Boyle asked.

"Yes, I believe they are. Everything is being carried out according to your instructions."

As Boyle had assumed, Pass knew what to do after their conversation on January 5. They both believed that they could rely on the loyalty and the traditional code of silence in the face of outsiders, as well as the fear of reprisals, with the other union conspirators. As far as the gunmen were concerned, the union boss still believed that his name had been left out of the planning; he thought only Pass and Turnblazer knew his role in the plot.

Even if there'd been a slip, or educated guesses, the killers didn't have anything with which to pin their actions on him or anything that could be proved against Pass. The one chink in the armor was the R&I Committee as the source of the blood money. If the investigators found out it was a hoax and got one of the field representatives or pensioners to admit it, that could spell trouble.

However, Pass had already moved to shore up that defense. He knew that they might someday need to "prove" the committee existed starting in 1968 and that the committee members had worked that year and into 1969. They needed something more than just his letters to Boyle requesting reimbursement money.

Pass decided to create vouchers for the reimbursements going back to 1968. He then had Roark, who'd worked for him for more than twenty years and could be trusted, copy and place the vouchers in the District 19 files.

He also got together with Turnblazer, and together they decided that they would put the R&I Committee to work for real. It would demonstrate that the recruitment efforts in Harlan and Bell Counties were real and ongoing.

Boyle was pleased with his man's efforts. However, another wrench was thrown into the mix that night. Pass was in his hotel room listening to the ten o'clock news when it was announced that three men from Cleveland had been arrested and charged with the murders of the Yablonskis. He caught the suspects' names: Vealey, Martin, and Gilly. Only the last one was familiar to him—Paul Gilly, the son-in-law of Silous Huddleston.

The next morning, he met with Boyle who had also seen the newscast. "Do you know them?" Boyle asked.

Pass answered that he didn't know them.

"Do you think they're Prater's guys?" Boyle asked.

"I don't know, but I think so," Pass replied.

Law enforcement nabbing the killers so easily wasn't good news. But Boyle didn't panic. He had an idea on how to use the IEB meeting to further improve the credibility of the R&I Committee.

On January 22, 1970, in the afternoon, the meeting room was swirling with the news about the Yablonski murders and suspects having been arrested. But if anybody had any thoughts about union involvement in the slayings, they were keeping them out of earshot of Tony Boyle and his enforcer Albert Pass.

After some regular business was handled, Boyle was ready to go forward with his idea. He invited Pass to come to the podium to tell those present about the "great work" done by the R&I Committee members.

On cue, Pass strode to the microphone where he gave an impassioned account of how the R&I Committee had been formed at the 1968 UMWA convention in Denver for the purpose of recruiting non-union mineworkers in District 19. The committee had worked throughout 1968 and into 1969, he said, and though it had been dormant since the fall while the political campaign was going on, it had been reactivated. The members were now back working hard to spread "the gospel of unionism."

After Pass finished, Boyle walked back to the podium where he initiated a standing ovation for his friend's speech. Now there would be "witnesses" who would be aware of the history and efforts of the R&I Committee. But he had one more notion about how to use Pass's speech.

The only other person who supposedly knew about the murder plot and Boyle's role was Turnblazer. Normally, he would have attended the IEB meeting as the president of District 19, but he'd been attending hearings in the Kentucky legislature and Boyle had told him to stay there.

After the IEB meeting adjourned, Boyle asked for a copy of the minutes, something he usually never bothered with. He pulled the pages from the transcript that described Pass's speech about the R&I Committee. "Give this to Turnblazer," he told his henchman, "so he'll know the story."

CHAPTER SEVENTEEN

ON THE BANKS OF THE MONONGAHELA

JANUARY 24–27, 1970

Special Agent William "Bill" Curtis of the FBI stood on the steep slope above the Monongahela River looking down at the dark waters that swirled beneath a hole chopped in the ice. A rope line manned by a team that stood on the shore disappeared into the water where somewhere below a diver searched the murky bottom.

Tall, clean-cut, square-jawed, college-educated, and handsome, Curtis could have been a poster boy for the FBI. Assigned to the Pittsburgh office, he was one of a dozen agents—as well as a bevy of federal auditors in Washington, D.C. and Kentucky and Pennsylvania State Police officers and investigators—actively working the Yablonski case.

Based on Vealey's statement, on January 21, Curtis had led the search at the overlook, the vantage point behind the Yablonski home. It had snowed in the three weeks between the murders and the confession, but it wasn't hard to find empty beer and whiskey bottles—of the make and quantity described by the suspect—and other debris. The litter was carefully preserved and sent off to the FBI lab for fingerprint analysis.

The following day, an FBI supervisor, Charles Groenthal, the top FBI expert at fingerprint analysis who had examined more than two million prints in his career and testified at more than a hundred trials, reported his findings from the evidence gathered at the overlook. He had detected latent prints for two of the suspects. Two for Vealey—one on a Stroh's beer can and one on a cardboard box that had contained a bottle of Seagram's whisky—and one for Buddy Martin on a Stroh's beer can. Groenthal concluded that Martin had been eating potato chips and oil from the chips on his fingers had helped preserve the print.

Groenthal would also come through with another fingerprint identification that would further corroborate Vealey's confession. On January 23, Agent Calvin Durst drove to the West Brownsville Hotel where Vealey said he and Gilly stayed the night after Christmas. Miraculously, nearly a month later the room had still not been cleaned, and he was able to gather more for the fingerprint expert to examine. Groenthal did not disappoint either, finding Gilly's prints on a bottle of Sprite that had been left in the room.

Vealey had also described their leaving the Clarksville area after the murders during a snowstorm, heading west on Route 88. He said Gilly drove while he rode in the front passenger seat and Martin slept in the back.

Along the way they stopped twice. Once to throw three film cannisters down a hillside a few miles north of California, Pennsylvania. Gilly had taken them from the house as a sort of "proof" that they'd been there, but Martin demanded he get rid of them in case they got pulled over. The cannisters were spotted from the air and recovered by Schifko of the Pennsylvania State Police.

The second stop was the place above the Monongahela where Curtis now stood looking at the scene below. It was here, according to Vealey, that Martin had thrown the murder weapons into the water—a chrome-plated, pearl-handled .38 caliber revolver and an M1 carbine.

Three days earlier, on January 24, Senior Chief Machinist's Mate Fred Schunk, a master diver on loan from the U.S. Navy, donned diving equipment and entered a hole that had been chopped in the ice with fire axes. Just getting in the river was an act of courage and fortitude. On a nice warm sunny day, battling the current and trying to see through the murky water would have been a challenge. But the air temperature when Schunk went in was fourteen degrees, and below the surface the water was so dark that a flashlight was of little use.

Schunk was in the water, described later as "shilt"—a combination of "shit" and "silt"[32]—for about an hour, and it was beginning to look like the search was coming up empty when the diver returned to the surface. He was holding the revolver Vealey described and handed it to an incredulous FBI agent.

After that incredible find, Schunk was no longer available and was replaced by FBI agent Kenneth Russell, himself a master diver. For two days, Russell battled the currents and the elements searching for the carbine with no luck. But on this day, as Curtis watched, the diver's hand emerged from the water; in it, he held a carbine.

So far, everything Vealey described about the murders and fleeing the scene had checked out. The case against the three killers was overwhelming with Vealey's confession, though he could still refuse to testify and jeopardize the prosecution. But more than just the three hitmen, the evidence had continued to implicate union officials in the UMWA.

Still, Curtis knew that it would take all the evidence, and as many confessions and witnesses, as could be found and corroborated to make a case that went beyond the gunmen. Even then, getting to someone as powerful and influential as Boyle could take years and as many trials as there were defendants.

There was also the location to contend with. The murders had gone down in the heart of coal country where the UMWA was the single most influential political and cultural force. It was known to have politicians, judges, and law enforcement in its back pocket, and could afford the best lawyers money could buy. Nor was the union above intimidating witnesses and ensuring loyalty through violence and bribes.

---

32   Lewis, *Murder by Contract.*

Indeed, the UMWA was the most powerful union in the United States, the model for the Teamsters Union and United Auto Workers. It exerted considerable influence on national, regional, and local elections. Presidential candidates had been known to consult Lewis and ask for his endorsement. And despite warnings about the potential for violence during the recent union election, the U.S. Departments of Labor and Justice had declined to get involved rather than taking on Boyle.

Up against that sort of muscle and political power, the person responsible for prosecuting the Yablonski murders was currently the district attorney of Washington County where the crimes occurred. Curtis doubted that that individual was up to this task.

District Attorney Jess Costa was a nice guy and an able administrator. But Washington was a sleepy county and not used to "big city crime." Costa operated with a part-time staff, and most of his cases didn't rise above misdemeanors and minor felonies. Murder, when it rarely happened, tended to be the garden variety kind— domestic disputes, robbery gone wrong, or unintended in the heat of the moment. Not the cold-blooded, paid assassination of a former UMWA presidential candidate, as well as his wife and daughter.

It was going to take a special prosecutor, and a special kind of prosecutor. As he drove away from the Monongahela, Curtis wondered who had the ability and tenacity to take on such a complex, high-profile case in coal country. Who had the ability to pull all the evidentiary pieces together and make them fit into a coherent picture? Who knew how to play his cards right to get suspects to flip and reluctant witnesses to step forward?

Just dealing with the disparate law enforcement agencies involved would be a monumental task given the traditional rivalry between the FBI and "the locals." Getting them all to work together as a single team and keep it all on track for however long it took was going to be a Herculean task.

The FBI agent didn't envy whoever went up against Boyle and the UMWA. He wondered if there was someone who was just as tough as "Tough Tony" on the side of justice.

CHAPTER EIGHTEEN

"SCANDALOUSLY INACCURATE"

MARCH 9, 1970

As Tony Boyle stood behind a bevy of microphones, his face contorted into a mask of rage while he waved a fourteen-page statement during a hastily called press conference at the National Press Club building in Washington, D.C. "I came here today to set the record straight, to give you the facts."

Those facts, he snarled, were that neither he nor the union had done anything wrong during the 1969 election campaign, nor had anything to do with the murder of Jock Yablonski and his family. "I swear to Almighty God that I'm telling the truth," he said holding up his right hand.

The press conference had been arranged by a public relations firm hired by the union on the heels of allegations of Boyle's involvement in the Yablonski murders.

After the IEB meeting in January, Boyle and Pass were satisfied that they'd covered their bases. The history of the R&I Committee had been established with the IEB members and put on the record in the official transcript of Pass's speech, and the R&I Committee members had been put to work doing real proselytizing.

A month later, Pass gave the transcript to Turnblazer, who asked what happened to the money from the R&I kickback scheme. "It went to a good cause," Pass told him and offered no further explanation. Nor had Turnblazer asked for one.

They'd left Pass's letters to Boyle in the national headquarters files and the vouchers and cashed checks in the District 19 files for the federal auditors to find. Indeed, they wanted the investigators to notice them. With the blood money accounted for as a legitimate union expense, there were no other links back to Boyle.

However, there was troubling news. The arrest of the so-called "Hillbilly Hitmen" had been followed by more bad news. First, there were rumors that one of the assassins was spilling his guts to the FBI. That seemed to be confirmed when Annette Gilly, who Pass told Boyle was the wife of one of the killers, Paul Gilly, was indicted in early February for the Yablonski murders in Washington County.

Two weeks later, Silous Huddleston, the guy Prater had used to find the killers, was indicted on federal charges. The arrest warrant accused him of violating Yablonski's civil rights by having him murdered. He'd subsequently been charged in Washington County for the murders.

The arrests, particularly of Huddleston because of his direct ties to the union, were even more ominous because a couple days earlier, Boyle was summoned to the office of Labor Secretary Shultz. There he'd been informed that the department was going to file suit to overturn the election on grounds of fraud and campaign irregularities.

The Labor Department actions were the result of that troublemaking lawyer Joe Rauh and a new group of agitators called Miners for Democracy that had formed after the funerals. The chief organizers of the group were Rauh, the Yablonski brothers Kenneth and Chip, and some of Yablonski's campaign staff. Its membership included most of the miners in the West Virginia chapter of the Black Lung Association, miners who walked off the job in protest after the murders, and several union leaders at the local level.

Their first order of business was to get the Department of Labor to overturn the 1969 election results. Now, Shultz said he was going to court to do that.

Boyle decided he needed to go on the offensive by hiring the public relations firm. They decided to call the press conference at the National Press Club headquarters building.

Whatever the firm thought would be accomplished by putting Boyle in front of a bunch of reporters, they had no idea that Boyle would go on a two-hour rant.

Flailing his arms and shouting, Boyle said he and the UMWA were the victims of "outrageously and scandalously inaccurate" charges, "Communist-style duplicity" by the government, and "reckless journalism."[33]

Boyle complained that Shultz told him during the meeting that the union would have a chance to answer the allegations before the department took any action. But, the union boss complained, the labor secretary didn't tell him the lawsuit paperwork had already been filed in federal court. He said he didn't learn that bit of news until Shultz left their meeting and held his own press conference where he announced the lawsuit.

After two hours of hurling bitter recriminations and insisting upon his and the union's innocence, Boyle was nearly out of steam at his press conference when a reporter asked a question that both alarmed him and sent him over the top again. The newsman asked about a "secret committee" of pensioners that had supposedly been given checks to cash for work they had not done and then illegally funneled the money back for political campaigns.

"There is nothing secret about the United Mine Workers," he shouted at the reporter. "There is nothing secret about what they are doing!"

Boyle was rattled. Obviously, somebody was talking; even if, judging by the reporter's question, they didn't know the real purpose of the R&I Committee reimbursements. His response was to put the

---

33   Ben A. Franklin, "Boyle Denies All Charges; He Assails U.S.
      and Media," *New York Times*, March 10, 1970.

word out that everybody needed to "stick to the story." If they did, it wouldn't matter how big an army of FBI agents, federal auditors, and local cops were assigned to the case.

He might not have been as confident if he'd known the man who would be leading that army.

CHAPTER NINETEEN

RUNNING THE SHOW

"I want a deal!"

Beetle-browed and cursed with a perpetual five-o'clock shadow, Claude Vealey did his best to look confident, as if he was holding all the cards. He'd just been escorted by two U.S. marshals into the office of Bob Krupansky, chief of the U.S. Department of Justice's Cleveland office. Now, he expected to be offered leniency in exchange for his testimony against his two cohorts.

Although he'd given the FBI a detailed confession a few weeks earlier, and signed it, he knew from the defense attorney appointed to his case that it wasn't worth the paper it was printed on if he wouldn't testify. An FBI agent could have been sworn in to read it on the record during a trial, but juries weren't keen on confessions from admitted killers, especially those who turn on their co-conspirators to save their own skin, especially if the defense later put them on the stand to say they'd been coerced.

The room was filled with law enforcement officers and government lawyers. In addition to Krupansky, also present was Tom Henderson, a U.S deputy attorney general from the department's national office in Washington, FBI agents Bill Curtis and Joe Masterson, Pennsylvania police investigators Bob Dugan and Elmer Schifko, and Jess Costa, the Washington County district attorney. But Vealey's attention was drawn to a short, slightly built man with bulging eyes, prominent nose, and receding hairline the others seemed to be deferring to. His name was Richard A. Sprague, the chief assistant district attorney out of the Philadelphia District Attorney's Office.

DA Costa had recognized that he didn't have the experience or resources to take on the case, even with the assistance of the FBI, local law enforcement, and the Pennsylvania State Police. He was also being inundated with entreaties from local attorneys who wanted to be named special prosecutor. They all knew this was going to be a high-profile case with national exposure and trying the case would garner a lot of publicity good for the resume. Whoever he chose was going to make the others unhappy.

What's more, Chip and Kenneth Yablonski had been lobbying for a special prosecutor to be appointed. As attorneys, they knew that the case was beyond the capabilities of Costa, or any other lawyer in Washington County. It was going to take someone who could handle the national publicity and political pressure. Someone who was capable of not just convicting the three gunmen but going after the man at the top of the United Mine Workers of America.

Happy to pass the burden on, Costa asked Philadelphia DA Arlen Specter if Sprague, his chief assistant district attorney and number-two man in the office, could be appointed special prosecutor. Specter agreed.

A graduate of Pennsylvania Carey Law School, Sprague had done nothing there that indicated he would have a stellar career. Classwork bored him, and he was admittedly not a good student. But in the courtroom, he was a master tactician, detail-oriented, and a genius at creating the dramatic moment that would stick with juries.

Sprague had a well-deserved reputation in Philadelphia and state-wide with both law enforcement and the public who liked his tough "law and order" demeanor and for seeking the death penalty in first degree murder cases. In his seventeen years with the Philadelphia district attorney's office, he'd successfully tried to verdict hundreds of cases, including scores of capital intentional first-degree murder cases. In sixty-five of those cases, the defendants were convicted of first-degree murder; the only defendant who escaped the first-degree conviction was found guilty of second-degree murder.

Known for his intense trial preparation, Sprague lived and breathed whatever case he was trying until he knew every detail and was ready for any contingency the defense might come up with. After each day's courtroom proceedings were finished, he would meet with his staff, law enforcement and whoever else he deemed important, to essentially run through a dress rehearsal for the following day.

Although he prosecuted many notable murder cases, there was one in particular that cemented his legend among both prosecutors and defense attorneys. The case involved the disappearance of a woman who the police believed was murdered by her husband. However, no body had been found, nor was there any evidence of a murder in the couple's home. The only indication of foul play initially was when the woman's neighbors grew concerned after she had not been seen for several days and called the police.

In spite of the lack of a body, the police arrested the husband who was subsequently indicted by a grand jury at Sprague's direction for first degree murder. The husband claimed that following an argument, she'd simply left the house and disappeared. But Sprague reasoned that she wouldn't have left her bridgework on the bedroom dresser, as well as her handbag and cosmetics.

Right up to the end, court observers thought it was going to be a tossup on whether the defendant would be convicted. During closing arguments, the defense lawyer contended that the lack of a corpse was grounds for acquittal. He suggested that the victim could walk through the door at the back of the courtroom at any minute.

On cue, a tall, well-dressed, middle-aged woman who matched the description of the missing wife walked into the back of the courtroom and stood there as if trying to decide where to sit. She made enough of an entrance that almost everyone in the courtroom, including the jurors, turned to watch her.

Having made his point, the defense attorney acknowledged that she was not the defendant's wife. But, he said, the fact that every person in the courtroom turned to look at her and wondered for a moment meant Sprague had not proved the Commonwealth's case beyond a reasonable doubt.

Sprague, however, was undaunted by the defense attorney's theatrics. Rising to give his closing argument, he said, "Yes, you all turned and looked, but two people in the courtroom did not. I did not because I was looking at the defendant."

The clever prosecutor then turned toward the defense table and pointed. "And the defendant did not turn and look because he knows she's dead."

The verdict came back "guilty," and the defendant was sentenced to death.[34]

It was the sort of gamesmanship Sprague, an accomplished chess player, was known for—setting up his opponent, or leading them into setting themselves up, and then springing the trap. He possessed an extraordinarily sharp mind and had total recall, never using notes during his courtroom appearances. Armed with a tremendous knowledge of criminal law, he was often described by colleagues and opponents as driven when it came to prosecuting murderers.

Sprague had a commanding physical presence in the courtroom. His deep stentorian voice and stern, totally in charge demeaner kept the jurors' rapt attention. He could be merciless as he tore apart hostile witnesses on the stand, but he did it without yelling or histrionics. Not that he wasn't capable of raising his voice at just the right moment, but more often than not his tone was that of the voice of reason. And he always addressed his colleagues on the defense side of the aisle cordially, also exhibiting professional respect to the presiding judge.

Like a stage actor who hits all his marks, Sprague knew how to work a courtroom. He never turned his back on the jury whether he was approaching them, crossing the well of the court to a white board, or walking back to the prosecution table. He also insisted on handing exhibits to jurors, establishing physical contact.

Although he had no political ambitions, Sprague certainly had an ego and a competitive streak. He was pleased when he was chosen as the special prosecutor for a case with national implications and played at the highest level against what he thought would be

---

34   As recounted by Sprague to Robert K. Tanenbaum, 2020.

formidable opponents on the defense side. Of course, if he failed, the fall would be precipitous as well, but he looked forward to the challenge.

Sprague hit the ground running and was quickly up to speed by mid-March 1970. After reading Vealey's confession, he'd visited the murder scene starting with the vantage point on the hill behind the Yablonski house. FBI Agent Curtis had shown him where the beer and whiskey bottles, as well as the associated trash and cigarette butts, had been tossed. He wanted to be able to picture in his mind the killers as they'd waited for the lights to go out in the house and their victims to fall asleep.

Sprague then went down to the house where the Yablonski brothers were waiting to enter the premises with him. But to their consternation, he told them to wait outside while he went in with Curtis and state patrol investigators Schifko and Dugan. He walked through the kitchen and the study and then up the stairs to the bedrooms where the murders occurred.

The rooms had not been cleaned or altered. The blood was still dark and thick on the bedding and walls; the stench of death permeated the air. He'd seen the crime photographs and could picture the bodies as they'd been found: twenty-five-year-old Charlotte, her hair in curlers for a New Year's Eve party she'd never attend, lying on her side; her mother, Margaret, on her back; and Jock on the floor next to the bed, slumped against the wall, a shotgun just out of reach.

Sprague went from the murder scene to the spot along the Monongahela River and peered down at the place where the divers had found the guns. *Incredible police work*, he thought.

The evidence against the gunmen was overwhelming. It kept piling up, too. Such was the case of the film cannisters that Vealey had described Gilly taking from the house and then throwing into a field at Martin's insistence; they'd been examined by Groenthal who determined that Jock Yablonski's fingerprints were on them.

Unlike the Yablonski brothers, Sprague had not immediately jumped to the conclusion that Tony Boyle ordered the hit. But he didn't disbelieve it. Before the murders occurred, he was aware from the Philadelphia media that the campaign for the UMWA presidency was a bitter one with both sides accusing the other of corruption. He'd also heard of Joe Rauh and knew that the well-regarded labor lawyer had complained to the Department of Labor that his client was in danger from the union hierarchy.

There were certainly indications that the union president was involved, including the statements from Phillips and Vealey that the murders had been ordered because Yablonski had gotten on the wrong side of "some guy named Tony." Federal agents like Bill Curtis and other law enforcement obviously believed it could only mean Boyle. But Sprague wanted to arrive at that conclusion on his own, strictly based on the immutable evidence, which could not be refuted.

It was clear that the killers had been working for someone in the union who had paid for their heinous act. The three, dubbed "The Hillbilly Hitmen" by the press as tidbits about their clumsy efforts and nondescript backgrounds made it into the public arena, had not exactly been circumspect. Within days of the murders, Martin and Vealey had freely spent what they'd earned for the assassinations— Martin bought a used car from a salesman the FBI had already contacted, and Vealey boasted at the bar about spending blood money.

In all honesty, Sprague was surprised that such rank amateurs had been hired for a high-profile assassination. Whoever ordered the hit had to know the murder was sure to bring the national spotlight and amped up law enforcement efforts to catch the killers.

If Boyle was involved, Sprague couldn't fathom why he had not hired professional killers who would have accomplished the job efficiently, without leaving a bunch of evidence or opening their mouths about it. Instead, they would have scattered across the country, or hopped the first plane to Sicily if Boyle had turned to the mob for assistance.

The only thing that made some sense was that Boyle was relying on the loyalty and discretion of the union men who had arranged for the killings. Curtis and other Pennsylvania-based lawmen had warned him what he'd be up against taking on the UMWA and possibly its leader in the heart of coal country. Tough, brought up with the belief that the union was infallible, and not particularly trusting of law enforcement, they had their own version of *omerta*, the Mafia code of secrecy.

The so-called Hillbilly Hitmen weren't union men, but one of them, Paul Gilly, was married to the daughter of Silous Huddleston, the president of a local in LaFollette, Tennessee. Both the daughter, twenty-nine-year-old Annette, and her father were thought to be the conduits between the killers and whoever hired them.

The evidence pointing to a top-down conspiracy ramped up when FBI agents who specialized in forensic accounting began looking into the financial records of District 19 and surrounding districts for the six months preceding December 31, 1969. The task meant examining hundreds of thousands of transactions involving millions of dollars. Reams of correspondence that piled together would have been five feet high.[35]

The search reaped dividends when the agents discovered two checks, each for $10,000, issued a week apart in September 1969. Each had been requested in letters sent from Albert Pass, the secretary-treasurer of District 19, to Tony Boyle. What drew the investigators' attention was that of all the myriad financial requests from the union's Canadian and U.S. districts to the national office, these were the only two made directly to Boyle, who had assigned them as well. All of the other requests had been sent to John P. Owens, the UMWA's secretary-treasurer.

Alerted by this irregularity, the agents tracked what happened to the $20,000 and found that all but $30 had been distributed in checks to twenty-three District 19 pensioners. While the payments did not prove the money was connected to the killers, the anomaly and timing of the transactions certainly were suspicious. According to Vealey and Phillips, they'd been involved in the murder plot beginning in September 1969.

If the agents' suspicions proved correct, they now had a money trail from Pass to Boyle back to Pass and from him to the pensioners. Pass was known to be a close confidant of the union president. And

---

35   Lewis, *Murder By Contract.*

if he was involved, chances were, so was William Turnblazer, an attorney and president of District 19, as well as a known confidant of Boyle. But they needed someone to break their silence.

By February 5, the FBI had dug up enough evidence for Costa to charge Annette Gilly with murder. Yet, though Krupansky and several of the agents had all tried talking to her, she wasn't giving them anything except the cold shoulder.

On February 25, U.S. Attorney Krupansky appeared before a federal grand jury in Cleveland and presented enough evidence to indict Silous Huddleston on federal charges of obstructing justice. Then on March 12, Costa filed a state criminal complaint charging him with murder. But the old, ill former coalminer wouldn't talk either, except to proclaim his innocence. Father and daughter were placed in custody and not allowed to communicate. That same day, Gilly and Martin, on advice of counsel, refused to agree to extradition back to Pennsylvania. And that's where things stood.

When he took on the case, Sprague had been intrigued by the challenge of pulling together a complicated case that crossed state lines and would rely on a plethora of law enforcement agencies including the FBI, the Pennsylvania State Police, the Washington County Sheriff's Office, and investigators in Ohio, Kentucky, and Tennessee. In particular, the FBI was known to other agencies as a "one-way street"—taking in information but giving little back. In fact, Costa had complained to him that the FBI wasn't sharing. Sprague was well aware that generally the FBI simply dismissed local law enforcement as too unsophisticated to be taken seriously.

Sprague's reputation had started to change that, particularly when the federal agents working with him saw the way his mind worked and how detail-oriented he could be. But he knew that prosecuting the three gunmen and then working his way up the ladder from there was going to be difficult enough without the various agencies pulling in different directions and working different agendas. He needed them all on the same page, which meant that one person— and only one—could be in charge of the investigation and prosecution.

So Sprague was pleased when Krupansky suggested that they meet at his office with the various agencies present when Vealey was brought in. He'd flown in that morning from Philadelphia with a plan to put his stamp on the investigation.

Vealey had made it clear to the FBI agents who spoken to him that he wanted a deal for his testimony; otherwise, he was going to fight extradition back to Pennsylvania and even backtrack on his confession. When he was brought into the room where Sprague and the others waited, it was obvious that he thought he had the leverage.

"I'll plead guilty and testify for you if you'll guarantee life imprisonment. No deal. No cooperation," Vealey said.

Sprague was pleased that on top of Vealey's mind was avoiding the death penalty. That was exactly what he wanted him, his cohorts, and everyone else up the ladder to be conscious of. But he wasn't giving Vealey anything. He looked at the thug, shook his head, and to everyone's surprise matter-of-factly said, "No deal."

As jaws around the room dropped, Sprague kept his eyes on the surprised killer. The prosecutor had several reasons for playing hardball. One was juries looked askance at killers who got deals to turn on other defendants. And defense attorneys always used such deals to attack the credibility of those witnesses.

Sprague also wanted to send a message to the co-conspirators. He was playing for keeps, and the death penalty was going to stay on the table.

He was well aware that convicting the three killers wasn't going to be a slam dunk, especially without the confession and testimony of one of them. But if he had any hope of working his way through all the layers to reach Boyle, he was going to have to put the fear of God into the others and hope they'd roll over.

"Mr. Vealey," he continued, "if you think you're going to bargain with me, you're paddling up the wrong creek. Plead guilty and cooperate, and I'll take that into consideration when your case is disposed of ultimately. But I won't bargain with you."

It took a moment for comprehension to register on Vealey's dumb face, but then he scowled. "You're asking me to do something for nothing, Mr. Sprague. You're not offering me anything."

Sprague nodded. He figured that the FBI agents who had been talking to Vealey had probably indicated he'd get a deal if he talked. "That's right Mr. Vealey."

"Then I won't offer nothin' either, Mr. Sprague."

The Philadelphia prosecutor turned to the U.S. marshals. "Take him out. If he's ever willing to cooperate, you can bring him back. But not 'til then."[36]

When the stunned killer had been escorted from the room, Krupansky turned to Sprague. "You're a tough man, Dick. We *need* this guy as a witness. What right have you to be *that* tough?"

Costa was beside himself. Lose the case, and, as the district attorney who swore Sprague in as special prosecutor, his career was done. But he'd agreed when they started that the Philadelphia prosecutor was calling the shots.

Sprague looked around the room at the shocked faces of "his" team. They might not have liked it, but he'd established two things: he was running the show, and as team captain, he expected all involved to work together and cooperate.

---

36   Ibid.

CHAPTER TWENTY

THE STAGE IS SET

It has been said that the wheels of justice turn slow but they grind exceedingly fine. Such was the case with Sprague's approach to the Yablonski murders. This was by design to give himself and his team time to prepare, gather evidence, and put pressure on suspects and witnesses to cooperate.

Two years would pass from that terrible night in December 1969 before Sprague would bring the first of the killers to trial. But in the meantime, he and his team did what they could to keep the pressure on the killers and the other conspirators.

In the spring of 1970, Albert Pass, William Turnblazer, Bill Prater, and the twenty-three pensioners who had received the checks identified by the FBI auditors were subpoenaed by U.S. Attorney Krupansky to appear before a federal grand jury in Cleveland. Every one of them swore under oath that they had nothing to do with the murders and that the pensioners belonged to the R&I Committee. They testified that the money was used to pay their expenses incurred on missions to recruit non-union miners into the UMWA fold.

Proving that the money was used to pay the killers could make or break the case against the union officials, including Boyle. And that was going to be tough as long as they all stuck to the story. But the grand jury hearing was a shot across the bow of the union president and his henchmen, as well as the pensioners, that Sprague and the feds were onto them. Plus, he knew they had all lied under oath, which could be used as leverage against them.

Following the grand jury presentation, FBI agents Wally Estill and Hank Quinn were assigned to stay after the pensioners. The agents were based in the Knoxville, Tennessee office and familiar with the culture of coal country, so they could relate to the old-timers. They met a unified resistance when they first began talking to the pensioners and the field representatives for District 19, but gradually, they began to gain the trust of the mountaineers, even if the old men still weren't spilling the beans.

The pressure wasn't just at the state level as the federal attorneys were active as well. In March 1971, Boyle was indicted for violating the Corrupt Practices Act on thirteen federal charges having to do with embezzling more than $49,000 in union funds to illegally contribute to the 1968 U.S. presidential campaign of Hubert Humphrey and several congressmen and senators.

In the meantime, Sprague and the rest of the team focused on preparing to try the three gunmen. He'd indicted all three on June 25, 1970 in Washington County for "intentional murder" which carried the possibility of death sentences. Silous Huddleston and Annette Gilly were kept in jail as material witnesses, and unable to communicate with each other. The possibility of being charged as part of the murder conspiracy remained hanging over their heads.

Meanwhile, the Hillbilly Hitmen, including Claude Vealey, who continued to hold out for a deal, fought extradition to Pennsylvania, which actually worked in Sprague's favor. If the gunmen and their attorneys had quickly agreed to be extradited to Pennsylvania, and insisted on a speedy trial, he doubted he would have been ready. Especially if Vealey refused to testify.

Sprague—and for that matter, the defense attorneys—knew that eventually the trio would lose their fight and be brought to Pennsylvania. So he was happy to let the defense file all the motions and request all the hearings they wanted in the meantime.

In December 1970, Vealey lost his extradition fight and was brought to Pennsylvania to stand trial in early spring for the murders of Jock, Margaret, and Charlotte Yablonski. He was slated to be the first of the Hillbilly Hitmen to face justice, including the possibility of the death sentence.

Sprague wasn't budging on offering Vealey a deal in exchange for his testimony, but he was worried. He needed one of the three to testify against the other two to break the case open. But Buddy Martin was still playing the tough guy, and Paul Gilly, who had to consider his wife and father-in-law, wasn't talking either. Vealey was the most likely as he'd already confessed though he maintained that without a deal he was not going to testify for the prosecution.

A request by the defense to delay the trial again, to June 23, 1971, worked in Sprague's favor. In addition to being able to continue working on other parts of the case, he knew that the additional time would just add pressure on Vealey. After nearly a year in jail, he couldn't know if his companions would turn on him to save their skins.

Vealey blinked first. The day before the trial was set to begin, he agreed to testify without a deal on the murder charge. He confessed in open court before Judge Charles Sweet, president of the Washington County Common Pleas Court, that he participated in the murders and stated that he would testify for the prosecution. The only "deal" he got was that Sprague dropped the burglary and grand larceny charges. They weren't important to the prosecutor, whose only goal was to convict the killers and any other co-conspirators of first-degree murder.

With Vealey onboard, Sprague turned his attention to the other two gunmen. He needed to decide whether to try them together, which would have saved time and money but it also raised strategic issues.

He wanted to be able to call James Charles Phillips to testify about the entire plot to kill Yablonski, including the time he met Huddleston and Annette Gilly, as well as references to Pass, Prater and "some guy named Tony." His testimony would demonstrate that the murders were planned months in advance and were not a burglary gone awry, which if believed might result in a lesser charge.

However, it wasn't until Phillips had left the conspiracy because of his distrust of Gilly that Buddy Martin entered in Phillips's place on December 29, 1969. Therefore, Martin was not part of all that Phillips had done and agreed to do in furtherance of the plan to murder Yablonski. Simply, Martin was not a party to any of Phillips's conduct. Therefore, Martin's defense attorney could be expected to object to Phillips's testimony regarding the conspiracy prior to Martin's entry into the case. Notwithstanding this legal hair-splitting, Sprague didn't want the trial judge to potentially discourage the jury from regarding Phillips's testimony as it related to Buddy Martin but regard it as admissible against Gilly should Martin and Gilly be tried together. To avoid that type of jury distraction, Sprague wanted to try Martin and Gilly separately. Also, by trying the two defendants separately, Sprague would have the opportunity to ask for the death penalty first against Martin and then against Gilly, which Sprague believed would unnerve the other conspirators to the point of deciding to cooperate with the prosecutor.

Accordingly, Sprague decided to try the two young men separately. He chose to go with Martin first. He was the toughest of the three gunmen and least likely to ever cooperate. On the other hand, if he was convicted and sentenced to be executed, Gilly might roll over.

CHAPTER TWENTY-ONE

MAYBE SOMETHING WORSE

NOVEMBER 9, 1971

Kenneth Yablonski sat quietly in the witness chair as he gathered himself. He'd just described for the jury what it was like arriving at his parents' home on January 5, 1970, hoping that a lack of communication and milk bottles piled at the door only meant that they were out of town. Not *something worse*. But on entering through the kitchen door, he saw Rascal, his mother's small white terrier.

On the witness stand, it took a moment before he was able to get past the memory and continue. Turning towards the jury box in Courtroom 1 of the old-timey, dilapidated courthouse in Washington, Pennsylvania, he choked back the tears and said, "I knew they wouldn't have left the dog."[37]

Standing in front of him, special prosecutor Sprague nodded empathetically. Nearly two years after the murders of Jock, Margaret, and Charlotte Yablonski, he had started the trial of the *Commonwealth of Pennsylvania vs. Aubran Wayne Martin* by calling Kenneth to the stand.

---

37   *Commonwealth of Pennsylvania vs. Aubran Wayne Martin.* All quoted testimony is taken
      from trial transcripts provided by Richard A. Sprague to Robert K. Tanenbaum.

A master of creating courtroom drama, Sprague knew how po-werful the young man's testimony would be. He didn't try to rush him, preferring to let Kenneth lead the jurors step-by-step towards the horror that awaited him that day.

Meanwhile, the accused, "Buddy" Martin, sat at the defense table listening to the court proceedings as if none of it really involved him. Only five foot six and dubbed "the baby-faced killer" by the press, Martin even had a fan club of young women who sat in the third row behind the defense table, giggling and sighing whenever their collegiate-looking heartthrob turned to smile or wink.[38]

At his side, his lawyer, a young and inexperienced attorney who'd volunteered to defend the first of the Hillbilly Hitmen, waited for his opportunity. He'd only been practicing law for five years, and this was just his second murder trial and a real plum due to the media attention.

This was no ordinary murder case. No burglary gone awry. No crime of passion. Nor were the bumbling, inept, but ultimately successful trio the only targets on Sprague's list of villains to be brought to justice. A list whose ultimate goal was to hold account-able "some guy named Tony," who Sprague now was convinced was "Tough Tony" Boyle.

So he'd started the People's case in the most dramatic way he could: with the testimony of the man who'd discovered the bodies of his slaughtered family. From the witness stand, Kenneth Yablonski told the five men and nine women jurors (including the two alternates) that after seeing the dog and knowing that *something worse* had happened, he'd left the kitchen. The house was hot, the temperature in the 80s, and "I got part way into the dining room when I smelled this odor."

"Can you describe that smell?" asked Sprague, who, at five foot seven with bulging eyes and a large nose, was not physically impressive though his rich, deep voice could hold juries enthralled.

---

38 Courtroom descriptions were taken from several sources, especially *Murder by Contract* and from Richard A. Sprague as told to Robert K. Tanenbaum, 2020.

"All I can say, sir, now, is that it was the odor of death," Yablonski replied. "I don't know any other way to describe it. It was horrible."

"Then what happened?"

"I stopped and turned to Bill and asked if he smelled anything. He said 'yes.'"

Without further prodding, Yablonski recounted stepping into the living room. "The house was in disarray. There were torn papers all around; the Christmas tree was still standing. I remember the papers more than anything. Papers laying on the floor. I didn't see anyone in the living room."

As Yablonski then recalled dashing up the stairs to the second floor, Sprague stopped him long enough to have him describe the layout of the bedrooms before gently urging him to continue. "Tell the jury what occurred."

With everyone in the courtroom listening raptly, Kenneth Yablonski reached the moment when he approached the open door of his parents' room. "I saw what appeared to be a very large body lying on the bed covered by a quilt.... I ran into the room. It looked too large to be my mother. I thought it must be my father.... The face was covered as though they pulled the cover over the face."

This was the "something worse" that Kenneth had feared. "I took the cover and pulled it back. I couldn't see the face because it was all black or dark, but I could see the long hair and that's when I realized it was my mother. I looked for my father. I didn't see him on the bed."

However, he knew that his dad snored and sometimes slept in another room. Panicking, he rushed to the bedroom across the hall that he'd once shared with his brother and looked in. "I ran in there looking for my father, and I saw my sister. She was lying face down on the bed next to the door, and there was just blood all over the bed. It was all around, and her body was sort of dark in color."

In shock and horror, he staggered away from the room where his dead sister, her hair in curlers, lay in a pool of blood and cried out to his friend Bill Stewart, who had remained downstairs. "Where's my dad? Where is he? What did they do to him?"

He got his answer when he returned to his parents' room and walked around the other side of the bed and saw his father. "He was off the bed in almost like a kneeling, collapsed sort of position, sort of like this," the young man said as he demonstrated, "propped up against the end table."

The shotgun lay on the floor next to his father. "I remember seeing a lot of blood," he continued.

Running back down the stairs, Kenneth told his friend Bill Stewart they needed to call the police. But when Yablonski picked up the telephone, there was no dial tone. "The line had been cut."

Nearly two years later, as Kenneth Yablonski left the witness stand, the courtroom was as silent as the telephone had been on that terrible morning of January 5, 1970.

CHAPTER TWENTY-TWO

THE HORRIBLE CREATURE

"The People call Claude Vealey," Sprague said turning to the side door through which witnesses in custody entered the courtroom.

Escorted by a pair of deputies, Claude Vealey entered the courtroom looking like a man on the way to his own funeral. Ever since it got out that he'd flipped and was the government's star witness—a witness without whose testimony the case would have been in jeopardy—rumors had swirled throughout coal country that there was a price on his head.

It was a threat law enforcement took seriously. A twenty-four-hour watch was kept on Vealey's cell while a closed-circuit television screen monitored anyone approaching. Sharpshooters armed with rifles stood at the windows of the courthouse corridor that the prisoner had to walk down to reach the courtroom. Surrounded by three sheriff's deputies and a U.S. marshal, Vealey was kept away from windows for fear that he'd be killed by a sniper.

The crowded courtroom was ringed with U.S. marshals, state police officers, and more deputies; plainclothes cops mingled with the spectators. Anyone entering the courtroom had to pass through a metal detector—an unusual precaution in November 1971—and all members of the press had to wear badges with their photos displayed.[39]

The precautions were an acknowledgement of the potential reach of the UMWA in coal country. However, Sprague had a different concern, one of public perception.

The prison barber had done his best to clean Vealey up, giving him a close shave and neatly trimming and combing the few hairs remaining on his balding, melon-shaped head. He'd been dressed in a clean white shirt, pressed slacks, and polished shoes. But there was only so much gilding of the lily in Vealey's case.

Although he'd grown a small moustache, his perpetual five-o'clock shadow stood out against his pale skin. And with his dull features and thick, black eyebrows, he still looked like a mugshot on a "Most Wanted" flier at the post office.

In terms of who looked the part of a murderous criminal, there was little doubt Vealey was the clear choice when compared to the neatly coifed, collegiately dressed, and movie star-handsome Buddy Martin whose fan club scowled and murmured angrily as their heartthrob's accuser took the stand and was sworn in. Sprague worried that one or more jury members might base their decision on appearances instead of the evidence, but there wasn't much he could do about it. The evidence would have to show that the case had nothing to do with who looked like a killer and who did not.

Sprague believed that if ever a defendant deserved the death penalty, Buddy Martin was that person. He had aided in the execution of three people, including a twenty-five-year-old woman looking forward to the next day's New Year's Eve party, for a few thousand dollars. But there was another reason Sprague had to make sure that Martin was convicted and sentenced to death.

If he was ever going to get to "some guy named Tony," Sprague needed to put the fear of God, in the form of the death penalty, in the other conspirators and get them to flip and become witnesses for the prosecution. Anything less than the death penalty for Martin, and they might be willing to take their chances.

---

39   Lewis, *Murder by Contract*.

It meant convicting Martin of "intentional murder." And to prove the charge, Sprague had to demonstrate that the defendant was a "willing, active participant and intentionally caused the deaths of the deceased." The indictment concisely stated: "the defendant with intent to cause the death of the deceaseds, caused the death of the deceaseds by shooting them to death."

After having Vealey introduce his two lawyers, Sprague wasted no time diving into the heart of the matter. "Did you take part in killing Jock Yablonski?"

"Yes," Vealey replied, his voice subdued.

"Did you take part in killing Margaret Yablonski?"

"Yes."

"Did you take part in killing Charlotte Yablonski?"

"Yes."

"Do you see anyone else in the courtroom who took part in the killing with you?"

Vealey looked over at the defense table. "Aubran Martin."

An angry murmur rose from the fan club as Martin smiled slightly and shook his head.

"Indicate and point him out to the jury."

Aiming a finger at Martin, Vealey replied, "Sitting over there at the table."

Sprague turned to the court reporter. "The record will reflect that the witness pointed to the defendant's table, to the defendant..." He then turned to look at the defense table. "You mean Martin over here?"

"Yes."

Knowing that the defense would try to make Vealey look like he was implicating Martin to get "a deal," Sprague noted that Vealey had pleaded guilty to the murders and was awaiting sentencing. "Has there been any deal or agreement made with you in order for you to plead guilty?"

"Just the charges dropped in this courtroom?"

"And what charges were those?"

"I believe armed robbery, burglary, and grand larceny."

Sprague then led Vealey through the plot that began in July 1969 with an offer to help kill an unidentified person for another unnamed person for $5,250. "When did you find out who was to be killed?"

"October 1969."

"And who told you?"

"Paul Gilly."

"Who were you to kill?"

"Joseph Yablonski."

Sprague next had Vealey describe the inept stalking and bungled attempts to complete the job prior to December by himself, Gilly, and James Charles Phillips.

"The first trip to Washington, D.C., from Washington, D.C. to Scranton, PA, from Scranton to Clarksville, from Clarksville to Cleveland."

When Vealey hesitated, Sprague prodded, "And subsequent trips?"

"We went back and forth from Cleveland to Clarksville.... I believe it was seven times all total."

"Did you have weapons with you on each of those occasions?"

"Yes."

Sprague then asked the witness to describe the various ways the co-conspirators discussed to kill Yablonski.

"We talked about poisoning," Vealey said. That entailed putting rat poison purchased by Paul Gilly's wife, Annette. But they decided against that plot as no one was quite sure how to get the poison on something Yablonski would eat.

"What other ways did you discuss?"

"Firebombing."

"What do you mean by firebombing?"

"Putting gasoline in a bottle, lighting it, and throwing it through a window."

"And what happened to that plan?"

"Just never did carry it through."

It was the same answer Vealey gave to the plot to blow up the Yablonski home with dynamite. Sprague didn't even bother to mention the James Bond-esque idea of injecting Yablonski's cigars with arsenic.

Sprague asked Vealey when and how Martin got involved in the plot. Up to this point, the jury had only heard the names Vealey, Gilly and Phillips.

Vealey recounted the December 29 meeting at the Family Tavern in Cleveland.

"Did you know Martin prior to December 29, 1969?"

"Yes."

"For how long a period of time?"

"Six months."

"Now when Gilly was talking to Martin on December 29, 1969, then what happened?"

"I came into the bar and Gilly said Martin was to be the third man on the killing," Vealey said so softly that Sprague asked him to speak up and repeat his answer.

Satisfied, Sprague continued, "What happened to Phillips?"

"He backed out."

"Is that why you were now getting a third man?"

"Yes."

"When Gilly said that Martin was to be the third man in the killing, what was then discussed?"

"Gilly told him who was to be killed."

Defense counsel objected to Vealey's last comments as hearsay, "He's talking about what somebody else said to Martin."

Judge Charles Sweet looked puzzled. "Isn't this conversation in Martin's presence and an act in furtherance of the conspiracy to murder the deceaseds?" he asked, because if so, it wouldn't be hearsay. Affable and fair, Sweet sometimes referred to himself as "just an old country judge," but he was sharp and didn't allow either side to mess with the decorum of his courtroom or question the legitimacy of his astute legal mind. He gently reminded counsel that these kinds of incriminating conversations are considered "overt acts in furtherance of the conspiracy" and clearly admissible.

"I wanted to make sure it was in Martin's presence," counsel said, somewhat sheepishly.

Sprague turned back to Vealey and repeated his question about who Gilly told Martin was to be killed.

"Joseph Yablonski was the one to be killed. He lived in Clarksville, Pennsylvania and there was $5,250 in money that would be split three ways."

"This was what Gilly said to Martin in your presence in that taproom?"

"Yes."

Having established that Martin knew the purpose of the job, as well as the intended victim, Sprague next led Vealey through the events of the next day, December 30, 1969, starting with Gilly picking him up. "He had a .38 revolver and an M1 carbine."

"Can you describe the .38 revolver?" Sprague asked.

"Chrome with white handles...the carbine was in the trunk, and the pistol was in the glove compartment."

"What happened next?"

"We went to Martin's house and picked him up."

"Whose car was this?"

"Paul Gilly's brother's. Gilly said he borrowed it from his brother to use."

"On the prior trip into Clarksville, what car had you used?" Sprague asked. He wanted to establish that the killers had used two different cars, which would be important later in the prosecution's case.

"We used Gilly's car except for the last two trips."

"When you say Gilly's car, can you describe that car to the jury?"

Vealey nodded and looked at the jurors. "A 1965 Chevrolet Caprice, maroon with a black vinyl top."

"Do you know why the switch in cars?"

"Gilly's car broke down on one of the trips to Clarksville and hadn't been fixed right."

Under Sprague's questioning, Vealey described stopping at the empty house Gilly recently purchased to practice with the guns in the basement. When they finished target practice, they got back in the car and headed for Clarksville where they arrived about three or four o'clock in the afternoon.

"When you got to Clarksville, did you at some point go to any vantage point?" Sprague asked. But before Vealey could answer, counsel objected.

"It's leading," the defense lawyer complained.

Again, Judge Sweet answered patiently, as if coaching a law student. "Well now, a leading question, Counselor, is one that suggests the answer, and I can't guess from that where they went, can you?"

"He said, 'Did you go to a vantage point?'" counsel argued.

Trying not to roll his eyes, Sprague countered. "I'm trying to avoid going into every little turn."

Judge Sweet agreed. "I don't think you've described the place you're asking about to such an extent it's leading. If he said, 'Did you go to the corner of Main and Beau Streets,' it would be. Go ahead."

Sprague nodded and looked at Vealey. "My question is when you got to Clarksville, at some point, did you go to any vantage point?"

"Yes, sir. It was a dirt road went up on the mountain…there was a wide spot on the road [from which] you could see the back of the Yablonskis' house and clear through to the driveaway."

Sprague showed Vealey a photograph taken from the vantage point. Vealey confirmed that it fairly and accurately portrayed the spot. Sprague then offered into evidence the photograph; the court accepted it, and it was marked as a Commonwealth Exhibit. He handed the photograph to the jury, paused for all jurors to review, then resumed his questioning.

"What did you do while you were parked at that spot?"

"We was drinking beer and whiskey."

"Could you determine who was there at home?"

"From the previous trips that we made, Gilly and I came to the conclusion all three people were home. Yablonski, his wife, and daughter."

"What was decided upon determining that Yablonski's wife and daughter were at home?"

"To go into the house and kill all three of them."

"Where was that decided?"

"While we were sitting in the car up on the hill."

"At the spot the jury observed on the picture?"

"Yes."

"Did all three of you agree to that?"

"Yes."

"Then what happened?"

"We drank the one six-pack of beer. We drove into Clarksville and bought another one."

"Then what happened?"

"We drank that and half the pint of whiskey, and then we drove down to the Yablonski house."

"Approximately what time was this?"

"About one o'clock in the morning."

Step-by-murderous step, Sprague had Vealey recount what happened next and who did what. The witness told the jurors that when they got out of the car and approached the house, Martin was carrying the carbine and he had the .38 revolver. He described how they cut the telephone lines and disabled the cars.

"Why was it done?"

"In case anyone got out of the house they couldn't get away in the cars to warn anyone."

Vealey discussed in detail how they'd removed a door to enter the house where they were greeted by a friendly dog. They'd then taken off their shoes and checked the downstairs to make sure no one was there. Although all the lights were off in the home, the floodlights that Kenneth Yablonski had persuaded his dad to erect provided enough light from the outside.

"Now, was anything discussed as to who would do what?" Sprague asked.

"Martin took the .38 and said he would kill the girl. I took the M1. I was supposed to kill Yablonski and his wife."

The courtroom again fell silent in horror as Vealey described the cold-blooded murders of the Yablonskis with no more emotion than if he'd been reading a newspaper account. At the top of the stairs were three bedrooms—two of them with their doors open, a third with the door shut. Vealey said he looked through the doorway of the one in the middle, but no one was sleeping there. He then peered into the master bedroom from which rumbled the loud snores of Jock Yablonski.

Meanwhile, Martin twisted the knob and quietly opened the third door. The room was dark, and it took him a moment for his eyes to adjust and see the figure of the daughter lying on the bed.

Just twenty-five years old, Charlotte lay on her side with one arm stretched above her head, her hair in curlers in preparation for a New Year's Eve party she planned to attend.

The killers had agreed that they would fire simultaneously. So, Vealey readied the carbine and waited as Martin in the other room crept over to the sleeping girl.

Martin pointed the revolver at the top of Charlotte's head and, from a distance of about four inches, pulled the trigger twice in rapid succession. One bullet struck her skull in the middle, slanting down through her brain, and shattering an eyeball before exiting through her jaw. The second also went through her skull, striking her jaw before passing out and through her arm. She died instantly.

However, Vealey and Gilly were having no such success. As the latter hung back a few feet, the former aimed at the Yablonskis, and when the first of Martin's shots blasted open the night, he pulled the trigger. Nothing happened.

At the same time, the woman sat up in the bed and started screaming, while the man scrambled to reach a shotgun next to the bed. "I panicked and started fooling with it and I pushed the button and the clip fell out of it," Vealey explained.

"Then what happened?" Sprague asked.

"Gilly came and took the rifle, picked the clip up and started fooling with it, trying to get it to work.... He got it to fire once then it jammed again."

"Then what happened?"

"Martin stepped over into the bedroom door of the Yablonskis' and finished emptying the pistol at Mr. and Mrs. Yablonski."

Two bullets struck Margaret, who stopped screaming and fell back onto the bed. Two others hit Jock who slipped off the bed and collapsed against the nightstand.

The three killers stood for a moment listening to a gurgling sound coming from Jock. Then Vealey took the revolver from Martin and stepped out of the room to reload it. He returned and walking over to the mortally wounded man and shot him three more times, including the coup de grâce in the forehead.

"Why?"

"Mr. Yablonski was making a gurgling sound. I thought he was still alive."

"What did you want to do?"

"Finish him."

With the room smelling of blood and gun smoke, Martin walked over to a dresser and took the money lying on top, $240, which they split three ways. They then ransacked the house looking for money and other valuables before getting back in the car for the return trip to Cleveland.

"Was anything else taken from the house?"

"Later I learned Gilly took cannisters of some film or tape out of the house."

The three killers drove into Clarksville onto Route 88, headed for Pittsburgh. Just past Fredericktown, they stopped on a bridge over the river. "Martin and I tossed the guns in the river."

"Then what?"

"I threw the wire cutters in the river and the extra ammunition," Vealey said.

As they drove down the road, they started tossing the gloves they'd used out of the car one at a time. Then Gilly pulled the cannisters from his coat pocket and said he got them from the desk downstairs. "I told him to get rid of them because they could be traced. I threw them over a guardrail as we drove."

At this point, Sprague had the cannisters marked for identification as Commonwealth Exhibits.

"What happened when you got back to Cleveland?

"Gilly dropped Martin and I off at a bar on East Seventy-Ninth when he went to get the money."

"What time of day was this?"

"About eight o'clock in the morning. Martin and I sat in there, drinking, shooting pool. We waited about two hours, and Gilly came back with the money."

"Had you done anything else in the meantime while waiting for Gilly to come back with the money?"

"I went up the street to a barber shop and got a haircut. Then I went to a clothing store and bought some new clothes and a new pair of shoes."

"What happened when Gilly met you back at the bar?"

"We went into the back room where the pool table was, and Gilly gave Martin and me an envelope."

"How much money was supposed to be in your envelope?"

"A thousand dollars."

"How much was supposed to be in Martin's envelope?"

"$1,700."

"Why was Martin to have $1,700 and you $1,000?"

"Gilly put up $750 to get me out of jail in Youngstown, Ohio in October."

"He was deducting money you owed him."

"Yes."

Vealey testified that the men split up. He went home and opened his envelope, which contained $1,700. But Martin soon showed up and they exchanged envelopes.

Sprague then abruptly turned to defense counsel and said simply, "Cross-examine."

Under Sprague's direct examination, Vealey had testified for nearly six hours. Following on Kenneth Yablonski's emotional testimony, the one-two punch was devastating to the defense in spite of the leanings of Martin's fan club.

As a result, counsel's cross-examination of Vealey was comparatively short and inconsequential. His only hope was to portray Vealey as a liar who was cooperating to save himself from the death penalty and for profit.

During cross-examination, counsel brought up that Vealey had asked about getting a $20,000 reward for the arrest and conviction of the Yablonski family's killers. Vealey admitted it and said that FBI Agent Masterson told him he would be eligible.

"You believed him, Claude, didn't you?" counsel asked.

"At the time I believed him," Vealey replied, "but I changed my mind after. You see, he told me to keep this offer to myself. There was just me and him in the room together."

"So now you don't think you're going to get the twenty thousand dollars?"

"No. All I'm getting is what I got; the armed robbery, burglary, and grand larceny charges dropped, and the FBI said they'd not let me get the death penalty."

Counsel had pressed Vealey about a variety of small issues, including his criminal association with Martin—even tried to get him to admit that he had been angry with the defendant after leaving him during a burglary in Kentucky. Vealey denied being angry and the attorney had to move on.

When the young defense attorney had no better luck making any significant progress with his other lines of questioning. Judge Sweet grew impatient and urged him to move on. At that point, counsel gave up, "No more questions."

Sprague's redirect was short, sweet, and to the point, "Is there any doubt, Mr. Vealey, when you were in the Yablonski home, one of those who did the shooting with the .38 was this defendant, Martin?"

"No, sir. There is not."

"What was Martin's job?"

"He was to do the killing with myself."[40]

Later, after Vealey had been excused, *Associated Press* reporter Lee Linder interviewed a member of the "Buddy Martin Fan Club" who had attended the trial since voir dire began. She asked for anonymity because, like many of the other fans, she was playing hooky from school, but otherwise, she was more than willing to gush about the defendant.

---

40 *Commonwealth of Pennsylvania vs. Aubran Wayne Martin.*

"Buddy's so cute," the pretty young woman declared. "He couldn't possibly have done those awful things that horrible creature said he did."

Linder jumped to the conclusion that she was referring to Sprague as "the horrible creature."

"Oh no," she corrected him. "Mr. Sprague's cute. I mean that awful Vealey."[41]

---

41   Lewis, *Murder by Contract.*

CHAPTER TWENTY-THREE

THE CLASSIC
COUP DE GRÂCE

Sprague then called Washington County's coroner, Farrell Jackson, who took the stand to recount the horror he'd witnessed on January 5, 1970. A lifelong friend of Jock Yablonski, Jackson described seeing his body, the shotgun next to it, and Margaret's body beneath a cover, "It appeared someone had tried to cover it."

Lastly, he was directed by State Patrol investigator Dugan to the room where Charlotte's body lay on its side. "There were curlers in her hair," he said. The statement had a visceral impact on the jurors.

"There was a lot of blood, and it was difficult for me to tell from the state of the body where she was shot. But I did identify her as Charlotte Yablonski. I knew her well."

State Trooper Dugan had followed Jackson to the stand where Sprague asked him to identify several grisly crime scene photographs. After a short battle with counsel over the admittance of the more graphic photos, the prosecutor handed them to the jury "so they can understand and follow the testimony." As the photographs were passed from one juror to the next, their faces turned grim and ashen, and some appeared to be on the edge of crying.

Dr. Ernest L. Abernathy, the county's chief pathologist, followed Dugan to the stand where he added to Jackson's crime scene in more graphic language.

"When you say an odor of decomposition, exactly what do you mean, Doctor?" Sprague asked him at one point.

"I mean, sir, the smell of rotting flesh."

Several of the jurors recoiled at the description as did the Yablonski brothers who sat in the pew behind the prosecution table. It was the effect Sprague wanted, but it would get worse.

Using his own body to demonstrate, Abernathy describe the wounds suffered by each of the victims. Two shots to the top of her head from close range to Charlotte. Both of them fatal.

Margaret was shot in the left side of her chest, "which would have been fatal," and a second hit her right shoulder. Jock was hit five times: one struck the radial artery in his arm that was bloody but "would not have been fatal if treated immediately;" another struck his aorta and "definitely" would have been fatal; a third bullet struck him in the ribcage and was not fatal; the fourth passed through his neck from right to left, and "I think would have been fatal;" and last, a shot to his forehead, "also fatal."

"How would you describe this last shot, Doctor?" Sprague asked.

Abernathy paused for a moment before answering. "Sir, this could have been the classic coup de grâce."

Sprague's question wasn't just for dramatic purposes. He wanted the jury to recall Vealey's testimony about hearing Jock "gurgling" and why he shot Jock again. *I thought he was still alive.*

After counsel waived cross-examination of Abernathy, Judge Sweet announced over the defense attorney's protests that testimony would continue into the evening. Sprague didn't bat an eye and started trotting out a rollcall of witnesses, some of whom only spent a few minutes on the witness stand.

Chip Yablonski's sister-in-law Helen Slosarik, the last person to see the victims alive, described a wholesome family evening talking about the Christmas holidays and playing with Rascal. When she left the house about 10 p.m., Charlotte had her hair in curlers and was looking forward to the next day's New Year's Eve party.

Next up was Bill Stewart, who accompanied his friend Kenneth Yablonski to the house on that horrible morning. He spent five minutes on the stand and was followed by Pennsylvania State

Patrol investigator Elmer Schifko. He talked about finding the film cannisters.

Sprague next called the two divers, Senior Chief Machinist Mate Fred Schunk and FBI Agent Kenneth Russell, one after the other to testify about finding the chrome-plated .38 revolver with the pearl handle and then the M1 carbine in the murky, freezing Monongahela River. Each identified a weapon Sprague showed them.

Over the next hour, a steady stream of FBI agents and state police investigators climbed up into the witness stand and testified about their expertise in such fields as ballistics and fingerprints. All of it to corroborate previous testimony and nail shut the state's case.

A different sort of witness was then called. Donald Bran was a used car salesman whose car lot was a short distance from the Family Tavern. He identified Martin as the man who'd walked into his place of business with his girlfriend and purchased a car from him on December 31, 1969.

"How'd they pay for it?" Sprague asked.

"Cash. About $940, including tax, title, and plates."

After the used-car salesman stepped down, Sprague called FBI Agent William "Bill" Curtis to the stand. Of all the federal agents, the Philadelphia prosecutor had come to consider Curtis from the Bureau's Pittsburgh office as his "right hand man." He'd not only been one of the major investigators but had acted as a conduit between his agency, the local law enforcement, and the U.S. Attorney's Office throughout the investigation. He sat in the row directly behind the prosecutor's table—able to respond immediately to any requests—during the Martin trial.

This time, Curtis was on the stand for less than five minutes to testify about locating the beer cans and bottles. It was obvious that the Hillbilly Hitmen had quite a party gearing up for murder—not that the law would allow them to use that as a defense for their actions.

Just prior to a break in the evening's proceedings, Sprague called Arthur R. Feeney, chief of the License Plate Record Division for the Ohio State Bureau of Motor Vehicles. He would be on the stand for less than two minutes.

"Mr. Feeney, at my request did you check the 1969 automobile registration in the state of Ohio for license plate number CX457?"

"Yes."

"What does the registration show?"

"It shows that the car is registered in the name of Annette Gilly, 1846 Penrose Street, East Cleveland—a '65 Chevrolet four-door sedan."

The jury could guess that the car had something to do with the murderers. But they'd have to wait to learn the importance of the license plate number.

After a short coffee break, Sprague called Edna Faye Gilly, the wife of Paul Gilly's older brother, William, to the stand. There was little love lost between the sisters-in-law. Most of the Gilly family, including Paul's brothers, were good, law-abiding citizens. Paul was a different story and so, according to her sister-in-law, was Annette.[42]

Under Sprague's questioning, Edna testified that on December 30, 1969, Annette called asking if she could borrow one of her husband's cars. Annette said she wanted to visit family in Akron.

"I told her she was borrowing the car quite a bit," Edna said, noting her husband worked the night shift and was sleeping. "I wasn't waking Bill up. She could wait 'til he did." She then hung up.

Annette called back a little later and asked again. This time Edna woke her husband who said Annette could use the car—a blue Chevrolet—if she had it back by 9:30 that night.

"Did she keep her promise?" Sprague asked.

"No, sir. She made up a couple of telephone calls to us the next morning before she brought it home," Edna replied. "That was somewhere between 10:30 and 11:30 a.m."

"Did you notice anything unusual about the car after it had been returned?"

"The car was muddy inside and there was a bottle of whiskey, a quilt on the back seat, a 1970 calendar from a filling station in Cambridge, Ohio, and there were six Payday candy bars that had never been opened."

---

42   Lewis, *Murder by Contract*.

Sprague was tying Edna Gilly's testimony to Vealey's testimony about not using Paul's Caprice. It was one thing for a self-confessed killer hoping to escape the death penalty to implicate his co-conspirators, another when an upstanding citizen like Edna, with nothing to gain, corroborated his story.

After she stepped down, Sprague recalled Kenneth Yablonski back to the stand to recount the evening of December 18, 1969, when he arrived at his parents' house and was told by his father that two men had shown up at the house who he thought wanted to kill him. He recalled going to search for the visitors with his dad and Jock's friend, Karl Kafton.

"Just as we got across a bridge near the Koremooth Tavern, my father said, 'I'll bet that's the car.' On the side of the road was a Chevrolet; it was maroon with a dark top," Kenneth testified. "We made a U-turn and looked at the license plate. It was Ohio, CX457. I wrote it down and went back to my parents' home."

Karl Kafton followed Kenneth Yablonski to the stand. He was asked, "Did you note the license plate of the car you and the others saw?"

"Yes, sir, I wrote it down the first time on a memo pad I carried with me. Then when we got back to Jock's, I wrote it down again on a yellow tablet in his den."

Sprague handed Kafton a small white pad and a large-lined yellow tablet. "I show you the letter-writing pad, Mr. Kafton, which has on it, 'Ohio CX457,' and ask you if you can identify it and the writing?"

"Yes, sir, that's the pad I carried to take notes on," the big, former, West Virginia coalminer replied. "The license number is written in green ink, the kind I have in my pen."

"Now, I show you a yellow pad with 'Ohio CX457' written on it and ask if you can identify that writing?"

"I can. The tablet was Jock's; the writing on it is mine."

Sprague then talked Kafton through his efforts to trace the license plate to the car's owner and his call to Annette Gilly. He explained the situation to the state trooper who asked if Yablonski needed protection and, if so, he'd send a car out. "But Jock said it wouldn't be necessary."

Finally, after thirteen hours and thirty-one witnesses, Judge Sweet, at last, turned to the audience and said the court would recess for the day, "So go to the hotel, have a snack, get a good night's sleep, and be back tomorrow at nine thirty. We're all tired now; it's been a long, long day."

CHAPTER TWENTY-FOUR

A CALCULATED RISK

NOVEMBER 10, 1971

Dressed in a conservative blue suit with a red-and-gold striped tie, the youthful-looking defendant placed his left hand on the Bible and raised his right hand. He swore he'd tell the truth, the whole truth, and nothing but the truth.

"Mr. Martin," counsel began, "what is your full name?"

"Aubran Wayne Martin, sir," he replied.

"Have you a nickname?"

"Yes, sir. I've been called Buddy ever since I can remember. An uncle give it to me when I was real small."

It had taken another five hours and a half dozen witnesses to wrap up the prosecution case that morning and into the afternoon. The last of the testimony consisted of a steady stream of technical experts in ballistics, firearms, and fingerprints, including Charles Groenthal who was recalled to the stand to identify latent prints of all three killers on the cans and bottles found at the vantage point, which Sprague had lined up on a bench for the jury to see.

At about 2:30 p.m. Sprague finished and turned to Sweet. "Your Honor," he'd said, "that's the Commonwealth's case."

After a short break, counsel had started the defense case by calling his client to the stand, where Martin did his theatrical best to look young, innocent, and, to his fan club anyway, cute. Over Sprague's protests and Sweet's admonishments to keep it short, counsel began by getting his client to describe how he lived with his common-law wife and helped support her three kids. But sadly, he'd only completed seventh grade.

His answer to the next question about how he supported himself wasn't quite so innocent: "By stealing."

Having Martin admit to his criminal history was a calculated risk. Defendants can't be forced to testify, and judges will warn juries that failure to do so should not be taken as an admission of guilt. However, if the defendant does choose to testify, they are subject to cross-examination by the prosecution. That makes their criminal history, which would otherwise be kept from the jurors, fair game.

However, counsel's strategy was to portray Martin as a poorly educated, small-time thief. But not a murderer.

Then, he got to the meat of his cross-examination. Under his questioning, Martin said he'd met Paul Gilly at his restaurant in 1968. The association was a criminal one in which Gilly "bought the stuff I stole...we also did a job together near LaFollette, Tennessee— me, Paul, and Claude." Annette Gilly had been along for the ride on that one.

"She wasn't in on the burglary, which was supposed to be from a man Paul said had fifty thousand dollars in cash he was holding back from his income tax. We was also supposed to take any papers we found."[43]

Counsel moved on to how Martin met Vealey, again making no attempt to disguise his criminal history. "I first met Claude in the basement of Gilly's restaurant in July or August of 1969. Me and

---

43 This was the robbery of Ted Q. Wilson, an attorney from Winfield, Tennessee for the Southern Labor Union who was supposed to be targeted for assassination before the contract was switched back to Jock Yablonski. Martin was apparently unaware of the murder scheme at the time of the burglary. It was not a mystery to Paul Gilly, who'd been told of the plot by Silous Huddleston.

two other individuals were down there," the defendant said. "We had just come back from a burglary, and we had a bunch of guns, a coin collection, and some odds and ends.

"We was sitting down there, discussing how much we wanted for the coin collection and how much the guns was worth. Claude and someone else come down in the basement and whoever it was introduced me to Vealey."

Martin went on to explain that he and Vealey then proceeded to commit "twenty-five, maybe thirty, burglary jobs."

His attorney then asked if he remembered any in particular but got an unexpected answer. Counsel wanted him to mention the burglary in Youngstown, Ohio he went on with Vealey and James Charles Phillips. In that burglary, Martin had been the getaway driver and didn't go into the house, which was the point counsel wanted to make to the jury.

However, Martin, confused, blurted out, "Sir, do you mean the one in Clarksville?" He was talking about the site of the Yablonski murders.

Counsel shook his head. "Forget Clarksville..."

Sprague shot to his feet. "Your Honor, I object to 'forgetting Clarksville...'"

Realizing the mistake, counsel corrected himself, "I mean, for the time being."

Judge Sweet sighed and shook his head. "Counsel, that does seem an unhappy choice of words."

Moving on, counsel coaxed Martin into recounting the Youngstown, Ohio burglary. The point the attorney was trying to make was that the defendant had stayed outside in the car. However, the young counselor was about to blunder into a tactical mistake, though it wasn't immediately apparent.

"Buddy, were most of the crimes you committed burglaries?"

"Most of them, yes, sir."

"What were the others?"

"Well, I have stole things—you know, like when I was younger—cars, you know, stealing tires and stuff like that."

"Any other crimes you ever committed?"

As Martin answered, neither he nor his attorney noticed that not only had Sprague jotted something down on a legal pad, but Judge Sweet had made a note to himself.

"Resisting arrest and disorderly conduct and traffic violations," Martin ignored.

Having allowed the defense to go on with this line of questioning because some of it was marginally related to Martin's relationship with Vealey, Sweet finally grew tired of it and Sprague's repeated relevancy objections. He urged the lawyer to get to the point.

Martin described the meeting he had with Paul Gilly on December 29 at the Family Tavern. He said that Gilly invited him to go on a burglary in Tennessee with him and Vealey. At first, he declined because the last Tennessee burglary didn't work out; Gilly guaranteed him $2,000 and so he'd agreed.

About that time, he said, Vealey showed up at the tavern and Gilly told him that Martin would be joining them. That led to a side conversation between Gilly and Vealey. "It was like Vealey didn't want me to go along because ever since I run off and left him at that burglary down in Youngstown," Martin testified. "He more or less didn't want to have nothing to do with me."

A few questions later, Martin described how the next day he spent part of the day drinking beer with Gilly. They then picked up Vealey and drove to a house owned by Gilly where they practiced shooting a .38 revolver and a M1 carbine in the basement. He described the target practice as "just something to do."

Later, they got in a car Gilly had borrowed to drive to Tennessee for the burglary. Or so Martin thought. But after they'd been on the road for five or ten minutes, he realized they weren't heading in the right direction. That's when Gilly told him the burglary target was actually in Pennsylvania.

"Are you sure, Buddy, that he said the 'burglary'?" counsel asked.

"Yes, sir, I'm positive those were his words," Martin replied. The others said they didn't tell him the truth because it was such a big job, and he had a habit of telling his common-law wife where he was going when he went on a burglary.

When the trio reached Fredericktown, Pennsylvania a few miles north of Clarksville, they spent some time barhopping and buying liquor. "We left Fredericktown and drove to Clarksville and went past a residence," Martin testified. "I didn't know the name of the residence then." He shook his head sadly. "But I know now."

"Whose was it, Buddy?"

"It was Yablonskis'."

Up to this point in his testimony, Martin's chronology of events leading from his joining the conspirators and traveling to Pennsylvania did not differ much from Vealey's. The exception was that he claimed not to have known the real purpose of the trip or where they were going until they were on the road.

In addition to using Martin's testimony to portray his client as an unwitting participant in a murder scheme, counsel had gone to lengths to emphasize the small-time nature of his criminal activities. He'd also made a point of Martin describing how he'd been drinking since morning, including after the trio got to Clarksville. The drinking had continued at the vantage point behind the Yablonski house, including a trip into town to replenish their supplies of alcohol.

Only at this point did Martin's version of events veer sharply from Vealey's. He said that when they drove to the Yablonski property, they'd parked "two football fields" from the house with a row of trees between it and the car.

According to Martin, Gilly told him he was to remain with the car and keep a lookout for trouble. He said he then saw the other two take the revolver and carbine and depart for the house.

"Did they tell you they were going to kill anyone?" counsel asked.

"No, sir. They did not."

At that point, Martin, who calmly listened to his attorney and then looked at the jury when he spoke, said he that he dozed off.

"What happened next, Buddy?"

"The car door opened, and Paul was cussing at me," Martin recalled with a sheepish look as if describing getting caught with his hand in a cookie jar. "He said, 'I told you I'd give you two thousand dollars to come down here on a burglary and you fall asleep. What would've happened if the police come by? I shouldn't give you a dime!'"

At this point, Martin's story returned to the same basic account as Vealey's regarding the return trip to Cleveland, including stopping to throw the weapons in the river, and the film cannisters down a hillside. He claimed that he slept most of the way home and didn't hear the other two discuss murdering anyone.

Although there was apparently no $50,000 coin collection, Gilly had paid him the $2,000 he'd promised. The generosity surprised him.

Martin claimed to have not learned about the murders until some days later when a very drunk Claude Vealey came into the Family Tavern and told him to come outside to talk. "So we went out and sat in my car. We was listening to the radio, like a newscast, and it said something about people being killed in Pennsylvania. I didn't pay no attention to it.

"Then Claude says, 'Look, I'm going to tell you something for your own good. Don't tell nobody you was in the state of Pennsylvania because me and Paul killed them people.' And I said, 'What people?' And he says, 'Why them people they said on the radio was killed.'"

Martin said he thought Vealey was joking or trying to frighten him. "But then Vealey says, 'No, I'm serious. Don't tell nobody you was in Pennsylvania. If the FBI or police officers question you and you tell them you was sittin' in the car, that makes you part of it regardless, and you get put in the electric chair!'"

Then, as Vealey opened to door of the car to get out, he warned Martin. "Don't forget, Buddy, if you ever get up and testify about any of us was involved, you have a wife and three kids. They can be slaughtered in the same fashion that them people was in Pennsylvania."

Even with the threat, Martin said he wasn't sure Vealey was telling the truth until Gilly confirmed it. The ringleader issued his own warning that in addition to his father-in-law Silous Huddleston, a known union enforcer, someone higher in the coalminers union ordered the contract killing.

"Paul says to me, 'Buddy, you know there's high, important people backing it up. If you ever go to the police and tell on us, and if the police get us before we can do anything, we got people will see your family massacred.'"

Martin said he believed the threats were real. To protect himself from the killers, he purposefully got himself arrested for burglary. He was in that Ohio jail cell when FBI agents arrested him for participating in the Yablonski murders and moved him to the federal courthouse in Cleveland for questioning.

After having Martin repeat that he was unaware of any plan to kill the Yablonskis on December 29, 1969, counsel rested his case. Considering what the young defense attorney had to work with, he presented a viable defense. Against overwhelming evidence and Sprague's methodical presentation of the prosecution case, he'd managed to portray his client as a small-time thief who was duped into participating in a murder contract in Pennsylvania instead of a burglary in Tennessee.

Poor "Buddy," as he'd insisted on calling him throughout the trial, drank a lot of alcohol and passed out in the car while the two assassins went into the house. He believed until being threatened by Vealey and Gilly that they'd committed a burglary, not murder.

This is where counsel's "calculated risk" came into play. Even if he weren't the shooter, but acted for the purpose and in furtherance of committing the underlying felony and death that resulted, Martin would be still be guilty of felony murder, particularly because he knew that his codefendants were armed with deadly weapons.

Conceding that he believed they were at the house to commit an armed burglary made him guilty of "felony murder," the legal concept that even if he didn't pull the trigger, he'd participated in the legally stipulated felony that led to murder. It was a charge a prosecutor would use, for example, to go after a wheelman of the getaway car from a robbery in which a storeowner had been killed.

Sprague knew that in order for the death penalty to apply, the prosecutor had to prove intentional murder.

If the jury believed the story about parking "one or two football fields away" from the house and behind a line of trees, it was even conceivable that he might not have heard the gunshots. Especially if he was sleeping off a drinking binge in the backseat of the car.

Counsel's hope was that admitting to felony murder would save his client's life. It might even let him serve time and get out of prison someday.

Sprague wasn't about to settle. He wanted Martin convicted of "intentional murder" and sentenced to death. He didn't believe a word of Martin's story and felt that a death sentence was the appropriate punishment for the cold-blooded murder of the Yablonski family. And he wanted to send a message to the other conspirators.

In order to have the best, maybe only, chance for a death sentence, Sprague knew he would have to prove beyond a reasonable doubt that the defendant was a willing, active participant and "intentionally caused the deaths of the deceaseds." But he would have to wait until the next day as Sweet adjourned for the afternoon.

CHAPTER TWENTY-FIVE

"GOOD AT PLANNING AND SCHEMING"

DECEMBER 12, 1971

The next morning, Sprague began his quest by reexamining Martin's criminal past, which eventually led to Martin admitting that he was "good at planning and scheming."

The questions seemed no more than an attack on Martin's moral character. But the prosecutor had another purpose. "According to you, Mr. Martin, Gilly and Vealey tricked you, didn't they?"

Martin nodded at what he thought was a softball question. "Yes, sir, I would say I was tricked."

"Weren't you angry about that? They roped you into a murder, didn't they?"

Martin nodded. "Yes, sir, I'm pretty angry about it, yes I am."

"When the FBI agents came and asked you about it you didn't tell them you'd been tricked into a murder, did you?"

The young man in the witness box frowned. "No, sir, I didn't tell them nothin.'"

"And after you even heard that Vealey had opened up on you, you still didn't call or send for the FBI and tell them, 'Hey, wait a minute, he's the guy that tricked me into this,' did you?"

"No, sir. What the FBI told me, I wasn't sure was the truth or not. I didn't want to implicate anybody; I didn't want to get my family killed."

Only now did it become clear why Sprague made a point of Martin not marrying his girlfriend. "And by your family, you mean this girl you never got a license to marry, but you were living common-law with?"

"Yes, sir."

"Are you still scared for her?"

"Yes, sir, I am," Martin said, looking wide-eyed at the jurors.

Sprague raised his eyebrows as he turned to the jurors. "But it doesn't stop you from telling the story now?"

Martin's face flushed with anger. "Sir, I will never testify at one of the trials. I don't care if I stay in jail for a hundred years; I will never get up and say anything about them."

Sprague had made his point. If it meant saving his own skin, Martin was willing to implicate his two companions, even if it endangered his girlfriend.

Satisfied, Sprague changed course. He asked Martin if he'd ever carried a gun when participating in a burglary.

Martin admitted that he had sometimes. But it was just to frighten the homeowner if they returned during the crime.

"Was a rifle ever taken by any of your friends on a burglary until the Yablonski job?" Sprague asked.

"No, sir, I never remember anyone carrying a rifle."

Sprague changed direction again. "By the way," he began, "when you, Vealey, and Phillips committed this burglary in Youngstown, Ohio, you ran out on them, didn't you?"

"Yes, sir, I did."

"So, Mr. Martin, you're telling this jury under oath that, having run out on Vealey in a burglary in Ohio, Vealey was going to let you sit as the driver of a getaway car at the Yablonski home?"

Realizing what the prosecutor was getting at, Martin hesitated. Sprague asked him, raising his voice for the first time, "Is that what you're telling the jury?"

Martin still didn't answer as he looked back and forth between the jury and Sprague. "Would you say that again, please?" he stammered.

"Didn't you hear me?" Sprague asked.

"I heard you, sir, but I kind of got lost with the question."

Sprague shook his head. "You're getting upset, I think. My question is, are you telling this jury that after a burglary committed in Youngstown, Ohio, where you ran out on Vealey and left him to be caught by police, Vealey would let you be the driver of a getaway car on the Yablonski job? Is that what you're telling the jury?"

Martin swallowed hard. "From the impression I got, sir, it wasn't up to Vealey. It seemed like everything Paul said went."

While the answer was not outside of the realm of possibilities, Martin's obvious discomfiture when answering made it seem manufactured. Sensing the moment was right, Sprague challenged the defense portrayal of Martin as a soft-spoken young man who—yes, maybe stole things and even resisted arrest—wasn't really violent.

"Your lawyer asked you, 'Did you commit any job other than burglaries?' You remember that?"

"Yes, sir."

"You didn't give a full answer, did you?"

Martin shrugged. "I give him it to the best of my recollection."

Sprague nodded. "Do you know what a firebombing is?" The question got the attention of everyone in the courtroom.

Counsel leaped to his feet. "Objection, Your Honor! Your Honor, I have Mr. Martin's record, and there is no indication he was ever involved in a firebombing. Unless Mr. Sprague can show me otherwise, I say that the remark is prejudicial."

This was the danger of a defendant taking the stand and then compounding that with his attorney asking a question that had not been carefully thought out. Normally, Sprague would have been limited to asking Martin about crimes for which he had been convicted. Questions about what he was suspected of doing would have been off limits.

However, counsel had left the door open with the way he had framed one of his questions. The judge now addressed that. "Counselor, I made a note this morning when you asked the question,

'Are there any other crimes you ever committed?' I think you got an answer concerning disorderly conduct and resisting arrest. It is my recollection you asked the general question, 'Were there any other crimes you ever committed?' Did you ask that question?"

Counsel looked stricken. "I may have, Your Honor."

"Well then, if you asked that, didn't you open him up generally?" The defense lawyer shook his head. "I think not."

Judge Sweet sighed then asked the two lawyers to approach his dais for a sidebar conversation out of hearing of the jury.

"Your Honor," Sprague said after they'd gathered, "defense counsel asked his client, on the stand, whether or not he committed any crimes besides burglaries and received an answer. It is clear that counsel, in direct examination of his own client, did not limit the question to what the defendant had been arrested for or convicted of."

Sprague handed the judge a sheet of paper. "I have, and defense counsel has received, a copy of a statement from Claude Vealey, in his own handwriting and signed by Vealey, how this defendant tried to solicit Vealey to be Martin's driver, at which time Martin was to go and firebomb a house, which in fact occurred and someone, a young child, was killed.

"Vealey related how Martin told him what he was being paid for the job, and the offer of money to participate." Vealey had not participated but only because he "slept in."

The firebombing and death of the child was a real event that took place a few minutes after midnight on September 24, 1969. The Cleveland Police Homicide Department considered it an open case but believed that Martin was the man responsible for throwing the incendiary.

Sprague went on, "Let me say this, also, Your Honor. Counsel's attack and approach in this case is to try to paint his client as a nonviolent little pansy who commits burglaries but would not dream of violence. As soon as he's asked about other crimes that go into the area of violence, it is inappropriate and improper for the Court to exclude it."

With that said, Sweet agreed and denied the defense objection. The attorneys returned to their places, and Sprague continued his line of questioning, "All right, Mr. Martin, do you know what a firebomb is?"

"Yes, sir. It's a container with gasoline in it, a rag stuffed inside so you can light it."

"What happens when you light it? It explodes, doesn't it?"

Martin shook his head. "It just burns," he said and then added his knowledge was entirely from having seen televised reports of riots in Cleveland.

"In the summer of 1969, did you come to Claude Vealey and ask him to drive a car for you to an address in the vicinity of Eighty-Seventh or Eighty-Eighth Street, Cleveland?" Sprague asked.

"No, sir, I did not."

"And didn't you subsequently tell Vealey all about what happened when you threw the firebomb in that home?"

Martin, eyes large with feigned innocence, answered quietly, "No, sir, I did not."

"You're sure of that?"

"Yes, sir, I am."

Sprague stood for a moment staring up at the witness like he couldn't believe what he was hearing. "That's as true as everything else you say on this stand?"

"Yes, sir, it is."

Leaving his client open to Sprague's questions about being a suspect in the firebombing murder had been a huge gaffe by the defense attorney. It was also a demonstration of Sprague's legendary ability to recall even the smallest details of a case. He was able to exploit counsel's mistake because he recalled Vealey's statement about the firebombing. It wasn't something he ever expected to be able to use in the trial, but when presented with the opportunity, he'd seized it.

After two hours of intense questioning, Sprague had presented a tough case to beat. But except for the flash of anger when asked about implicating Vealey and Gilly in his testimony, he had not cracked Martin's veneer of small-time criminal being made a scapegoat for someone else's crimes. The firebombing testimony was good, but it was also the word of a known liar, Vealey, against the defendant's.

Sprague returned to Martin's testimony about practicing with the murder weapons as "just something to do" before they left to commit the burglary. "On any other burglaries you went on, Mr. Martin, did you do target practicing before the job?"

"No, sir, this was the first time."

"Were you going hunting that day?" Sprague asked, hesitating a moment before adding, "For human beings, Mr. Martin?"

Counsel objected to Sprague's description, but Sweet replied, "Counselor, we're trying a murder case."

"But, Your Honor," the defense attorney complained, "hunting for human beings?"

"What do you want me to do?" the judge asked.

"Strike the question," counsel replied.

"Motion denied; exception noted."

With that out of the way, Sprague asked, "Vealey's your friend, isn't he?"

Martin scowled. "He was, sir."

"Do you know why he would lie against you?"

"Yes, sir, I do. He knew the FBI offered him ten or twenty thousand dollars, and if he didn't come up with a good story, he couldn't get it. Plus, he figured how he would get only life in prison if he went and made his story sound good enough."

Sprague raised his eyebrows as if surprised by the answer. "You think, Mr. Martin, that Vealey's story that he went in to finish Yablonski off after you shot him that he reloaded the gun after you, helps him?"

"Yes, sir, because he won't get the electric chair."

Looking at the defendant with a slight smile, Sprague shot back, "I suppose you know what will happen to you, Buddy, if you don't make up a good story."

The statement clearly hit Martin hard. He winced and sat back in the witness chair as if he'd been pushed.

Sprague turned the witness back over to his defense attorney. But redirect was short and, it seemed, lacking much certainty.

On rebuttal, Sprague recalled Vealey to the stand to ask him more questions about Martin's violent nature. After the invitation to help firebomb the house, "did Martin ever discuss with you the use of a machine gun or a shotgun?"

Vealey nodded. "Yes, sir, both. Martin told me he shot up the front of Cindy's Tavern on the West Side of Cleveland with a machine gun and that he shot out a guy's apartment he thought stole a gun from him."

Dismissing Vealey, Sprague next called Pennsylvania State Police Sergeant Robert Dugan to the stand. He had a trap laid for the defense and Dugan was in on it.

Sprague handed the officer a photograph. "Sergeant Dugan, referring to the vantage point—the area pictured in this photograph marked for identification as a Commonwealth Exhibit—did you go there in January 1970?"

"Yes, sir, I did."

"From there were you able to see the Yablonski home?"

"Yes, I was. There was no obstruction in the view of that home; the house sits out all by itself."

"Thank you, Sergeant," Sprague said and turned to the defense table. "Cross-examine, Counselor."

The young defense attorney walked confidently to the stand and right into the trap. "Sergeant Dugan, that day when you and I went up to the vantage point, could you see the Yablonski home?"

"Not very well, sir."

"And what time of the day was this?"

"I don't recall exactly; it was probably late afternoon."

"You couldn't see the Yablonski house too well, is that correct?"

"Yes, sir."

Counsel took his seat looking like he'd scored a major point. But Sprague knew how the defense attorney would question the police sergeant and sprang his trap.

"Sergeant Dugan, was there a difference between the foliage on the trees this time of the year and in January 1970?"

"Yes, sir. There were leaves on the trees at the time counsel and I went up there. In January of 1970, the trees were bare."

It was a small win but one that illustrated Sprague's ability to anticipate a defense attorney's questions and, in this case, made the defense attorney looked unprepared.

After that humiliation, counsel hoped to call one last witness—an old friend of Jock's who would testify that Yablonski did, in fact, have a coin collection valued at $50,000 that he kept at the house. It would back up the reason Martin gave for the "burglary."

However, Sweet notified the defense attorney that he was aware that the witness had once been convicted of jury tampering in Washington County. That fact, said the judge, would be fair game for Sprague's cross-examination.

Having just been spanked, counsel decided not to expose himself again. He rested the defense's case.

CHAPTER TWENTY-SIX

"WELL, THAT'S ONE DOWN"

It was 11 a.m., and after a quick break, Judge Sweet told the jurors that the case was entering its final stage—closing arguments, followed by the court's charge—before they began deliberations. "These are important to you because this is where the attorneys pull together facts and theories and explain why various pieces of evidence are significant," he explained, "and give you reasons as to whom you should believe and whom you should not believe."

First up was defense counsel who launched into an attack on the prosecution's principal witness, Claude Vealey. It was his only chance. If the jurors rejected the venal, admitted killer's testimony, the prosecution's case against Martin would fall apart.

"Would you believe Claude Vealey, a demented criminal with an insane mind, a confessed murderer?" Counsel asked, pacing slowly in front of the jury box. "Would you believe the kind of testimony you got from such a man? Here is a murderer who determined, if he was going down the drain, his old pal Buddy Martin was going down the drain with him."

Most of the rest of his closing argument was in a similar vein and lasted a half hour. He finished by leaning over the jury rail as he read an excerpt from a magazine article that described in horrific detail an execution by electric chair.

As the jury had listened attentively, Martin seemed restless. He kept turning in his seat to glance towards the back of the courtroom as if expecting to see someone he knew. At last, he shrugged his shoulders and turned around to listen to his attorney's final appeal for mercy.

"Death," counsel said, "is final; it is irrevocable; it is the ultimate. What if, someday, Claude Vealey comes forward and says, 'I lied.' We could not bring Buddy Martin back."

Conceding that his client was probably guilty of felony murder, the defense attorney argued that the prosecution had not proved beyond a reasonable doubt that he was guilty of first-degree intentional murder and deserved the death penalty. "Buddy Martin will never, ever get out of jail," he said. "But don't take away all he has left—his life."

When counsel finished and took his seat, Sprague rose and walked over to stand in front of the jurors, looking each in their eyes before starting. "Any verdict but first-degree murder," he said at last, "would be a disgrace. All defense counsel is doing is trying to throw dust in your eyes. If you acquit Martin, Buddy Martin, the next thing he'll do is go out and tell his friends how he fooled you. Don't let him do that!"

Turning to look at Martin, he asked, "Why do you think those other two murderers, Claude Vealey and Paul Gilly, got hold of Martin after that other guy Phillips backed out?" He paused to let the jurors weigh the question before answering it himself. "I'll tell you why. They wanted a tough punk who wouldn't care two hoots for a human life, and they got one, Buddy Martin. You're dealing with a cold-blooded thug who murdered three people, three persons from this community—your community. These were assassins in the night."

As methodically as he had presented the case, Sprague demonstrated how the pieces fit together and corroborated Vealey's story.

It didn't take long. After speaking for less than an hour, Sprague told the jurors that there was only one just verdict. Guilty of first-degree murder.

When Sprague took his seat, Sweet turned to the jurors and gave the usual instructions including what constitutes reasonable doubt. "Reasonable doubt is not a fanciful or capricious doubt, or possible doubt," he said. "It is a doubt arising from the evidence and of such a nature that, if arising in your ordinary business affairs, would cause you to hesitate and restrain you from acting."

Martin's excuse that he was intoxicated "has no legal significance as bearing upon the degree of his crime," Sweet said. They could also use the evidence about the firebombing when weighing the defendant's effort to portray himself as non-violent.

When he finished, Sweet sent the jury to deliberate. The courtroom was then cleared of spectators, including the eight members of the Buddy Martin Fan Club who giggled when Martin smiled and winked at them. Counsel and his wife left arm in arm while the press scurried to pay phones to call their stories in.

Sprague found an empty room in the courthouse to play chess with Special Agent Curtis. If he was worried, he didn't let it show.

It took the jury of seven females and five males one hour and twelve minutes to let the court's bailiff know that they had reached a verdict. When word got out, there was a rush of spectators to get back to the courtroom.

When the lawyers were present and Martin seated at the defense table, Sweet instructed the bailiff to bring the jurors in. As they entered none of them looked at the defendant but instead kept their eyes on the judge.

Asked if they'd reached a verdict, the jury foreman answered, "We have," and handed over to the court clerk three slips of paper, one for each of the charges.

Sweet accepted the papers as everyone in the courtroom fell completely silent. The lawyers and Martin stood.

The jurist silently read the jury's decision and then looked up. He cleared his throat and announced that in the matter of the Commonwealth of Pennsylvania versus Aubran Wayne Martin for the murder of Joseph Albert "Jock" Yablonski there was a verdict. "And now, to wit, November 12, 1971, we the jurors empaneled in the above case, find the defendant guilty of murder in the first degree."

Although deeply relieved, Sprague didn't react. In their seats, the Yablonski brothers nodded grimly.

Martin's face remained impassive, but he raised his arm and patted his attorney's shoulder.

Sweet then read the jury verdicts for the deaths of Margaret and Charlotte Yablonski. Two more counts of murder in the first degree.

All that remained was the sentencing hearing. Sprague wanted to get started right away. But defense counsel was visibly shaken and pleaded for a delay, which Sweet granted.

When court resumed the following morning, Martin, perhaps as a last act of defiance, had ditched the Ivy League conservative suits he'd been wearing to court. His eyes hidden behind sunglasses, he sported a bright gold shirt, colored slacks, and a canary-yellow scarf.

Neither counsel nor Sprague presented any more evidence at the death penalty hearing. The former asked for mercy, Sprague for death. It took only forty-five minutes for the jurors to come back with their decision.

Called to his feet, Martin smiled as Judge Sweet announced the jury's verdict. They'd sentenced Aubran Wayne "Buddy" Martin to die by electric chair.

"Well, that's one down," Sprague told noted investigative journalist Arthur H. Lewis on the plane ride back to Philadelphia. "Now I'll get the rest of those murdering bastards, maybe even Tony himself."[44]

---

44   Lewis, *Murder by Contract.*

CHAPTER TWENTY-SEVEN

THE CAPTAIN
OF THE SHIP

FEBRUARY 28, 1972

The trial of Paul Gilly was essentially a replay of the Martin trial with a few notable additions. The defense had again waived its opening statement, and Sprague's was mostly dedicated to describing Gilly as "the captain of the ship" who had recruited, led, and paid his two associates.

After that, Sprague trotted out the same lineup of witnesses, starting with Kenneth Yablonski's description of finding "something worse" at his parents' home and then methodically working his way through the lineup of FBI agents and police officers, the coroner, the medical examiner, the two divers, the fingerprint expert, and Vealey. The latter had been brought to the courthouse under the same tight security measures that had accompanied his appearance in the Martin trial.

This time there was no Paul Gilly Fan Club of giggling, star-struck, young women. And the defendant's demeanor was a far cry from Martin's bravado.

Throughout the proceedings, Gilly sat meekly between his defense counsel—two experienced attorneys—his face pale and his body language scared and defeated. He rarely looked up during testimony except for furtive glances at Sprague, who clearly frightened him, his attorneys, and witnesses. Occasionally, he turned to steal a glance at his brothers and their wives who sat behind the defense table, but mostly, he kept his eyes down and shoulders hunched.

The first of the notable additions was James Charles Phillips, who had since been convicted of felony child sexual abuse for raping his girlfriend's four-year-old daughter. He testified about the initial efforts to locate and kill Yablonski, including the trip to Washington, D.C. and Chip Yablonski's house.

Shaking his head, Phillips recounted breaking into the Yablonski home in Clarksville and being left behind by Gilly. It had led to his quitting the conspiracy. By the time he left the witness stand, he'd not only condemned his former friend, but implicated Silous Huddleston, Annette Gilly, William Prater, and "some guy named Tony."

The other wrinkle in the witnesses' testimony was Sprague calling now-sixteen-year-old Kathy Jo Rygle to describe how on Thanksgiving Day, 1969, she was playing a license plate game with her cousin at her house near the Yablonski home.

At a prep session prior to the Gilly trial, Sprague and the team were discussing the yellow legal pad found on Jock's desk with the Ohio license plate CX457 jotted down when one of the state troopers spoke up. He'd heard that some girls in the Yablonski neighborhood played a game of taking down license plates of cars that passed their house.

It was a long shot, bordering on a moonshot more than two years after that Thanksgiving, but on the chance that the girls were playing their game that day, Sprague asked investigator Bob Dugan to canvas the homes in the area.

Dugan checked dozens of possibilities on the way to the Yablonski home from Clarksville. He hit paydirt when Kathy Rygle came to the door of her parents' house and said that, why yes, she and her cousin sometimes played that game. And yes, she recalled that they'd been playing on Thanksgiving 1969. In fact, she still had the notebook they'd used to record the make, model, and license plates of cars that drove past.

"Kathy, where were you on Thanksgiving Day of 1969?" Sprague asked the bright, dark-haired teenager on the stand.

"I was in my house, sir," she said, adding that she lived near the Yablonski residence.

"You were thirteen years old at the time?"

"Yes, sir. Well, almost."

"Were you alone?"

"No, sir. I was with my cousin Patty; she was twelve. We were playing games, but we got tired of that and started to take down license numbers."

"Is that a game, too?"

"Kind of, sir. Patty and I watched cars going past, and we'd take down the license numbers and the states, the kind and color of the automobiles."

Sprague held up a white piece of paper and showed it to Rygle. "Is this where you wrote down those numbers and descriptions of the cars that passed by?"

"Yes, sir."

"The very same paper?"

"Yes, sir."

Sprague nodded. "Now, Kathy I'm going to ask you to look at that piece of paper and read to the jury the license plate number of the fifth car down and the description of the car."

"Sir, it says, 'maroon, black-top Caprice, Ohio license CX457'"

As it turned out, Kathy Rygle wasn't the only one in the area who wrote down license plate numbers and kept the evidence. Sprague called John Joseph Price, who'd been tending bar at the Koremooth Tavern on December 18, 1969.

"While I was behind the bar, a couple of strangers come in," Price began when Sprague asked him if he recalled anything in particular about that day. "They were annoying me."

"Can you see any of the men in this courtroom?" Sprague asked.

"Him," Price said, pointing at Gilly. He said that besides not liking the pair, he thought they might be there to rob the bar. So, he asked a bar patron to go outside and take down the car's license plate number.

"What was the make of the car and license plate number?"

"A 1965 Chevrolet sedan, CX457," Price said.

Sprague's last witness was Special Agent John Calvin Durst who, on January 23, 1970, found the empty Sprite bottle in Room 2 at the West Brownsville Hotel. Durst testified that he'd turned the bottle over to the Bureau's fingerprint expert, Charles Groenthal, who identified prints on the bottle as belonging to Paul Gilly.

With that, Sprague rested his case. During the prosecution's case, the defense made little progress challenging its witnesses. One of the defense attorneys grilled Vealey for more than two hours but got nowhere.

Nor was the defense case much more effective. They didn't dare put Gilly on the stand for fear that he would fold under Sprague's withering cross examination. They restricted their case to calling character witnesses, mostly his brothers and a nephew.

The Gillys were a law-abiding, hard-working family who had been shocked by the testimony about Paul's criminal life even before the murders. But his brothers and nephew stuck by him, describing him as a kind, good-hearted man who loved his family and was good to his parents.

Sprague took it easy on the character witnesses. Their testimony wouldn't have an effect on whether the jury believed Paul Gilly was guilty, or even whether the murder was premeditated. The prosecution case had demonstrated that Gilly and his compatriots had stalked Yablonski for months before killing him.

Even defense counsel didn't really argue for his client's innocence so much as plead for mercy. "You, ladies and gentlemen of the jury, have a godlike power to grant Paul Gilly life or give him death. Somehow, someday, we're going to realize enough blood has already been spilled in the Yablonski case."

After summing up the Commonwealth's case for the jurors, Sprague turned to look at the Yablonski brothers. "There sit Jock and Margaret's two sons, whose parents and sister have been wiped off the face of the earth." He then pointed to Gilly, who shrank further into his seat. "And right over there sits the man who hired and released two rattlesnakes to exterminate them. God help you and the rest of us if you flinch from your duty."

The jury began its deliberations at 2 p.m.; six and a half hours later, they reached a decision. The seven men and five women determined that Paul Gilly was guilty on three counts of "murder in the first degree."

Standing in front of Judge Sweet, Gilly's pale face grew even more ashen, and it appeared that his attorney had to hold him up. His family sobbed softly in their seats as Judge Sweet recessed until the morning.

The next day, it took the jury slightly less than two hours to come back with its sentence: death in the electric chair.

As the sentence was pronounced, Gilly leaped to his feet and looked at the jurors. "Oh my God," he cried, "what have you done to me?" He was then half-carried out of the courtroom by two deputy sheriffs, giving his family a last wave before the door closed.

Walking down the hall with Sprague, Kenneth Yablonski said, "That's one more bastard. Congratulations Dick."

But Sprague shook his head. "That's not in order yet, Ken. Wait until I finish the job."[45]

---

45   Lewis, *Murder by Contract.*

CHAPTER TWENTY-EIGHT

GENTLE PRESSURE

The road to finishing the job was paved with the conviction of Paul Gilly. Sprague had taken care of business with the Hillbilly Hitmen—two of them were facing death in the electric chair and the third life was behind bars awaiting sentencing after his usefulness as a prosecution witness concluded.

The tough Philadelphia prosecutor hoped that the convictions and subsequent sentences had put the fear of God in the rest of the conspirators. He knew that to get much further he needed confessions from one or more of them, as well as from members of the Research & Information Committee.

FBI agents Wally Estill and Hank Quinn had an informant who'd told them about how the pensioners had been told to cash the checks and then kick back the money to the six field reps, who then passed the money onto Prater and Pass. The informant told them that some of those field representatives were angry that they were being told by Prater and Pass to contribute to a defense fund for Silous Huddleston.

Working off that information the agents kept up what they called "gentle pressure" on the tough old men who made up the R&I Committee. They'd treated the mountaineers with respect and had been welcomed in their homes, even praying with them. But to a man, the pensioners and field reps, stuck to their story.

The agents understood why. They were afraid that they'd lose their pensions and health benefits, and there was always the fear of violence in Bloody Harlan and Bell Counties. Combined with an ingrained loyalty to the union, it was going to take more time.

In the meantime, Sprague thought that Huddleston and his daughter, Annette Gilly, might cave after Paul was convicted. Huddleston was next up for trial in April. But so far neither father nor daughter had been willing to cooperate.

Special agents Bill Curtis and Joe Masterson were told to keep up the pressure on Annette, but she wasn't the usual thirty-two-year-old woman who was easily frightened by police accusations. Talking to her, the agents were aware of her rough beginnings in Oneida. But she wasn't some innocent victim.

Marrying Paul Gilly, she was not just aware of his criminal activities buying and selling stolen property, especially guns, and burglaries; she'd participated. According to Vealey and Phillips, she was the conduit between her father and her husband for the Yablonski murders. She was tough as nails and not about to "snitch," especially if there was nothing in it for her.

Silous Huddleston was of like mind. He'd done plenty of dirty work for the union over the years, most of which he'd gotten away with. He was well-versed in the "gospel" of the UMWA and his loyalty to the union, and its leadership, was without question. Especially when they were threatened by a "traitor" like Jock Yablonski.

Still, father and daughter could see what was coming. It was Annette who caved first. Curtis and Masterson had kept reminding her of the death sentence that had been handed down to her husband and Martin, and at last it worked. On March 21, Curtis called Sprague to tell him that she was ready to talk.

The news came as a big relief to Sprague. He'd been determined not to offer a "deal" to Annette. But he was worried that without her testimony, he might not be able to convict her dad, much less anyone further up such as Prater, Pass, and hopefully Boyle.

Now that she was cooperating, Sprague told the agents to treat her with kid gloves. He had her brought to the confines of Philadelphia, but instead of housing her in the city jail, he put her up at the Sheraton, where she was allowed to order room service while a police officer stood guard outside her door.

Even though she'd agreed to talk, Annette wasn't very forthcoming at first. But after a few days, she gave a complete, signed confession. She also agreed to plead guilty to murder and testify against her father, Prater, and Pass. She didn't have more than a hunch that Boyle was involved, but Sprague was convinced that if he could convict the others, he'd be able to reach the union boss. The only "deal" he had to give her in exchange for her testimony was an agreement not to seek the death penalty.

Sprague made sure that word of Annette's confession got back to Huddleston's lawyers. The attorneys responded by trying an end-around to avoid having to deal with Sprague, who they knew would play hardball. Instead, they approached Assistant U.S. Attorney Henderson looking for a deal.

This was the second time a defendant's lawyer tried to avoid Sprague. The first had been Paul Gilly's lawyer who also tried to work something out with Henderson. But as he had then, the assistant U.S. attorney listened to what Huddleston's lawyers had to say. Their demands included all charges being dropped against their client in exchange for his testimony against the other conspirators. The defense attorneys said Silous also wanted the $50,000 reward the union had offered for the apprehension and conviction of the killers.

The federal prosecutor had laughed that off and said, for the second time, the lawyers would have to talk to Sprague. It was the Philadelphia prosecutor's show, and even if Henderson agreed to drop federal charges of violating the Yablonskis' civil rights— essentially the federal murder charge—he had no authority to drop charges brought by the Commonwealth of Pennsylvania.

With no other option, Huddleston's lawyers called Sprague, demanding a deal. However, with Annette's confession, Sprague was sure he'd convict her dad and was even less inclined to make any concessions beyond not pressing for the death penalty.

Huddleston didn't go for it. He was willing to take his chances at trial which was set to begin April 17, 1972.

A week before the trial, Sprague flew into the Allegheny County airport where he was met by Annette's attorney. They then drove to the city of Washington and Judge Sweet's courtroom for her arraignment.

Statuesque, blue-eyed Annette arrived wearing a conservative dark-blue suit and white blouse with light blue high heels, her copious platinum blonde hair teased up in the fashion of the day. She was accompanied by the tightest security yet.

A motorcade of state police and sheriff's vehicles had escorted her and her guards from a motel where she'd been kept overnight. When the vehicles pulled up, a dozen officers jumped out with their weapons out and eyes on surrounding rooftops. She was immediately surrounded and hidden from view by plainclothes officers and deputies armed with submachine guns, shotguns, and carbines.

The level of security was indicative of the importance Sprague placed on Annette's testimony. It also demonstrated fears among law enforcement in Washington County about the reach and willingness of the UMWA union to commit violence to protect itself.

As they stood in front of Sweet's dais, Annette towered over District Attorney Costa. Sprague read the first of the three murder charges against her. Sweet then focused his attention on the young woman.

"How say you, Mrs. Gilly, guilty or not guilty?" the judge asked.

"I am guilty, Your Honor," she replied.

After she answered the same way to the other charges, Sprague turned to her and asked, "Did you, Annette Gilly, conspire with others to cause the death of Joseph A. 'Jock' Yablonski, his wife, Margaret, and daughter, Charlotte?"

"Yes, sir, I did."

Then it was the judge's turn. "Are you aware, Mrs. Gilly, that you have taken an irreparable step? You have waived your right to trial by court or jury and those precious rights contained in the Sixth Amendment which I will read to you now. Do you understand?"

"Yes, Your Honor," she replied.

Annette had been told by her attorney that even though the death penalty was off the table, she could still be sentenced to life in prison for each murder count. She nodded and, her voice barely audible, said, "Yes, Your Honor, I am."

Judge Sweet then told Sprague to call his witness. He summoned Agent Curtis to the stand, where he testified that Annette Gilly had confessed to the murders. But he didn't reveal the contents of her thirty-two-page confession.

Withholding the contents was part of Sprague's strategy. He didn't want the union leadership knowing what she'd said until Henderson had a chance to get a federal indictment for Prater and have him arrested before he could go into hiding.

As soon as he got the word from Sprague after court recessed, Henderson, who was waiting in the federal building in Pittsburgh, immediately obtained the federal indictment for Prater on a charge of violating Jock Yablonski's civil rights. He then called FBI Agent Estill in Knoxville and told him to arrest Prater.

With Agent Quinn, Agent Estill drove to LaFollette, Tennessee, where they arrested a surprised William Prater at his home in front of his wife. The mother of five sons and two daughters, who had no inkling of her husband's illegal activities, was stunned as her husband was handcuffed and led away.

The federal charge meant that Prater could be extradited immediately to Pennsylvania. He was flown to Pittsburgh and incarcerated on $200,000 bail.

Annette Gilly's full confession wasn't revealed in open court until the morning of April 13 and the arraignment of Silous Huddleston. It was read to the court at that time by Agent Curtis after Sprague called him to the stand.

Annette wasn't present in the courtroom. But her father was— sitting in a wheelchair, wheezing for breath due to black lung disease and looking like somebody's grumpy old grandfather.

Reading from the transcript of Annette's confession, Curtis began: "I, Annette Gilly...wish to state that I, with six others, took part in the plan to murder Joseph Yablonski between July 1969 and February 1970. To carry out these plans I made trips to LaFollette, Tennessee to get arsenic for this murder. I made telephone calls from Cleveland, Ohio to LaFollette, Tennessee to obtain information from a person, which was then relayed to me by another individual to aid in the murder.

"I first learned of the plan to murder Joseph Yablonski as a result of a meeting my father, Silous Huddleston, had with William J. Prater and Albert Pass. My father told me that during the course of this meeting it was agreed upon that something had to be done about Yablonski fast.

"My father decided to come to Cleveland to get someone to commit a murder. He came by bus so there would be no record of his arrival. This was in July or August of 1969. Paul, my husband, and I picked him up at the station and took him home. My father stayed approximately one week and during that time he and Paul had numerous conversations.

"Paul told me that my father wanted him to find people to kill a man named Joseph Yablonski, and Paul said there would be five thousand dollars paid for the job."[46]

While downplaying her role and even at times portraying herself as merely an observer, Annette laid out what she knew of the conspiracy. With a few new revelations, much of her confession filled in the blanks around the previous testimony of Vealey and Phillips regarding the stalking of Yablonski and the murders.

Ever since her arrest, she'd been sequestered in jail and unaware of what had been said at the trials of Martin and her husband. As such, a defense attorney couldn't claim that she'd tailored her statement after reading press reports or talking to anyone else, including her father.

"When Paul got home from this trip, he told me he, Phillips, and Vealey had been to Yablonski's son's house." She also recounted his story about Vealey and Phillips going into the Yablonski home on Halloween and making sandwiches.

"I knew the purpose of those trips was to locate and murder a union official who lived in Clarksville, a man named Jock Yablonski."

---

46   Transcript of Annette Gilly's confession as given to FBI
      Special Agent William L. Curtis, April 1972.

There was a brief moment of levity when Agent Curtis read a passage regarding the killers' travels together. "When my husband came back from these places, he complained about how dirty Vealey was and how bad he smelled. They all had to sleep in the car, and they were all cold and hungry."

In her statement, Annette recalled what happened after the December 18, 1969 when Vealey and her husband met Yablonski at his front door. "While Paul was gone on one trip, I received a telephone call from a man who said he was a Pennsylvania state policeman. He asked me about Paul and said he, Paul, might be a witness to an accident. I asked if Paul was all right, and he said yes. He asked if Paul was looking for work, and I said no, he was a painter.

"Approximately five minutes later, Paul called me, and I related what had happened and he assured me he was all right and would be home in a few minutes. He did come home, but it was two or three hours later."

According to her statement, when Paul got home, he told her that they watched the Yablonski house and when the women drove away, he and Vealey decided the time had come to act. It was planned that Vealey upon Paul's signal would shoot and kill Yablonski when he came to the door. But Paul never gave the signal and instead talked to their intended target about jobs and then left. "As they were driving away, the women returned."

Right after Christmas, her father told Paul that the murder had to be "expedited" or that a Pennsylvania UMWA district would get it done another way. It was a matter of pride. "My father said that District 19 had never let the union down, and they weren't going to now."

As Curtis read the transcript, Huddleston watched and listened raptly. Occasionally he shook his head, but courtroom observers didn't see any open display of anger or surprise at his daughter's perfidy.

Except for a few minor details, Annette's account mirrored the testimony of Phillips and especially Vealey, corroborating and even elaborating on some aspects that the two conspirators hadn't known.

For example, on the fateful day of December 30, her husband told her to borrow a car from his brother. "He didn't want to use our car since the license number was known."

Vealey didn't know that was the reason they took a different car to Pennsylvania. He'd testified that he'd been told by Gilly that it was because the Caprice broke down. Differences in the stories, even minor ones, actually gave credibility to her account.

When Paul came back the next morning, Annette told Curtis, he woke her up. "I got up, plugged in the coffee pot, and went into the bathroom where I found Paul sitting on the edge of the bathtub.

"Paul said, 'All three are dead.' I didn't say anything, but I knew who he meant."

Later, after she'd returned the borrowed car, her husband told her about the murders. Initially, according to her statement, they only intended to kill Jock, which was why they disabled the cars and cut the telephone line so that the women couldn't get away or call the police. But "Martin went into the girl's room, panicked, and shot her.

"Paul and Vealey were in the master bedroom when Martin fired and the woman in the bedroom screamed. Vealey shot her, and she fell back. Yablonski tried to run. Paul fired once but said he missed. Martin and Vealey then fired more shots at them, killing them."

Some of what she said was new to Sprague and the investigators, such as how the news about the murders got back to conspirators in the union. "On January 4 or 5, 1970, Paul received a call from my father at which time Paul made small talk but then stated, 'I finished the church.' This was a code which would tell my father the murder had been done.

"A day or two later, the bodies were found, and it was all over the radio and television."

On January 9 or 10 her father asked her to come to LaFollette. When she arrived, she asked for the rest of the money. Silous took $5,000 out of an envelope, kept $1,000, and handed her the rest. Annette pocketed $400 or $500 and brought the rest back to her husband, who didn't tell his fellow killers about the additional amount.

Corroborating the testimony of Vealey and Phillips, as well as what other testimony and evidence showed, was important. However, what really caught the attention of Sprague and the investigators was what she said about the involvement of her father, William Prater, and Albert Pass.

"On one occasion," Curtis told the court as he read from the affidavit, "my father and I went to Mr. Prater's house for the specific purpose of asking Bill whether or not, in the event someone additional to Yablonski was killed, the union would pay.... Bill answered he didn't care if the whole family or the whole town was killed, as long as the job was done. Mr. Prater said they could run Yablonski down with an airplane if necessary."

Her father, she said, just wanted to be sure that if anyone else was killed, the union would still pay. "My father told Prater that if the union didn't pay, my father would be next in line to be killed."

At some point in the fall of 1969, she said, her husband told her that he wasn't happy dealing with just her father. He wanted to be assured by someone higher up in the union that the murder was sanctioned. "Arrangements were made, and my father and Paul went to meet Bill Prater."

Even that wasn't enough for her husband. "Paul wanted to see someone higher than Prater in the United Mine Workers union. Arrangements were made the next day for Paul, my father, and Bill Prater to meet Albert Pass, who was secretary-treasurer of District 19.

"I asked Paul and my father if I could go with them; however, both said no. My father said that Pass wouldn't want me there because he did not trust women."

When her husband returned from that meeting, he told her that he'd been promised a high-paying union job, and that they'd give his father, Henry Gilly, a pension. "I also believe that at this time an additional $5,000 was promised upon completion of the job."

The third $5,000 was delivered by a man who flew in from Washington, D.C., she said. "My father stated that after they obtained the money, Prater, Albert Pass, and a fourth man (in the basement of Prater's house) 'wiped' the money off on both sides with rags to remove all fingerprints.... My father informed me of this to show how careful and cautious the union was over this matter.

"During this same period of time, my father told me that the Yablonski murder had the approval of the 'big man.' To me, that meant Tony Boyle, president of the United Mine Workers."

In her confession, Annette told Curtis that when the assassination was being arranged, she and Paul weren't supposed to know who they were dealing with except her father. Silous, she said, was only supposed to deal with Bill Prater, and he in turn with Albert Pass. "According to this arrangement, those that Paul hired, Claude Vealey, James Charles Phillips, and later Aubran Wayne Martin, were not to know who was involved except Paul and me."

Just before his arrest, her husband told her that if something happened to him to remember four names: Titler, Owens, Pass, and Prater. "I asked why I should remember them, and he told me I'd know when the time was right."

After Paul's arrest, her father came to Cleveland to testify before the grand jury. "While there he told me that with the union, the sky was the limit, unless I talked, then the grave was the limit.

"When I heard Phillips had talked, I asked my father what would the union do about Phillips. He said they'd kill him."

After reading Annette's statement to the court, Curtis was dismissed and the arraignment was concluded. It didn't take long for word of her confession to get back to union headquarters in Washington, D.C. Within hours, Edward Carey, the general counsel for the union, called a press conference where he "categorically" denied that Boyle or anyone else in the union had anything to do with the Yablonski murders.

CHAPTER TWENTY-NINE

CULTURALLY INGRAINED LOYALTY

APRIL 17, 1972

It took until after a week of jury selection and the day his trial was supposed to begin for Silous Huddleston to throw in the towel. The million-dollar defense he felt he'd been promised by Prater had never materialized. A little over $23,000 had been raised from field reps and pensioners to pay for a couple of decent lawyers, but the national office didn't contribute a dime.

Silous felt betrayed and with his daughter's confession still ringing in his ears, he decided to forgo a trial and take his chances by testifying for the People. His lawyers got word to Sprague right before the trial was about to start.

Agents Curtis and Masterson took the old man over to a Ramada Inn and put him up in a room, a big change from the jail cells he'd been kept in since his arrest. There the agents interrogated Huddleston for nearly two weeks before they felt they'd wrung every detail from him.

Even though he confessed and said he wanted to "clear his conscience," he wasn't particularly remorseful about Yablonski's death and the deaths of the two women. He still considered Boyle's rival a traitor out to destroy the union, and the women were collateral damage, in the wrong place at the wrong time...their beds.

Based on Huddleston's statement, the U.S. attorney in Cleveland presided over the Federal Grand Jury that indicted Albert Pass for violating Jock Yablonski's civil rights. That started the ball rolling for several other events.

Waiting for word of the indictment in District 19 Middlesboro, Kentucky on May 2 were FBI agents Wally Estill and Kitchen. They were parked a short distance from Pass's home. When they got word, they drove up to the house and arrested the secretary-treasurer of the District.

The agents felt sorry for his wife, who packed his bag and kissed him goodbye. She would be left alone to care for their adult daughter who had been bedridden with cerebral palsy since childhood. But the lawmen had no such feelings for the man who arranged for the slaughter of the Yablonski family.

On May 3, Huddleston was arraigned in Judge Sweet's courtroom. "How do you plead to the three charges of murder and one of conspiracy?"

"I plead guilty, sir."

Sprague then informed the court that the only concessions made to Huddleston were that provided he testify truthfully, the prosecution would not seek the death penalty and would recommend that the federal charges be dropped. He then called Agent Curtis to the stand to once again read a statement into the record.

"I, with seven other people, took part in the plans to murder Joseph Yablonski. From June 1969 to February 1970, I met with a number of these people and agreed to find others to commit the murder. I also obtained the money to pay the others before and after the murder. I made numerous telephone calls to Cleveland, relaying information from those who had the money to those who were to do the killing."

In his confession, Huddleston explained that after he'd arranged with his son-in-law Paul Gilly to get some of "his boys" to kill Yablonski, he then called Bill Prater and told him that he had a man looking for accomplices.

"Prater, Albert Pass, and I were the only people who knew about the plan to commit this murder. A short time later, Paul told me he had the boys to do the job. I told this to Prater and asked him how my boys would get paid, and he said he'd let me know."

"Two or three days after, Bill Prater and I met with Albert Pass and Albert asked if my boys would do it. I said, 'Yes,' but they wanted to know when they'd be paid. Albert said he'd consider it official when he heard news of the death on the radio or television."

Huddleston said that when he asked Pass how the assassins could find Jock, the secretary-treasurer drew a line on a map showing the location of the UMWA headquarters in Washington, D.C. There was a small park that Yablonski would pass on his way to the building and Pass suggested they could shoot him there and get away. He also mentioned that when Yablonski was in Washington, D.C. he stayed at his son Chip's house.

There was also a meeting with Prater and Pass at the District 19 office in Middlesboro. Huddleston expressed concern that the killers didn't know what Jock looked like and might shoot the wrong guy. Pass then looked through a copy of the *UMW Journal* and located a photo of Jock standing with two other union officials. Pass drew an arrow marking Yablonski on the photo.

Huddleston didn't have much to say directly about Boyle, other than Pass traveled regularly to Washington, D.C. to speak to the union boss. Some of his statements only touched on the union boss's involvement in a peripheral way, such as the time in mid-November 1969 that Prater called and said Pass was returning from Washington, D.C. and wanted to meet with them at the Knoxville airport. When they met Pass, Huddleston said, he told them to call off the murder for at least thirty days after the December 9 election.

As he sat listening to Curtis read Huddleston's statement, Sprague was pleased at how well it corroborated the confessions of Vealy, Phillips and Annette Gilly, but also added details that expanded on what the others had to say. Especially about the involvement of Prater and Pass. It didn't give him Boyle, not yet, but it was a start on connecting the dots from the killers to those who set the conspiracy in motion.

"Shortly after Christmas 1969, Bill Prater drove to my house. I went out to the car and he showed me an envelope. He told me there was five thousand in it and said they would pay five thousand more if my boys would murder Yablonski before the first of the year."

Huddleston recalled waiting anxiously for news that the murders had been accomplished. Then his son-in-law called to say he'd finished painting the church, but the old man wasn't sure what that meant until January 5 when he saw the news on the television.

A few minutes later, he got a call from Prater. "Bill asked me if I'd heard the news and I told him I had," Curtis said reading from the transcript. "He says, 'What they do, slaughter the whole family?'" But other than that question, his friend never expressed any regrets about the deaths of Margaret and Charlotte.

Huddleston voiced some bitterness that the million-dollar defense fund he'd been promised never materialized. One of his other daughters asked Prater about it, he said. "He told her it was a figure of speech."

CHAPTER THIRTY

A MAJOR BREAKTHROUGH

As important as Huddleston's confession was linking the killers to the conspirators further up the food chain, there was another aspect to his statement that provided the key to breaking the case open. And that was to give the agents the man, Dave Brandenburg, who could reveal the truth regarding the twenty-three pensioners and six field reps who made up the Research & Information Committee.

Sprague and the feds had long been sure that the $20,000 paid to the pensioners for their recruiting expenses was actually used to pay the Yablonski killers. The informant told them that the members cashed the checks and then kicked back the money to the field reps who in turn gave it to Prater then onto Pass. The informant had also said that the men weren't happy about being told to contribute some of their wages for Huddleston's defense.

Huddleston's confession gave Sprague and the others insight into the pressure being put on the R&I Committee members by the union. According to his statement, at one point shortly after the murders were discovered, he was trying to figure out what to do with an additional $9,000 he'd been given by Prater to pay the killers. He was worried that the FBI was watching him and might find the incriminating money on him before he could give it to the assassins.

About that time, he'd been contacted on another matter by Dave Brandenburg, one of the twenty-three pensioners and the minister of the small Fundamentalist Free Pentecostal Church of God in his remote coal mining community of Peabody Hollow near Lick Creek in Kentucky. During their conversation, Huddleston said, he'd asked the minister to hold onto $8,000 for him until he asked for it back.

"Dave asked why I didn't put it in a bank, and I told him I couldn't because the FBI was watching me and those boys (the killers) hadn't been paid. He said, 'Oh that money!' I knew he realized this was the murder money. Dave said if I hadn't told him what the money was for, he'd have held it for me; now he couldn't; it was 'blood money.'"

However, the Rev. Brandenburg, who had a new teenaged wife to keep happy, was persuaded to help after he was told he could keep five hundred, and if Huddleston didn't pick it up in three weeks, he could take another $500. For a man receiving a $150 monthly pension from the union, the extra cash was too tempting.

Huddleston had then driven to Brandenburg's isolated home in the woods. He gave the money to the pensioner, who took out $500 and put the rest in a five-gallon bucket, where he told Huddleston it would be until he returned for it.

After Annette's arrest, Huddleston collected the money so that he could give $2,500 to her lawyers. Three days later, he was arrested, too.

The information about Brandenburg gave the prosecution team a name who might prove to be a weak link in the R&I Committee, whose members were under pressure from the FBI and the union. According to Huddleston's statement, after the field reps and R&I members were subpoenaed to appear in front of the federal grand jury in Cleveland, Prater met with several of them at Brandenburg's house. The purpose was to make sure that they were all on the same page for the grand jury and the "stick to the story" mantra.

Huddleston said he also met with Prater, and together they had visited the homes of several R&I members. "Bill told them the Labor Department was conducting an investigation and federal agents would probably be out to ask about the union checks they received.

"Bill said that if they were asked what type of work they'd done to earn the money, they should say they had been doing organization work. Bill also told them what to say when they were asked how they spent their money."

Agents Estill and Quinn had spoken to Brandenburg in the past when applying their gentle pressure. They found him to be a friendly and religious man, of the sort that handled poisonous snakes as part of the religious service, a practice that had started in Appalachia in the early twentieth century.

Like the other R&I members, he'd insisted that the committee was legitimate and that the checks he'd received were to compensate him for expenses he'd incurred. He denied that there was any kickback scheme.

However, if Huddleston was telling the truth, Brandenburg knew that the money had been given back to union officials and that he knew it was "blood money." By doing that, and then helping Huddleston hide the money, he'd moved himself from a possibly unwitting participant to a conspirator in the case.

Having "cleared his conscience," Huddleston suggested that the feds bring Brandenburg to him. Wally Estill flew the preacher to Knoxville where they were met by Curtis and assistant U.S. Attorney Henderson, who took him to the Ramada Inn where Huddleston waited.

The two men were cordial with each other. Most of the day, Huddleston did the lion's share of the talking while the feds remained quiet—before the preacher loosened up and finally confessed. It took a bit longer still before he agreed to help them persuade other members of the R&I Committee to cooperate.

It was a major breakthrough. Estill and Quinn had spent thousands of hours trying to convince the stubborn old men, most of them sick with black lung or ailing from injuries incurred in the mines, to tell the truth about the R&I Committee. They would spend thousands of hours more now, even when accompanied by Dave Brandenburg, who urged the pensioners and field reps to come clean.

None of it came easy. Some of that was fear of reprisals from Tony Boyle and his loyal supporters. With a word, the president or Pass could take away their $150-a-month pensions and health benefits. Most of the pensioners had no other income, and facing black lung and other mining-related illnesses without medical benefits was the stuff nightmares were made of.

However, it wasn't just fear that kept the R&I Committee members quiet. It was also culturally ingrained loyalty and a union man's instinct to close ranks with his brothers, especially against threats from the outside. Beyond that was several hundred years going back to the Ulster Plantation and then onto the wilderness of what would become the United States in which they looked out for each other because no one else was going to. That sort of cultural connection had instilled an almost fanatical loyalty to other "brothers" in the union.

The men of that generation from the backwoods and dirt-poor towns of Appalachia had very little formal education, often no more than the third or fourth grade. But they'd toiled, and sometimes died, in the mines together, often since childhood. They went to the same churches, were buried in the same cemeteries generation after generation. They'd lived most of their lives on the edge of poverty, in constant danger, and many would die young from black lung and mine disasters, but it was still better than what they and their fathers had before the union.

All of their lives they'd been told that the union was the only entity looking out for them and their families. Not the owners or operators. Not law enforcement or politicians. Certainly not the federal government. No one had their backs except the UMWA and its leaders, starting with the immortal John L. Lewis and his hand-picked successor "Tough Tony" Boyle.

In that regard, Boyle's rhetoric during the campaign for UMWA president set the stage for the tragedy that followed and the difficulty the murder investigation team had bringing the guilty to justice. In speeches, as well as through the union journal, Boyle had portrayed Jock Yablonski as a "traitor," someone who was in bed with the oil and gas companies. His rival wanted to take away pensions and was out to destroy the union, he said. Not every union man believed it, but many did, especially from the rabidly loyal union men in Harlan and Bell Counties of District 19.

Coal country was a violent land and blood had been spilled both for and against the union. The killers may have been paid assassins, but they weren't the only men who would have killed a "traitor" who threatened to destroy the union. Such an act wasn't seen as murder, it was self-defense.

Union man Silous Huddleston had summed up the feeling of many others when he concluded his statement to the FBI agents that Curtis read to the court. "I believe Jock Yablonski was controlled by outsiders who wanted to destroy the union. He tried to get all the pensioners out of it so they would not be entitled to their pensions. They fought hard to get these and without them, they might as well be dead. I participated in the plan to murder Jock to keep him from destroying the union."

The irony was that Yablonski was one of them. He'd gone to work in the mines as an adolescent, lost his father to a mine accident, breathed the same coal dust, and stood on the picket lines with his UMWA brethren in the days of the gun thugs and corrupt sheriffs siding with the owners. When there was trouble in coal country, John L. Lewis had called upon him and his oratory skills to bring the rebels and non-union miners into the fold.

In truth, there was no evidence that he was anything but a loyal union man; he'd even admitted having been part of the hierarchy he'd labeled as corrupt when he announced himself as a reform candidate. But Boyle was a consummate liar with the full resources of the union, including its magazine at his disposal.

However, his illicit activities were catching up to him. In March 1972, in Federal Court, Boyle was convicted of thirteen felonies for violating the Corrupt Practices Act. Boyle was sentenced to a five-year prison term and fined $179,500 with an additional fine of $49,500 to pay back the union. He was out on appeal, but who knew for how long?

In the meantime, Boyle wasn't too concerned when Annette Gilly and Silous Huddleston flipped. They had no proof of his involvement, and his spokesman denied it every time it was brought up by the press. But Bill Prater and Albert Pass were both in jail in Pennsylvania and charged with murder by Sprague. That was troubling.

Making matters worse, Boyle was also being challenged for his position as the president of the UMWA. In May 1972, federal judge William B. Bryant ruled in favor of the lawsuit brought by Miners for Democracy, the Yablonski brothers, and Joe Rauh. He threw out the results of the 1969 UMWA election and instructed the union to schedule another election to be held in the first eight days of December 1972. He also decreed that the Department of Labor should oversee the election to ensure fairness.

Over the weekend of May 26–28, 1972, Miners for Democracy delegates met in Wheeling, West Virginia where they nominated Arnold Miller, a former miner and leader of the Black Lung Association who had worked for the Yablonski campaign, as their candidate to face Boyle.

Boyle had heard reports that R&I Committee members were under pressure from the FBI. Indeed, he'd heard one of them, Dave Brandenburg, had confessed and was traveling with FBI agents. They were going house-to-house to talk to other members, though so far, the others had not cracked.

Yet, just as the justice train was picking up speed, Sprague suffered a strategic setback. In June 1972, ruling on a case known as *Furman v. Georgia*, the U.S. Supreme Court struck down the death penalty in a narrow five to four decision. It didn't mean the death penalty would never again be a punishment, but the court stated that before it could be reinstated, states had to deal with inconsistencies in how it was applied. Accordingly, the court found the bifurcated procedure requiring two trials, one to decide guilt or innocence, the other to determine if the death penalty should be ordered. The Supreme Court now held that if the accused was found guilty, the death penalty would be mandatory. (In 1975, the court reversed, going back to the pre-*Furman v. Georgia* process.)

However, the ruling meant that Aubran Wayne "Buddy" Martin was no longer on death row awaiting execution, and instead he was serving three consecutive life sentences. It also meant that Gilly, who had not yet been formally sentenced by Judge Sweet pending appeals, also no longer had to fear the electric chair.

The cudgel that Sprague had been holding over the conspirators in the hope that they would turn on each other was gone. Conviction of first-degree murder still meant life without parole in prison. But while killers might proclaim that they'd prefer a quick death to a lifetime behind bars, prison did not hold the same visceral fear of being put down like an old dog through lethal injection, the electric chair, or hanging.

Without the threat of the death penalty, Sprague's clout had lessened. However, in the end, something more powerful than even the threat of death would replace it.

CHAPTER THIRTY-ONE

A FOOLISH AND STUPID MISTAKE

MARCH 13, 1973

Pale and haggard after three years in prison, Paul Gilly looked down from the witness stand at the defendant, William Prater, and then back to special prosecutor Richard A. Sprague. The thirty-seven-year-old former housepainter, restaurant owner, and paid killer had just spent the past hour testifying about his role in the stalking and murder of Jock Yablonski, as well as explaining the roles of his wife, Annette, and father-in-law Silous Huddleston. He was a nervous wreck.

At the defense table, William Jackson Prater, a fifty-two-year-old, well-built man with close-cropped gray hair, listened intently with a look on his face that said, "What has this got to do with me?" Occasionally, he glanced to the spectator seats where his wife, grown sons, and teen-aged daughter sat, shrugging as if none of the testimony made any sense.

After several delays and some added twists to the Commonwealth's case, the trial of District 19 field rep Prater had finally got underway on Monday, March 6, 1973 with jury selection. His defense attorney, H. David Rothman—a tall, respected trial lawyer from Pittsburgh with an old-fashioned handle-bar moustache—had successfully lobbied Judge Sweet for a change in venue to Erie, Pennsylvania. The new judge, Edward H. Carney, ran a more business-like courtroom than the affable Sweet but was no less knowledgeable about the law or fair and courteous to both sides.

The front page of the *Erie Morning News* was dominated by a story about the trial and a smaller article that ran under the headline: "Sprague vs. Rothman: A Study in Contrasts." In that story, the reporter described Rothman as "slow, deliberate, soft-spoken." Of the twenty-five murder cases he'd been involved in, "He modestly says: 'My batting average is better than .500.'"

The reporter described Sprague as "dynamic, challenging loud.... Sprague, who carries a national reputation as one of the most colorful, hard-hitting, untiring prosecutors in the land, has prosecuted sixty-seven murder cases. All were convictions."[47]

After the all-white jury of seven women and five men, plus two alternates, was seated on Thursday, March 9, Sprague began his opening statement by describing the crimes as "the assassination of a family." He'd then ticked off the evidence that would prove beyond a reasonable doubt the defendant was guilty of three counts of first-degree murder. He noted where and when the murders took place, when the bodies were found and by who, and the wounds on each of the victims.

Then Sprague briefly went over the conspirators' futile attempts to stalk and kill Jock Yablonski in the fall of 1969 and how finally, on the night of December 30, 1969, they lay in wait on the vantage point behind the Yablonski home before completing their horrific task.

Up to that point, Sprague had kept to the same script as the first two trials of the gunmen Martin and Gilly. But at that point in his opening statement he began to dig into where this trial would deviate from the others as he step-by-step turned attention to the conspirators who put the killers up to their heinous act.

---

47   Jeff Pinski, *Erie Morning News*, March 6, 1973.

"To find out who hired them," he said, standing as always facing the jurors, "we need to start at the end to find the beginning." He then told the panel what they could expect to hear from the killer Claude Vealey, conspirator James Charles Phillips, and Annette Gilly, "who pleaded guilty to participating and arranging the murders."

They'd also hear from Silous Huddleston, he said, who'd tell them that Prater was the man who asked him to find the killers. And that Prater was the conduit through which the money flowed from District 19 secretary-treasurer Albert Pass to Huddleston to the killers.

Further testimony would show that Pass had written letters to Tony Boyle asking for $20,000—ostensibly to pay twenty-three District 19 pensioners who belonged to a "fictious" committee for their expenses. He pointed out that Pass had never written directly to Boyle for money, instead making such requests to the UMWA secretary-treasurer Bill Owens. The UMWA president had then personally contacted the union comptroller and told him to send the money to Pass.

Those pensioners, he said, were told to kick the money back to Prater. And they were under orders from Pass not to tell anyone. The pensioners lied to the FBI and to the grand jury. "They feared their pensions would be cut off and their medical benefits as well."

Just before Thanksgiving 1969, the prosecutor continued, Prater contacted Huddleston and told him that Boyle was going to win the election and to hold up on the murder plot until later. The defendant told the old man, "We don't want anyone to think Yablonski was killed so that Boyle could win the election.

"Then after the election, the defendant Prater told Huddleston, 'The contract is back on. Go ahead and get it done; have them kill Yablonski. But get it done before the first of the year.'"

Testimony would further indicate, Sprague said, that Prater told Huddleston not to call him when the murders were accomplished. "I'll hear about it on the TV and radio news." On January 5, 1970, when the bodies were found and the murders were reported nationwide, Prater was watching TV and called Albert Pass, who saw the same broadcast.

As Sprague spoke, the tenor of his opening, as with the entire strategy, began to subtly change from concentrating on the gunmen and lower-level conspirators to the upper echelons. Through the first two trials, he had not brought Albert Pass much into the picture, and much less was said about Tony Boyle, other than vague references about "some guy named Tony" by Phillips and Vealey.

It wasn't until Annette Gilly's statement was read aloud in court during her arraignment, and reported in the press, that the name "Tony Boyle" was directly tied by the prosecution to the murder of the Yablonskis.

Joe Rauh and the Miners for Democracy had kept up the pressure with various lawsuits.

Then in December 1972, Boyle lost the UMWA presidential election to Miller: 70,373 votes to 56,334. It was the most closely regulated union election in American history and as bitterly fought by Boyle as his efforts against Yablonski.

Flying nearly every weekend from his headquarters in Washington, D.C. to the coal fields and mining towns, Boyle had launched a scorched-earth campaign, railing against his opponent as a "communist," blasting the government for interfering in union affairs, and even continuing to slander Yablonski, who he saw as the root of all his problems.

"This is what Adolf Hitler did when he took over and destroyed that country," he said at one rally. "He started by destroying the labor leaders and the labor organizations, and then he destroyed the churches, and then he built those incinerators, and he burned his own people. Some of 'em alive."

Every chance he got he invoked the name of John L. Lewis and his place as the rightful heir to the UMWA throne. "I'm telling you for your own good. If you don't listen, then take your gamble," he railed in another speech. "Lewis said that out of the five hundred thousand men he could have named, he chose me, and he said he made no mistake. I sincerely believe you owe me your support for what I've done these nine years."

When questioned about the murders of the Yablonski family and allegations of his involvement, Boyle would fly off the handle.

"I saved Jock Yablonski three or four times when Lewis was going to fire him," he told a reporter for the *New York Times* during the campaign. He then complained about Yablonski's alleged corruption, his disloyalty, and those who would make Boyle's slain rival out to be "a saint, a martyr."[48]

In the end it didn't matter, for the first time in American history a rank-and-file insurgent was elected over an incumbent union president. However, that didn't mean the old lion was toothless. There were still plenty of UMWA members, including prosecution witness Silous Huddleston, who still considered him the rightful president. The 56,334 who had voted for the old union boss either didn't think he was guilty of conspiring to kill Yablonski and his family, or they believed his rival had betrayed the union and deserved what happened to him.

However, Boyle had to focus on stopping Sprague. He made it clear to his minions, the defense attorneys, and the prosecution that the Prater trial was his line in the stand. Rothman was Prater's lawyer but Boyle was calling the shots. Not only were Pass and District 19 president William Turnblazer on the defense witness list, so was Boyle.

Sprague welcomed Boyle's team to go all in. It would mean they would all be exposed to cross-examination, and he could use their responses to expose their lies and condemn Prater. What's more, their testimony could later be used to trip them up at their own trials.

It was a real risk for Boyle and the others, but Sprague understood the reasoning. They both knew that if Prater was found guilty, Boyle was in trouble. It would mean that based on the evidence, a jury had made the leap from finding the gunmen guilty to believing that union officials had put them up to it. And the further up the chain of command Sprague moved, the closer he would get to Boyle.

However, if Sprague lost, it might also spell doom for his pursuit of the union conspirators. Although there was a massive amount

---

48   Laurence Leamer, "The United Mine Workers holds an election," *New York Times*, November 26, 1972.

of evidence pinning the murders on the killers, there was far less proving who put them up to it. The prosecution witnesses were "corrupt"—killers, liars, and others who the jury could be persuaded had reason to implicate others for their own benefit. And because conviction would take a unanimous decision by the jury, all it would take was one to decide the prosecution had not proved its case beyond a reasonable doubt.

The prosecution case was strong, but it was no sure thing. And a loss by either side in the Prater trial could mean a knockout blow to any future prosecutions. With that in mind, both sides were determined to win here.

"Ultimately, the death of Jock Yablonski is going to go back to the beginning," Sprague told the jury. "William Jackson Prater, the defendant, is not the beginning. There is a conduit along the way. You cannot pass by this conduit; each link has to be uncovered.

"Huddleston will tell you how the defendant and Albert Pass, 'the boss man,' related that they want Jock Yablonski killed. You're going to hear how, with the union election apparently won by Boyle, Prater, right afterward, got back to Huddleston and said, 'The contract's on; go ahead and get it done. Have them kill Yablonski.'

"You're going to hear how twenty thousand dollars was transferred, on Tony Boyle's orders, to Pass, the twenty thousand offered to the assassins in the murder of Jock Yablonski."

After Sprague concluded his opening statement, Rothman declined to give one on behalf of the defense. The prosecutor then launched into his case, calling for the third time his first witness, Kenneth Yablonski, to the stand to describe finding his slaughtered family. *Something worse...*

From there, the first part of the case against Prater had not differed much from the first two trials. Fitting the pieces of the puzzle together one at a time, Sprague called his lineup of witnesses. The coroner and pathologist with the horrible photographs of decomposing bodies. The divers who'd braved the icy Monongahela River in January 1970 to locate a pearl-handled revolver and M1 carbine. Karl Kaftan and Kathy Rygle, who was now seventeen years old, and the bartender at the Koremooth Tavern, who described how they'd almost serendipitously written down the Ohio license plate they'd seen on a maroon Chevrolet Caprice. Without that small piece, the investigators may have never found the guilty parties.

Inexorably, one witness would step down and another climb up to continue the onslaught. Aided by photographs, Agent Curtis pointed out the vantage point where the killers lurked, drinking beer and whiskey from bottles later found in the snow. He was followed by FBI fingerprint expert Charles Groenthal to link those bottles, as well as a film cannister and pop bottle, to the killers. Then it was time for Sprague to move on to the meat of his case.

In the first two trials, Claude Vealey appeared right after Kenneth Yablonski. But in this trial, Sprague had waited until after his other witnesses to call the thuggish killer. Vealey would open the door regarding the amassing of evidence against "the man named Tony" and much more.

Looking like prison food agreed with him, a pudgy Claude Vealey stepped into the witness stand and again recounted stalking Yablonski with Paul Gilly and James Charles Phillips. "Gilly said a man named 'Tony' was behind him."

Gilly had a UMWA magazine clipping, he said, with a photograph of three union officials standing together. An arrow had been drawn on the photograph to indicate the target.

Vealey's testimony implicated Annette Gilly and Silous Huddleston, but he didn't mention the defendant Prater.

The killer's testimony reached its climax with his methodical narrative of the executions of the Yablonski family. He concluded by describing getting rid of the guns and film cannisters on the way home, and then splitting up the money in Cleveland.

Next up was James Charles Phillips, now serving a life sentence for the rape of his former girlfriend's four-year-old daughter. After he repeated his role as one of the original conspirators, including the trip to Washington, D.C. and breaking into the Yablonski home on Halloween, he was hammered by Rothman, who needed to make both Vealey and the witness look like lying killers trying to save their own skins by going along with the prosecution's attempt to railroad Prater.

The defense attorney succeeded in portraying the pair as the venal creatures they were, but he could not shake them from their stories. Asked by Rothman why he quit the assassination team, Phillips shrugged and said, "Well, for one thing, sir, I couldn't see, like I said, killing the whole family. Stealing, yes, but I couldn't kill."

Up to this point in the prosecution's case, there had been little to differentiate it from the first two trials, though of course, it was all new to the jurors. But even Sprague had not seen the next witness coming until a few days earlier.

The previous Friday, March 9, Sprague received a call in his office after court recessed that was a complete surprise. The caller was William Gilly, an older brother of Paul Gilly. He wanted to know if he and his siblings could talk to Paul.

Sprague wasn't sure what it would accomplish. Gilly no longer had to worry about the death penalty, but he still faced three consecutive life sentences. The prosecutor made it clear to his brother that he wouldn't be offering any sort of deal, so there wasn't anything in it for the convicted killer. But if he wanted to try, he could.

As Sprague later heard the story, Paul's brothers talked to him on Saturday and Sunday about coming clean. They were good people, who had been shocked when they attended the trial and heard about Paul's criminal activities, even without his involvement in the Yablonski murders. Staunch churchgoers, they had traditional concepts of heaven and hell, and alone with their brother, they'd reminded him that their parents were old and wouldn't live much longer. Their mother and father were convinced that if Paul didn't confess to the murders and ask for forgiveness, the family wouldn't all be together in the hereafter.

At first, Paul balked and tried to protest his innocence again. Perhaps it was the shame that admitting to such a cold-blooded crime engendered. But his brothers didn't accept his lies, and gradually, he admitted his guilt. But he still didn't want to confess to the authorities or testify for fear of Tony Boyle and his henchmen. Even in prison, it would be dangerous to have "snitched" on union officials, and not just for him; it could mean retaliation against them, his family.

Paul's brothers said not to worry about them. They'd take care of themselves. It was the afterlife and the anguish of their elderly parents they cared about. At last, Paul gave in.

Late Sunday afternoon, Sprague received another call from William Gilly, who said his brother was willing to confess and testify. The prosecutor had Paul and William flown to Erie and brought to the motel where Sprague was staying during the trial.

Sprague started the meeting by reminding Paul that there would be no deal in exchange for his testimony. Glancing first at his brother who nodded, the convicted killer then gave his statement outlining his participation in the planning, stalking, and ultimate murder of Jock Yablonski and his family.

Obviously frightened, Gilly was called to the stand Tuesday. He began by testifying that his role in the conspiracy started when his wife, Annette, asked him to meet with her father Silous Huddleston about killing a man. He'd then hired Vealey and Phillips and with them searched for Yablonski, intending to kill him.

On the stand, Gilly reached the point in his story a week before the murders and a week after the killers were greenlighted to resume the murder plot. "Around December 21 or 22 I went with Silous to Prater's house in LaFollette," he said as he mopped the sweat from his face with a handkerchief. "Prater wanted to know why there were no results yet.

"He said to let Vealey do whatever he wanted to do, but just get the job done. It was important for District 19 to get it done through District 19. He said, 'Finish it. Kill Yablonski and whoever else was around. No more holdups.'"

In some ways, Gilly's testimony largely mirrored the accounts the jurors had already heard from Vealey and Phillips. It differed in that he was the leader, and that he was also the middleman between them and the union officials who wanted Yablonski killed. It also expanded on what Annette had told the jurors about how the plot began and the interactions with Huddleston.

However, the real coup for the prosecution was how Paul Gilly was able to bring Prater, Pass, and, to a lesser degree, Boyle into the conspiracy picture. "Silous said the money for the killing would come from District 19 in small units so no one could trace the money," he explained to the jurors. "He told me that Prater was arranging to supply the money. He further told me that the money would be distributed out in small checks and then put together by Albert Pass."

Satisfied with the money arrangements, Gilly said he then hired Vealey and Phillips. "Silous said he would tell Prater and Pass."

Gilly testified that the first time he met Prater was in early October 1969 after his team of assassins started getting cold feet and wanted to see some money. Huddleston had then arranged for him to meet Prater in the basement of the field rep's house. The two older men told him that the money was with Pass and that only he could authorize giving any to Paul, which was then arranged.

It was during that meeting, Gilly said, that Prater gave him a map of Washington, D.C. on which the location of the UMWA building was underlined. The jurors had already seen the map, which had been found in the Gilly's kitchen by FBI agents, when Sprague entered it into evidence during Vealey's testimony. It was also Prater, he said, who told him that Yablonski sometimes stayed at his son's house while in D.C.

On the stand, Gilly recounted how after Vealey and Phillips were arrested for burglary, he'd asked Huddleston for some of the money to bail them out. Huddleston said he needed to ask Prater for permission and that, in turn, Prater again had to get the okay from Pass.

Sprague asked Gilly how he got the photograph of Yablonski standing with the two other union officials on which an arrow had been drawn. The ringleader of the killers responded that it was brought up in a conversation with Prater in which he said he wasn't sure what Yablonski looked like. Then Prater recalled that he'd seen a photo of Yablonski in the union magazine and that he'd ask Pass for a copy. He was told that Pass drew the arrow pointing to the target, and then gave the photograph to Prater, who sent it to Huddleston, who mailed it to his son-in-law.

It was Prater who told him that Tony Boyle was behind the contract to kill Yablonski. "He and Silous were telling me how fair and great Tony Boyle was." And Boyle promised through Prater that Paul's father would receive a UMWA pension provided the team accomplished the murder.

Asked by Sprague why Yablonski was targeted, Gilly responded, "I was told by Prater that Mr. Yablonski was trying to wreck and destroy the union and its pension funds, and they wanted him killed."

"Did he say who wanted him killed?" Sprague asked the witness.

"Yes, sir, Tony Boyle," Gilly said. "He said Mr. Yablonski had filed some kind of suit in court and blocked Mr. Boyle where he couldn't help the pensioners."

"I want you to look at the defendant, Prater," Sprague said as he ended his questioning of Gilly about noon. "Is there any doubt in your mind that he is the man who helped arrange and pay for these murders?"

"No, sir," Gilly replied.

At one point in late December 1969, he continued, Prater summoned him from Cleveland to a meeting in the basement of the Prater home in LaFollette.

"Prater gave us new instructions—what to do, where to go," Gilly said. "It didn't make no difference what or how. We could do whatever we had to do to get the job done. Prater wanted some results done, or there would be someone else come from Kentucky to do it."

"Was anything said as to who was paying to get this done?" Sprague asked Gilly.

Gilly replied, "I don't know who said it, but at this time it was said that this was being done personally for Tony Boyle, through District 19."

At an earlier meeting with Prater in LaFollette in October 1969, Gilly testified, "Prater said it was agreed in District 19 that they would carry out this murder for Tony Boyle."

Gilly also said that Prater told him "he would verify that Tony Boyle personally said my father would get his pension—provided I would carry through and see that Mr. Yablonski was shot and killed."

During cross-examination, Rothman had to fall back on the strategy of attacking the witness's credibility, noting that Gilly was an admitted murderer who proclaimed his innocence even after his conviction. The defense attorney then tried to elicit that Gilly had not been "officially" sentenced because the death penalty had been deemed unconstitutional and was hoping for a deal. However, his argument was muted when at Sprague's suggestion, Judge Carney explained to the jurors that the delay in sentencing was not unusual.

Rothman also tried to make up some ground because of a discrepancy between Annette Gilly's confession and her husband's testimony. Annette told Agent Curtis her husband told her to remember four names—Titler, Owens, Prater, and Pass—if he was arrested. "He said I'd know what to do when the time came," she'd told the jurors.

However, Paul Gilly testified that he told his wife to memorize the names Prater, Pass, and Boyle. When questioned by the defense attorney on the stand, he was adamant those were the names he told her.

Rothman seemed to think he'd scored points with the jury. But the fact that Paul did not try to change his testimony to match his wife's actually countered the defense attorney's implication that FBI agents let him rehearse his testimony with his wife and his father-in-law.

Nearing the end of cross-examination, Rothman attempted to cast doubt on Gilly's change of heart. "When Vealey said to you, 'Let's kill them all,' why didn't you say, 'Fellows, let's get out of here?'"

Gilly hung his head before looking over to his family then back to the defense attorney. "Yes, sir, I could have done that. It was another foolish and stupid mistake, like I made all the way through. I been sick and sorry ever since and that's the truth. What makes it so bad is that I know I could have stopped it, but I didn't."

"What made you decide to kill Jock Yablonski?"

"A lot of persuasion of folks you listen to," Gilly replied, "and the pension that my father and a lot of others did not get and could not get."

"Didn't you believe there was another way, short of murder?" Mr. Rothman asked Gilly.

"No, sir, I didn't."

As the confessed killer stepped down from the witness stand, he looked again to where his brothers sat in the spectator section. With tears in their eyes, they nodded to each other, then he was escorted from the courtroom by deputy sheriffs.

CHAPTER THIRTY-TWO

AN UNLIKELY PROFILE IN COURAGE

After Gilly was removed from the courtroom, Sprague called his next witness, Edith Roark, the long-time bookkeeper for District 19. As he waited for the middle-aged woman to make her way to the witness stand, the prosecutor thought about the extraordinary roles serendipity and religion had played in the case so far. And he knew there was more to come.

It was one thing for the killers to have left evidence—fingerprints, the map and the magazine photograph, beer and whiskey bottles—lying around like dirty socks. They weren't known as the Hillbilly Hitmen because they'd impressed anybody with their criminal acumen.

However, some of the prosecution's best evidence seemed so fortunate that bordered on imagined heavenly intervention. How else to explain why three different people on two separate dates wrote down the license plate of an otherwise innocuous maroon Caprice? Not only that but two of them had held onto the otherwise meaningless evidence for two years!

Yet without Karl Kafton's notepad, investigators would not have been able to trace the visitors of December 18 back to Paul Gilly. Without that notepad, they may have never found the killers.

And Kathy Rygle's slip of paper from a game she was playing with her cousin not only corroborated the Kafton and the Koremooth Tavern bartender, it established that the murders were not some burglary-gone-awry. Three weeks apart between Rygle's game and the others' notes, it showed a premeditated plan to stalk and assassinate Jock Yablonski.

The extraordinary luck hadn't stopped there. Sprague thought that the divers locating the murder weapons in the dark, ice-cold Monongahela River was nothing short of a miracle.

Then, with the Prater trial already underway, and totally out of the blue, Paul Gilly decided to tell the truth. In years of trying murder cases, Sprague and I had occasionally run into a suspect whose conscience led him to confess. But never had a convicted killer agreed to testify against his co-conspirators having been convicted of three first-degree murder charges, likely to spend the rest of his life in prison, while having already served over a year in the penitentiary without even asking for leniency.

And why? Because his aged parents wanted to reunite the family in heaven and thought Paul wouldn't be allowed to join them if he didn't try to atone for his sins.

Sprague wondered what other surprises awaited.

As Roark placed her right hand on the Bible and was sworn in, Sprague prepared to begin the phase of the case that would have enormous ramifications not only for the man on trial, but for the conspirators still waiting. It would showcase the culture of Appalachia coal country and the United Mine Workers of America. And it would pit the fundamentalist faith of an impoverished, honest, and hard-working people against loyalty born in the bowels of the Earth, on the scraped mountaintops of Appalachia, and on the picket lines.

Before it was over, it would also feature the first showdown between the tenacious prosecutor from Philadelphia and the flamboyant "Tough Tony" Boyle, a product of the Montana coal fields and the union's struggles to survive and grow powerful. The fate of both men rested on the consciences of a bunch of old mountaineers who made up the faux R&I Committee.

Nearly from the beginning of the investigation, the FBI and Department of Labor auditors had focused on the two $10,000 checks that Albert Pass had requested directly from Tony Boyle in September 1969. The union stance was that the money was used to pay twenty-three District 19 pensioners who had been selected for the committee by six field representatives for expenses they incurred while recruiting non-union members into the UMWA fold. Proving it was "blood money" was the tough part.

The federal investigators had literally examined millions of pieces of correspondence and financial records. But the two checks requested by Pass had drawn their attention for a couple of reasons. First, there were no other instances of Pass asking Boyle directly for assistance, or Boyle personally authorizing such expenditures. All such requests had, for years, gone directly through Bill Owens, the long-time UMWA secretary-treasurer.

Another point that raised their suspicions was the timing of the requests and payments, the same period of time Paul Gilly and his first two accomplices, Claude Vealey and James Charles Phillips, began stalking Jock Yablonski. In their testimony, Vealey and Phillips confirmed the approximate dates they were recruited and connected the plot to Huddleston and, to a lesser degree, Prater. The timing had just been confirmed by Paul Gilly, who tied even further up the line to Prater, Pass, and Boyle.

As early as spring 1970, the FBI had been hearing from an informant who said pensioners had then kicked the money back to the representatives, who'd then given it to Pass, who had then given it to Prater. He'd also told them that the field representatives were angry that money was being withdrawn from their paychecks to pay for Huddleston's defense fund to the tune of a little more than $23,000. The press had even reported the kickbacks, which had been angrily denied by Boyle.

The investigation team from Sprague on down believed that the money had been used to pay the killers. But knowing that and proving it were two different animals. The key was the six field representatives and twenty-three pensioners, but they'd stuck to their stories through two grand juries and continuous "gentle pressure" from FBI agents Estill and Quinn.

However, that too had changed, and Sprague was about to exploit that opening. He set the stage by putting Roark on the stand.

Wearing tortoise shell glasses and toting a large brown handbag, the soft-spoken bookkeeper was an unlikely profile in courage. She'd worked for District 19 for twenty-five years, all of it under Albert Pass. She'd known Prater for much of that time as well. She had cause to fear violent reprisals for testifying, but she was there to tell the truth.

Roark began by agreeing with Sprague that she had typed the two letters dated September 24, 1969 and September 30, 1969, from Pass to Boyle. The second of these two letters "apologized" that the expenses had not been paid in a timely manner for the period between September 1968 "through September 1969." She said she'd signed both for Pass.

The bookkeeper testified that never before in her quarter of a century working for the district had Pass made a direct request for funds to Boyle. Or had Boyle personally, in her experience, responded to funding requests.

After verifying the deposit of $20,000 from the national organization into the Middlesboro District 19 bank account, Roark explained what had happened to the money. "On September 30, 1969, Mr. Pass supplied me with the names and amounts and instructed me to make out a check for each one named. On October 10, 1969, at Mr. Pass's orders, I did the same thing with twenty-three more checks."

Turned over for cross-examination, Rothman hardly bothered to question the bookkeeper. From start to finish, she was on the stand less than fifteen minutes.

The next prosecution witness, UMWA comptroller Howard Channel, took less time than that. His sole purpose was to tell the jury about Boyle's call directing him to deposit the two $10,000 checks in the District 19 account payable to Albert Pass.

"There never before had been a request for District 19 funds directly to Mr. Boyle," Channel said.

Arnold Miller, who'd won the election against Tony Boyle on December 8, 1972, had been a long-time friend and supporter of Yablonski. His testimony was also brief. He testified only that Yablonski intended to ask the Department of Labor to set aside the December 9, 1969 Boyle reelection due to Boyle's fraudulent practices.

The testimony wrapped up that day's court session. Sprague and his team left the courtroom to prep for the next day's session, which they knew would be pivotal not just in the current trial, but in those that followed.

CHAPTER THIRTY-THREE

"A DAY OF
RECKONIN' COMING"

MARCH 15, 1973

"The People call Noah Doss."

Looking like he expected to be attacked, Doss nervously approached the witness stand and was sworn in. He was one of the six field representatives who'd recruited a portion of the twenty-three members of the R&I Committee. But in spite of his fear, the sixty-one-year-old wasn't an unwilling witness, even if it had taken him awhile to reach that point.

The last time Doss testified under oath was in front of a grand jury in Pittsburgh. Like the others, he'd lied and stuck to the story: the R&I Committee was real; the checks given to the twenty-three pensioners, including the four men he'd recruited, had been to cover expenses—"basically sandwiches and gas"—they'd incurred while recruiting. There'd been no kickbacks.

However, the façade had crumbled, as religious faith and conscience—prodded by patient FBI agents—had won out over loyalty to the union. At least, the union as represented by Albert Pass and Tony Boyle.

With the repentant Reverend Dave Brandenburg acting as a go-between, Agents Estill and Quinn had continued their strategy of "gentle pressure" to reach out to the field representatives and pensioners. Week after week for months after the preacher's confession, they'd driven through some of the most impoverished counties in the United States to meet with the representatives and R&I Committee members.

Even though the agents knew that the men had perjured themselves in front of the grand juries and their obstinance protected a murderous administration, their reasons, while not excusing their misconduct, induced feelings of genuine understanding amongst the investigative team.

It had been nearly ten years since President Lyndon B. Johnson had announced the "War on Poverty" and visited Appalachia for photo ops and to demonstrate that poverty was not just an issue affecting black communities in the inner cities. But not much had changed in the tiny, isolated towns of coal country with their boarded-up shops and deteriorating buildings, or in the remote hills and dells of Bell and Harlan Counties where most of the R&I pensioners lived. Many of their homes were two-room shacks that lacked running water and were basically weathered slats that barely kept out the wind and cold. But as impoverished as they might be, they were a tough, proud people.

Most of the coal had played out in the areas where the pensioners lived, and the mines were closed or barely operating. The union locals had few, if any, active miners, and membership was almost entirely made up of men dependent on their $150 monthly pensions and miserly health benefits to survive.

It was a UMWA stronghold, and without Brandenburg, the FBI agents told Sprague they may have never reached the others. But even though the preacher had confessed that night in the motel room—including holding onto the "blood money" for Huddleston—it had still taken more persuasion to get him to testify and work with them to get the others to cooperate.

The agents had continued to take their time, especially Quinn, a corncob pipe–smoking good old boy from the hills of North

Carolina, who could quote scripture right back at the preacher as they smoked together on his ramshackle home's front porch. It worked as at last Brandenburg agreed to cooperate and talk to the others about telling the truth.

Prior to the preacher's confession, the agents had warned the field reps and committee members that they could be prosecuted for perjury for lying to the grand juries and even be charged with embezzlement for cashing the checks knowing that union funds were being used illegally. But they were aware that the tough old men weren't as afraid of prison as they were the hereafter.

So, they concentrated on appealing to their faith and their consciences. They befriended the men and, being devout Christians themselves, knelt with them in prayer in the living rooms and kitchens of their homes. Even before the reps and pensioners started to come around, they were all on a first name basis with the agents, who had an authentic fondness for the mountaineers, most of whom suffered from black lung or other mine-related injuries and illnesses.

With Brandenburg quoting scripture at them and the agents appealing to their sense of right and wrong, come around they did. Slowly at first, only admitting that there was a possibility that the R&I scheme *might* have happened the way the agents described, they started to cave. Then one by one, or sometimes a few at a time, they told the truth.

The R&I Committee didn't exist until September 1969, not 1968 as Boyle, Pass, and Prater claimed. Nor had they done any recruiting work until the committee was given real work after January 1970.

The field reps said they'd been told by Albert Pass to recruit pensioners whose loyalty was unquestioned. Those pensioners were then given two checks a few weeks apart and told to cash them and hand the money back to Prater and Pass. They'd been told the money was for campaigns for politicians friendly to the union. They knew using union funds for that purpose was illegal, but not until the Yablonski murders, and the disturbing reports in the news, did they realize there'd been a more sinister purpose.

Even then it wasn't an easy decision to talk to the authorities. Coming from Bell and "Bloody" Harlan Counties, they'd been on the front lines of the Coal Wars. They believed that John L. Lewis was infallible, and even if Tony Boyle wasn't on the same iconic level, he'd been their hero's choice to lead the union.

If Boyle said Yablonski was in league with oil and gas companies and wanted to destroy the union and do away with their pensions, then that was what they believed. Therefore, Yablonski was no better than a gun thug or Pinkerton man or corrupt cop.

Even if the slaughter of the two women troubled their consciences, there was the trepidation that if they broke ranks, with a word from Boyle or Pass their pensions and health benefits would be cut. And the fear of violent reprisals was not unwarranted. Three people shot in their sleep in a farmhouse in Clarksville, Pennsylvania was proof of how far union leadership was willing to go when threatened.

However, once the old men came clean, they were all in. This was exemplified when, rather than make the fed charged with delivering subpoenas for them to appear at the Prater trial drive all over the countryside, they met him as a group in the parking lot of a centralized grocery store.

On the morning of their scheduled court appearance in Erie, the old mountaineers had breakfast on the government's tab in the courthouse cafeteria—those who couldn't read the menu relying on their comrades to order—and appeared to be in good spirits. Some had even cheerfully called out "Good morning, Mr. Sprague" when they saw him pass through.

However, on the stand, Doss showed none of that cheer and mostly kept his head down and eyes averted as he was questioned. But he didn't waver in his testimony when he "went back to the beginning" and described Pass asking him to recruit pensioners for "a problem," which the secretary-treasurer explained was a lack of funds for political campaigns in the district.

"Mr. Pass asked me could I trust them and I said, 'Yes, sir, I think I can.' So, he instructed me to ask them if they would let him issue checks to them, cash them, and return the money to me so I could give it back to him. He told me if they was ever questioned, they was to say they worked for the money, and it was being given as a reimbursement on expenses they incurred while they were working."

Sprague let the genesis of the plan to raise money to pay the Yablonski killers sink in for the jurors who listened with rapt attention. "Had any of these men done any work for these checks, Mr. Doss?"

"Not to my knowledge, no, sir."

Sprague asked if Pass had told him what his men should do if federal authorities questioned them.

"He told me to keep telling the men that if they was ever questioned by anyone to say they spent the money on their selves. After the death of Joseph Yablonski, he would tell me regularly to keep in touch with them to see that they was telling the same thing."

Sprague didn't question the field rep for long before turning him over to cross-examination by Rothman. The defense attorney's first questions concentrated on how the pensioners felt about the candidacy of Yablonski against Boyle.

"Their local unions were all in favor of Mr. Tony Boyle.... The general feeling of the membership was that Mr. Yablonski wasn't qualified to lead the United Mine Workers of America."

Rothman moved on to make a case that the pensioners on the R&I Committee had always been active advocates for the union, including recruiting non-union members and manning picket lines during strikes.

"Sure," Doss agreed. "They was acting in the interest of the union, and they would talk to people from a non-union mine and try to urge them to join the union."

The defense attorney's next question was to elicit a response from Doss that it wouldn't have been unusual for the pensioners to be paid for expenses incurred while advocating for the union. But Sprague objected, which led to a sidebar conversation at the judge's dais.

"Are you claiming these men did not turn back the money?" he asked Rothman as the judge listened. "Let's get to the heart of it. If you end up conceding the money was turned back, all of this is a bunch of nonsense."

"I'm not conceding that, Mr. Sprague," Rothman shot back.

The judge then interceded. "Then you are interrogating the witness on the basis that they did work for him, were paid for it, and kept the money?"

"Yes, Judge, I am," Rothman agreed. The lineup of the field representatives and pensioners had been a devastating blow to the defense. His client's only hope was that he would convince the jury that the R&I Committee existed prior to 1969 and that the reimbursements were legitimate.

Judge Carney shrugged and denied Sprague's objection and let Rothman go ahead with his line of questioning.

Rothman then asked Doss if what he was saying now was the truth, since he'd lied to the grand juries in Cleveland and Pittsburgh. The clearly frightened field rep said that he'd been "afraid not to lie" because of the threat of reprisals from the UMWA leadership.

The defense attorney tried to turn that around by asking Doss if he was lying on the stand now because he was afraid that he might be prosecuted on federal charges of perjury.

Doss acknowledged that he was worried about federal charges for perjury and violating the Landrum-Griffin Act. But he insisted that he was telling the truth.

Rothman had scored points portraying Doss as a frightened man under tremendous pressure from prosecutors. But Sprague quickly addressed this by asking the witness, "Mr. Doss, why did you change your story?"

"As I said, there was pressures from lying and knowing there was a day of reckoning coming. It was just more than I could take, so I just decided I was going to tell the truth and get it off my chest."

After Doss stepped down, Sprague called each of the remaining five field representatives to the stand where essentially the same script was followed. He would get them to repeat that the R&I Committee was a hoax, that the R&I pensioners had been recruited based on their loyalty to the union, that they were paid for non-existent expenses, and that they kicked the cash back to the recruiters, which the recruiters in turn handed over to Pass.

After each man was handed over for cross-examination, Rothman would attack them as liars who couldn't be trusted. They were only testifying against his client now because they were afraid of federal charges.

However, no matter how hard the defense attorney went after them, they stuck to their story. Only this time, the story was true, and to a man they concluded their testimony saying they'd been afraid to tell the truth before for fear of reprisals, but they were doing so now to clear their consciences and get it off their chests.

CHAPTER THIRTY-FOUR

"HE WOULD RULE IT, OR HE WOULD BUST IT!"

MARCH 16, 1973

Laboring for breath even with the tube running out of his nose to an oxygen bottle, Silous Huddleston climbed onto the witness stand and settled into the chair with a slight smile on his face. He nodded to Prater who reacted with a scowl.

"Mr. Huddleston, did you help arrange and participate in the arrangements for the murder of Jock Yablonski?" Sprague asked jumping right to it.

"Yes, sir, I did."

The words were hardly out of Huddleston's mouth before Rothman was on his feet and asked to meet at the judge's dais with Sprague. He wanted to prevent the prosecutor from questioning Huddleston about the aborted plot to murder Ted Q. Wilson, the lawyer for the rival Southern Labor Union, prior to the Yablonski murders.

The defense attorney was concerned that rather than come across like a good, law-abiding family man who'd unfairly been targeted by the prosecution, his client was going to be connected to the plan to kill Wilson, thanks to Sprague's prosecution. Instead of an upstanding citizen, Prater would be a man who in the course of a year planned not one, but two, murders.

"Your Honor, the prior alleged plot to kill Wilson did not result in the arrest, the accusation, or the indictment of anybody," Rothman argued. "It establishes no course of conduct, and Mr. Sprague is attempting to say that the entire twenty thousand dollars related to two separate offenses."

The defense attorney was alluding to Sprague's expected contention that the original scheme to raise blood money through the fictious R&I Committee was originally meant to pay for Wilson's murder. And only later that was changed to Yablonski.

Rothman was correct in assuming that Sprague intended to attack his client's character. Well-dressed and handsome, with his distressed wife, daughter, and sons sitting behind him, Prater didn't appear to be a man who would condone murder. Turning slightly towards the defendant, Sprague added, "Here is a man who already agreed to hire people to kill another person."

Judge Carney agreed with Sprague. He cited case law that evidence of other crimes "is admissible when it tends to prove a common scheme, plan, or design embracing the commission of two or more crimes so related to each other, or to establish the identity of the person charged with the commission of the crime on trial."

With that out of the way, Sprague went back on the attack with rapid-fire questions to Huddleston. "Did you help turn over the money for the killing of Jock Yablonski?"

"Yes, sir."

"Who helped participate in these arrangements with you?"

"Bill Prater and Albert Pass."

Sprague then asked the witness if he saw Prater in the courtroom. Huddleston nodded and with a half-smile pointed at the defendant, who this time did not react, but behind him his wife and sons recoiled.

"Now, Mr. Huddleston, when was the first discussion between you, Prater, and Pass concerning the killing of anyone?"

Huddleston recalled that that discussion had occurred when he met Pass and Prater in the former's driveway, and the other two had asked if he could find someone to kill Wilson. "I told them I couldn't guarantee it, but I might find somebody to do it. Then my son-in-law, Paul Gilly, come to visit me. So I asked him if he knew somebody that would be interested in killing Ted Q. Wilson and he told me he had some boys to do the work."

Later, the three men had met in Pass's basement, where he was informed that the killing of Wilson had been called off. Instead, the "boys" were to murder Yablonski. The reason given was that Yablonski was working with Continental Oil to get rid of the union so that the company could take over coal country.

Most of the rest of Huddleston's testimony mirrored his confession about his role in arranging the murder of Yablonski. He also testified about the Reverend Brandenburg and the "blood money."

Just before a recess in the court proceeding, Huddleston wanted an opportunity to explain his motivation for participating in the conspiracy. "I didn't take orders from Albert Pass any more than I did from any official. If they asked me, if any of them asked me, 'Would you help settle a dispute?' 'Would you help organize a place, or help out the union?' I always done that. I done it for free, never accepted money for the things I done. I would go with Mr. Prater; I would go with any field worker to help because that was just the interest I had in the union."

After the recess, Rothman tried to shake Huddleston, but the old man stuck to his story and didn't try to make excuses. Indeed, despite saying that he wanted to clear his conscience by telling the truth, he didn't exhibit any remorse for the death of Jock Yablonski or mention the two murdered women.

Declaring that he was still proud to be a member of the United Mine Workers of America, he made it clear that he believed that Yablonski had been out to destroy the union. Prater and Pass told him that even after the election, Yablonski swore "he would rule it, or he would bust it!"

Although he'd held up well under questioning by the prosecution and defense, alternating sometimes between humor and anger,

Huddleston just seemed like a tired old man with black lung disease when he was finally dismissed. He seemed unsteady on his feet as he made his way down from the stand and was led out of the courtroom to be taken back to the Washington County Jail to await the next trial.

The testimony of Huddleston had occupied the entire day. But before it was over, Sprague called two more witnesses: Ted Q. Wilson to testify briefly about the burglary that Paul Gilly and Claude Vealey had admitted to committing with Buddy Martin, and then the manager of the Southern Central Bell Telephone Company.

The manager testified to the veracity of a record of a call between Prater's home and Pass's on January 5, 1970 at 6:15 p.m. Sprague made sure the jury did not miss the significance of the timing of the forty-two-second call. Just a few minutes before the call, the two men had been watching the television newscasts about the Yablonski murders.

After such a long day, much of it fraught with emotion, everyone was exhausted. But Judge Carney decided before adjourning for the day that they'd meet again the next morning, even though it was a Saturday.

CHAPTER THIRTY-FIVE

A HIGHER POWER

MARCH 17, 1973

As Sprague called each name, six old miners who'd been members of the R&I Committee, dressed in clean overalls and their hair and beards neatly combed, entered the courtroom. They looked around blinking as if surprised and somewhat taken aback by all the faces turned towards them. Then they'd shuffle, amble, or limp, depending upon their physical disabilities, to the witness stand to be sworn in as directed by Judge Carney.

Most coughed or wheezed as they gave their names, evidence of black lung disease. Often, they bore the scars of injuries from working in the mines—missing fingers or twisted backs and stiff necks—in obvious pains as they tried to find comfortable sitting positions. But despite the trepidation that was on many of their faces as they waited to be questioned, there was no question that they were strong, independent, proud men doing what they thought was right.

Speaking in the soft drawl of the Appalachian dialect, a speech pattern dominated by the Scots-Irish influence of the eighteenth century, each admitted that they'd lied to the grand juries in Cleveland and Pittsburgh about the existence of the R&I Committee. They had cashed the checks and given the money back to Prater. They'd been told that the money was for political campaigns supported by District 19, and that was good enough for them. At least, until they'd been convinced that the money was used for murder.

Questioning pensioner Bronce Waldroop, whose life history mirrored that of the others, Sprague asked, "Mr. Waldroop, did you tell the grand jury in Cleveland you gave the money back to Prater?"

"No, sir. I told them a big lie: that I used the money for my own self," said Waldroop, a frail black lung victim who listened with his left hand cupping an ear. He been born and raised in a small coal-mining town, dropping out of school and going into the coalmine while hardly more than a child. He'd married and raised his six children in that same town, and that's where he figured he'd die and be buried.

A lifelong member of the UMWA, he'd never been more than twenty-five miles from home until summoned before the grand juries and now the trial in Erie.

"Why did you lie to the grand juries?" Sprague asked.

"Mr. Prater told me to tell them that," Waldroop replied.

"Why did you listen and do what Mr. Prater told you to do?" Sprague asked.

"Because I got a hospital card and I draw benefits from the union," the old man responded. "If I didn't do what Mr. Prater said, I was afraid of being cut off."

On cross-examination, Rothman noted that since Waldroop's retirement as a miner in October 1968 due to medical issues, he'd occasionally participated in efforts to talk to non-union miners about the benefits of joining the UMWA. The defense attorney was trying to make the point that the R&I Committee was just an extension of those efforts.

The old man readily admitted the proselytizing but, he said, it wasn't as part of any non-existent R&I Committee. Nor had he incurred any expenses or asked for reimbursement for his activities; he'd cashed the two checks he'd been handed and then given the cash back to Prater.

As he would for each pensioner called to the stand by Sprague, Rothman tried to disparage their credibility and suggested that they were testifying because they were afraid of being charged with crimes. But sometimes, his questions only added to their trustworthiness, such as when he asked Waldroop why he'd changed his testimony from what he'd told the grand juries.

The old man shrugged and replied, "Sir, a Higher Power told me to."

The testimony template for each of the pensioners didn't deviate much. Under Sprague's questioning they explained how they'd been asked to cash checks and give the money back, but never did any work for which they needed to be reimbursed. They'd been told that the money was going to be used by District 19 for political campaigns. Then later to stick to the story when the FBI began coming around asking questions.

There was a brief moment of levity that illustrated the naivete of the old mountaineers, and probably went further than all the testimony to depict their native honesty. When Big Billy Lowe was called and walked into the courtroom, dressed in clean overalls like the others, he seemed surprised and a little frightened when he saw the full courtroom.

He glanced around, searching for someone he recognized, then smiled when he saw a familiar face. "Hello, Mr. Prater," he called out loudly, "how are you today?"

Prater shook his head, then smiled and responded, "Fine, Billy, how are you?"

It was the sort of guileless character trait of the men that Rothman had a difficult time diminishing. The old mountaineers came off as simple men, some of whom had signed their checks with an "X" and confessed not being able to read. Their matter-of-fact descriptions of the hard lives they'd lived, and their suffering due to black lung and other ailments, often had the jurors in tears.

They were members of the UMWA and proud of it. For the most part, they hailed from Harlan and Bell Counties in the very heart of union coal country and had stood up to gun thugs and corrupt cops who worked for the owners and operators. Most had supported Tony Boyle as the heir of their hero, John L. Lewis.

However, there was one "higher power" than even the UMWA that they answered to. As each of the half-dozen pensioners Sprague called testified, it became clear that they'd been caught between their loyalty to the union that had dominated their entire adult lives, and their consciences when they realized what the money had likely been used to accomplish.

The one pensioner whose appearance on the stand differed markedly from the others was the Reverend Dave Brandenburg. The miner-turned-preacher had used his time on the stand to show off his oratory skills, his voice booming across the courtroom, smiling at the jurors like they were his parishioners.

While much of his testimony mirrored the others as far as the basic facts went, he was the only one of them who'd known that the kickback scheme was intended to procure "blood money." Not only that, but he'd agreed to hold onto some of it for Silous Huddleston, who'd told him that he was afraid of being caught with it by the FBI agents. He admitted keeping a thousand of it for his troubles.

It was on these points that Rothman pounced. The defense attorney pointed out that Brandenburg, as well as the others, had signed affidavits presented to him by Prater on March 4, 1970 regarding his participation in the R&I Committee. The affidavits were filed in federal court in Washington, D.C. as part of the proceedings in the lawsuit filed by the Department of Labor against the UMWA challenging the results of the 1969 election.

At first, Brandenburg said he couldn't remember signing the affidavit. He finally admitted that he had, but his earlier denials made him look less than honest.

Rothman had then read the affidavit stating that beginning in October 1968, Brandenburg had received reimbursed expenses as a member of the R&I Committee. Further, he'd made reports of his efforts to his field representative while continuing in that capacity until September 30, 1969.

This was dangerous territory for Sprague. If the jurors believed that the pensioners had been telling the truth on the affidavits, then their testimony in court was false. The conclusion would then be that they were now lying to save their skins as part of a conspiracy by the federal government and the Commonwealth of Pennsylvania.

There was little Sprague could do with that line of questioning. He had to trust that the mountaineers were believed now and that the jury would understand why they lied to the grand juries and on the affidavits.

The testimony of the pensioners took up all of Saturday and part of Monday morning. When the last of them had stepped down and left the courthouse, Sprague called a different kind of witness. He had hoped to play a recording of the fiery speech Yablonski had given the day after he was cheated out of the union presidency. He believed that it was the final straw for Boyle who then decided to renew the contract on his rival's life.

However, Rothman had objected, arguing that the recording would inflame the jury, and Judge Carney agreed. So instead, Sprague asked Jeanne Rasmussen—the wife of Dr. Don Rasmussen, the well-known black lung researcher and activist—who had recorded the speech to read a transcript of it.

"Mr. Yablonski said, 'Working coalminers in this country aren't going to take this lying down,'" Jeanne read from the stand. "'We have contacted the Department of Labor, asking them to do certain things. Yesterday, the undersecretary of labor called me to read a letter saying there will be a conference to discuss the contents of our telegram of complaint that the election was rigged.

"'I intend to speak for those fifty thousand coalminers. I am not interested in bringing about a division in the United Mine Workers of America. I know the only way this union can go forward is to go united. So, this fight is going to go on! I say to you, let's stick together. We know all the thieves and the enemies.

"'All of those thieves and all of the enemies know how to get in touch with me.... Your candidate is not giving up. The fight is going to go on to bring about a union that's responsible to its members.'"

Sprague believed that announcing to the union membership and its leadership, that "the fight will go on" had signed Yablonski's death warrant. The thieves and enemies had indeed known how to get in touch with him, and his wife and his daughter.

CHAPTER THIRTY-SIX

"TOUGH TONY" BOYLE

MARCH 19, 1973

The night before he was to appear on the witness stand as a defense witness, "Tough Tony" Boyle flew into the Erie airport and departed the plane acting like he was Caesar returning to Rome after a victorious campaign. He grinned and waved to the media who'd been clued in about his arrival. Calling out to some of them by name, he'd then crossed the tarmac surrounded by a cordon of state troopers and deputy sheriffs.

As the now-former president of the UMWA was escorted to Sheriff Andrew Hanisek's car, he and his police escort passed Kenneth Yablonski and Jock's brother, Leon Yablonski. "Tony, you goddamned murderer," the younger Yablonski shouted.[49]

The Yablonskis were at the airport because they had just dropped attorney Joe Rauh off for a flight. Earlier that day, as the last prosecution witness before Sprague rested the prosecution's case, the crusading labor lawyer had testified about the lawsuits he'd filed on behalf of Jock Yablonski.

In doing so, he put to rest the contention that Jock wanted to block or deny pensions. It was one of the main accusations Boyle

---

49   Jeff Pinski, *Erie Morning News*, March 20, 1973.

had used against his rival during the campaign, and even after to the murder conspirators to justify the murder of Yablonski. Boyle had suggested that it was a possible motive for pensioners to want to harm his rival when he spoke to the FBI agents who spoke to him on January 9, 1970. But there was no such lawsuit, Rauh told the jurors.

After taking him from the airport, Sheriff Hanisek dropped Boyle off at a motel. After he'd checked in, he was taken by Rothman to visit Prater in the Washington County Jail.

"It was a touching scene," Rothman later told journalist Arthur Lewis.[50] "Prater actually cried. He seemed so grateful that Tony came to see him and was willing to testify on his behalf."

Reached by telephone in Washington, the former union president's lawyer said, "Tony Boyle has never wanted him killed and would not be a party to it. He so testified under oath before a Federal grand jury and will do so again."

With the jurors waiting in the deliberation room, and before calling Boyle to the stand, the next morning, Rothman asked the judge to rule on several issues. The first was the usual plea of defense attorneys following the prosecution's case to have the charges dismissed claiming that the prosecution had not proved its case. And if the judge didn't agree, to at least toss the charges pertaining to the murders of Margaret and Charlotte Yablonski, arguing that their deaths were not part of the conspiracy to kill Jock that Prater was alleged to have been part of but committed "spontaneously" by the killers.

After Carney quickly dismissed the first motion that the prosecution had not proved its case, Sprague made no attempt to hide his derision regarding the second request. "Obviously, in the design to murder Jock Yablonski the conspirators took the risk that anyone else who was around could well be killed to have them shut up," he said scornfully. "It would be absurd to say that there is not a responsibility by this defendant and the others for the deaths of

---

50   Lewis, *Murder by Contact.*

Margaret and Charlotte Yablonski. When you set out with a pack of rattlesnakes, you are responsible for what they do."

Judge Carney dismissed this motion as well and then asked Rothman to speak to his next two motions. The defense attorney asked that if, as expected, the judge would advise Boyle of his rights against self-incrimination and warn him that anything he said could be used against him at a future trial, it be done in the judge's chambers, away from the jury.

Rothman's concern was that the so-called "corrupt" witnesses—such as Paul Gilly, Claude Vealey, Silous Huddleston, and the pensioners, who had either been convicted or admitted lying to the grand juries—had been advised in front of the jury. But other "clean" witnesses, such as the FBI agents, Kathy Rygle, Karl Kafton, and Kenneth Yablonski, were not advised, as there was no need. The defense attorney argued that this created a distinction between the credibility of the two groups and would do so again if Boyle ended up in the first group.

Rothman's last request was that Sprague be prohibited from asking Boyle about his conviction on the federal charges because the conviction was being appealed.

Again, Sprague could hardly contain his disdain for Rothman's arguments. The so-called "corrupt" witnesses, all of them prosecution witnesses, had been advised of their rights in front of the jury and the prosecution had to live with whatever conclusions the jurors drew from that regarding their character and credibility. It was only right that Boyle be advised in the same way.

As to the last argument, Sprague pointed out that Boyle had been convicted and sentenced on the federal charges. "The fact that the case is now on appeal in the appellate courts is not a basis of refusing to admit that for the purpose of impeachment. He is not a defendant in this case, he is a witness."

Judge Carney ruled that Boyle would be advised of his rights in front of the jury just like the prosecution witnesses had been. He said he would wait to rule on whether Sprague could ask Boyle about his federal convictions until Rothman had a chance to provide him with Pennsylvania case law on the issue. The jury was then seated, and Rothman called Boyle as his first witness.

The bravado of the night before was gone when Boyle walked into the courtroom. "Tough Tony" seemed frail, his face pale and drawn as he slowly stepped up onto the witness stand. He looked like someone's tiny, kindly old grandfather and spoke quietly when identifying himself and giving his address in Washington, D.C.

After being advised of his rights and telling the judge, "I want to testify," Boyle spent the first part of his time on the stand talking about the R&I Committee. It all began, he said, when Albert Pass approached him in a hallway during the 1968 UMWA convention in Denver with the idea of using pensioners to recruit non-union miners in District 19.

"Mr. Boyle," Rothman asked, "what reason did Mr. Pass give you for the need to organize this committee?"

"Well, sir," Boyle said, looking at the jurors, "they had run into a great deal of difficulty over in those counties, Harlan and Bell, where local officials, the law enforcement officers and company thugs, as we call them, would run the organizers off. They thought they had to come up with this new name.... So, I was told to give the committee the name of 'Research and Information....' I told Albert Pass, I said, 'I'm in a hurry to get to the convention. I don't care what you call it as long as we get this done.'"

Boyle was next asked if anyone else was aware that this committee was being created. He nodded and said that a little later he ran into William Turnblazer, the president of District 19, on a stairway. "I said, 'Bill, I just had a conversation with Albert out there, and he is going to set up a Research and Information Committee to try to organize the unorganized miners.' Bill said, 'I know all about it; we have discussed it.'"

Having thus established that there were two witnesses to the formation of the R&I Committee, if the jury believed Boyle's recollection, Rothman moved on to answering why Boyle responded personally to Pass's requests for the two $10,000 checks to reimburse the pensioners on the committee.

Boyle began by stating he'd often received requests from district offices asking for financial help from the national office. He would then call the secretary-treasurer Bill Owens and tell him to send the money.

In this case, Pass had told him in September 1969 that he was late in reimbursing the pensioners for their five-dollar per day expenses they'd incurred during the year since the convention. Boyle said he was upset with Pass because "the union pays its bills on time."

Boyle noted that he'd reported the expenditures to the U.S. Department of Labor in April 1970. The document he'd signed for the department said it was for District 19's R&I Committee.

Towards the end of his questioning, Rothman asked Boyle about his relationship with Yablonski. Noting that they'd met in 1942 when John L. Lewis had called them both to Washington, D.C. to work for the national office, Boyle basically described Jock as a loved, but sometimes wayward, younger brother. He pointed out all the things he'd done for his rival—appointed him to important positions, and even made sure his friend got paid "more than average" when he got Yablonski on Labor's Non-Partisan League Board.

Shaking his head sadly, he then recounted how all of his largess had been met with betrayal when Yablonski planned to run for the presidency behind his back. Jock had then compounded his treachery when he announced his candidacy while accusing Boyle of corruption.

Wrapping up his testimony, Boyle noted that it was Yablonski who nominated Albert Pass to the International Executive Board of the UMWA. The implication was that Pass had no reason to want his benefactor killed.

As for William Prater, Boyle said he hardly knew him. "I saw him at committee meetings, conventions, or things of that nature, but he did not report to me."

After Rothman declared he had no more questions for the witness, Judge Carney declared a short recess. As he stepped down from the witness stand, Boyle was suddenly back to his bluster of the night before, waving and calling out to members of the press.

At the prosecution table, Sprague ignored the theatrics.

When Boyle returned to the witness stand to face cross-examination, his demeanor changed again. He was back to acting like a pitiful, little old man dreading a beat-down by a bully.

Sprague didn't disappoint him. During the recess, Judge Carney had ruled that the prosecutor could question the witness about his convictions, and Sprague dove right in. "Mr. Boyle, in March 1972, were you convicted in the Federal Courts of the United States of thirteen felonies?"

"I was found guilty, and the case is on appeal."

Ignoring the second part of the response, Sprague pointedly asked again, "You were found guilty of thirteen felonies in the federal courts, is that correct?"

Rothman objected saying that Sprague should be more specific about the nature of the charges. The judge sustained the objection and suggested, "Rather than 'thirteen felonies,' I think the type of crime should be placed before the witness."

Sprague shrugged and asked, "You were charged and convicted, were you not, of conversion of union funds?"

"The charge was conversion of union funds, but we never maintained they were union funds."

Again, Sprague ignored Boyle's excuse-making. "But you were convicted of conversion of union funds, were you not?"

"Absolutely."

"You are also convicted of violations of the Corrupt Practices Act, were you not?

Boyle got a confused look on his face. "I don't know whether that's part of the case or not."

Sprague looked incredulous. "Don't you know what you were convicted of?"

"I think that that was part of the case."

"Do you know what you were convicted of?"

After hemming and hawing and refusing to answer the question directly, the judge finally stepped in. "What was the violation called?" Carney asked.

"Violation of, I believe, the Corrupt Practices Act," Boyle answered.

"And you received a sentence did you not?" Sprague asked.

"I did."

"Of five years in prison?"

"Correct."

Sprague pointed out that the sentence also included a fine of $179,500 and restitution of $49,500 to the United Mineworkers for misappropriated funds.

As the prosecutor started to change to a different line of questioning, Judge Carney interrupted him and turned towards the jurors. "I would like to inform the jury of the reason for the admission of these questions and these answers. A conviction and sentence is a factor to be taken into consideration of the witness, in determining the credibility, the believability of the witness. This is the sole purpose for the admissibility of this evidence."

Invited to continue, Sprague asked Boyle if he knew Harrison Combs, an attorney on the staff of the UMWA. But Rothman objected, causing the judge to ask both attorneys to approach the dais.

Once there, Sprague told the judge that Combs had talked to Boyle about a matter related to the case. "I propose to ask this witness whether or not he had a conversation with Mr. Combs during which Boyle said that he talked about raising money for the defense of Albert Pass and told Combs that if he doesn't come through with Pass, Pass is going to implicate others, including him."

After Rothman objected again, Judge Carney said he'd allow Sprague to ask Boyle about Combs, but only if Sprague intended to call Combs to the stand as a rebuttal witness if Boyle denied the conversation. Rothman would then have the opportunity to cross-examine Combs.

Back in front of the witness, Sprague asked Boyle if "after the codefendant Pass was arrested in this case, did you have a conversation with Harrison Combs, Sr.?"

"You would have to be more specific," Boyle replied. "I had conversations with a lot of people after Pass was arrested."

"Did you talk to Mr. Combs about raising money for Albert Pass?"

"No, not that I recall."

"You did not talk to Combs about raising money for Albert Pass?"

"For what purpose?" Boyle asked.

"Did you talk to Combs about raising money for Pass for any purpose?"

"Not that I recall. No."

"Did you talk to Combs and say to Combs that you, Tony Boyle, better come forth and help Pass or else he is going to implicate others, including you?"

"No, I have no recollection of every making such a statement."

"Well, if you said something like that you would remember it?"

"I certainly would."

"And you didn't say it?"

"No."

"You are positive?"

"I am positive I never said it."

Sprague moved on by showing Boyle a photograph of himself shaking hands with Silous Huddleston. He asked if he knew the old miner.

Boyle said he knew Huddleston only from newspaper accounts of the Yablonski case. He said the photograph was from a convention and that he shook a lot of hands at such gatherings. But he didn't recall that incident or Huddleston.

Sprague asked Boyle about the lawsuits Yablonski and Rauh had filed after the election. Boyle said he couldn't remember much about them because they'd just been forwarded to the legal department. He said as president, he didn't deal with legal matters.

Sprague turned that around on him when he asked him to repeat the details of his meeting with Albert Pass at the 1968 UMWA convention in Denver.

"What makes that conversation stand out so clearly in your mind?" Sprague asked.

"Because of all that is happening about the Research and Information Committee."

"And that's why you now remember all of that?... I'm trying to find out why that one conversation with Pass stayed in your mind?"

"Well, there's a lot of things that stayed in my mind, there is a lot of things that don't stay in my mind. I think that's true with everyone."

"But not the suits Jock Yablonski filed against you?" Sprague asked sarcastically.

Sprague dove back into why Pass wrote to Boyle personally, something he'd never done before, asking for money to reimburse the pensioners. And why Boyle handled the request himself.

Again, Boyle asserted that he was angry with Pass for the delay when he asked for the first $10,000. "I bawled him out," he said.

Then when Pass asked for another $10,000, "I bawled him out again."

Sprague asked Boyle if he ever asked for an accounting of where the money had gone and what it had paid for. The witness replied that it was not his responsibility to get involved on that level.

Boyle essentially gave the same answer when he said he didn't ask William Turnblazer, the president of the district, about the men on the R&I Committee or the work they had supposedly done.

Sprague pointed out that Boyle had testified at the grand jury hearing in Pittsburgh that as president of the union he would always take up such matters with the president of a district.

"I don't recall saying that," Boyle responded.

After he approved the idea, Boyle said he didn't hear anything about the committee until Pass asked for money a year later. He said the whole R&I Committee was Pass's idea, as was the plan to keep it secret so that non-union mine owners wouldn't get wind of the recruiting efforts.

Subtly this testimony was the start of Boyle throwing his loyal vassal Pass to the wolves. If the committee was solely the idea of the secretary-treasurer of District 19, and possibly District 19 president William Turnblazer, and Boyle's only involvement was to approve it as a way to recruit non-union miners, then he wasn't part of a conspiracy to kill Yablonski.

However, Sprague wasn't letting him step back from a more direct and personal role. After Boyle testified that it wasn't unusual for him to receive requests for financial help such as Pass's from representatives of other districts, the prosecutor motioned to a man in a suit sitting in pew behind the prosecution table. "Stand up please. Do you know that gentleman?"

"Yes."

"Who is he?"

"He is connected with the Department of Labor."

Sprague introduced the man as an auditor with the department who participated in "an examination of all the papers of the union starting in March 1969."

"Is that not correct?" he asked Boyle.

"Yes, he made such an examination I am told," Boyle agreed. "I wasn't with him, but I am told he did."

"And do you know it to be a fact that he has not found one letter of request to you for funds, except the letters we are talking about in this case, in your own files?"

"No."

"You are saying that there were such letters, is that correct?"

Boyle, who appeared rattled, took a moment before answering, "I am saying that there were such letters."

"But not from Pass?"

"Not from Pass, from other people asking for money too."

"Did you ask Pass how well the committee succeeded with its recruiting efforts?"

"If he says I did, I did," Boyle said.

"I am not telling you what Pass says," Sprague retorted. "I said, 'Did you ask him?'"

"I don't recall."

"Are you worried about what Mr. Pass is saying?" Sprague asked.

"No," Boyle answered a little too quickly. He gathered himself then asked, "Worried about what? That Pass is saying that he paid them?"

Sprague pressed harder. "Did you say to Pass, 'Well, wait a minute, let's see the figures, the expense reports upon which you are figuring how much you owe?'"

"I don't ask for reports from districts," Boyle replied.

"You never saw any reports from this secret committee you approved?" Sprague asked incredulously.

When Boyle said he did not, Sprague changed directions again. He asked about a meeting between Boyle and Pass "on November 29 or 30, 1969" before a campaign speech in Madisonville, Kentucky. "Did you ask Suzanne to set up a meeting with Pass two hours before the speech?" he asked referring to Boyle's long-time assistant Suzanne Richards.

"Absolutely not."

When Sprague started to press Boyle about the meeting, Rothman objected that the questions were outside the scope of his direct examination and therefore not appropriate for cross-examination. Judge Carney appeared to be ready to sustain the objection, but Sprague asked to approach the bench for an on the record conference with counsel.

"If the court please," Sprague said once he and Rothman had gathered, "we are showing here a direct contact between this man and one of the codefendants, Albert Pass, at a meeting arranged by him on November 29 and 30 in Madisonville, Kentucky."

"Yes," Judge Carney agreed, "but how is it made relevant?"

"Boyle is denying that there was any conspiracy between him and Pass relating to the distribution of the monies to be used for this murder," Sprague said, "and I submit that on the cross-examination of this witness, all things connecting him with Pass become relevant."

"This is not a defendant, Your Honor," Rothman countered, referring to Pass.

The judge said that he didn't think that all things related to Pass were relevant. "But I do think that anything that would show that there was any more to it than setting up the committee for the purpose that it states is. Now, if this meeting will do that...."

Sprague jumped in. "Your Honor, we will have testimony showing that he arranged with Suzanne Richards to get ahold of Pass, and he arranged to go out to Madisonville and meet with Pass." Other testimony, he said, had already indicated this was the time when Boyle told Pass to hold up on the murder until after the election.

Rothman continued to object, and the judge sustained the objection. It ended Sprague's questioning on that particular point, but he quickly moved on to ask Boyle if he remembered the March

9, 1970 press conference he called at the National Press Club in Washington, D.C.

When Boyle nodded and said yes, Sprague asked, "And do you remember when the members of the press asked you if you arranged for the Research and Information Committee?"

Boyle said he didn't remember. "There was so many questions."

"A reporter called it a secret committee," Sprague reminded him.

Boyle responded that there was nothing "secret" about the committee. He said that now that Sprague jogged his memory, he remembered telling the press that he didn't handle money affairs of the union and that such matters were the purview of secretary-treasurer Owen's responsibility.

"You didn't say at the time that you were the one who authorized these funds?" Sprague asked.

Realizing that he was falling into a trap, after all, the press conference had been recorded by the press, Boyle shrugged and said, "I could have very well said that... I don't remember."

Sprague pressed on. "Now, after the defendant Pass and this defendant Prater were arrested, did you hear any reports that the funds, this twenty thousand dollars, had in some way been used to pay for the murders?"

Boyle replied that he only heard that accusation when he read it in the newspaper.

"After the arrest of Prater and Pass, did you thereafter hear that these pensioners were saying they had been made to kick back this money?"

Boyle said he never heard it directly. "I read about it in the newspapers."

With the witness looking more and more uncomfortable, Sprague kept hammering away. He asked Boyle why, as the president of the union, he didn't take more of an interest in whether the funds had been used for murder.

"I didn't believe then, and I don't believe now that the money was used for that purpose," Boyle said.

Sprague didn't try to hide his skepticism that Boyle took no interest in what was being reported in the press.

"There wasn't anything I could do about it," Boyle explained looking at the jurors. "And newspapers are not always correct."

Sprague questioned why he didn't ask for "any records" showing that the R&I Committee and the expenses were legitimate. But Boyle kept passing the responsibility on, insisting it was something that would have been handled by the union's legal department and that he didn't remember.

"You don't remember something that important?" Sprague asked.

"I stayed away from finances as much as I could," Boyle replied.

With Boyle beginning to tire, Sprague wasn't letting go. "Did you make any attempt to talk to the field reps or pensioners?"

"No, they are located in Tennessee," Boyle explained. "I am located in Washington, D.C."

"So, you made no attempt?"

"No," Boyle admitted. "I took for granted the money went to the people it was intended to be used for."

"Even ask to see the checks?"

Boyle repeated that it wasn't his responsibility.

Sprague switched directions again and asked Boyle who he was with when he heard about the Yablonski murders.

Boyle said he was alone in his office. "Until they came in with the teletype to tell me about the horrible thing that happened."

"And when did you next talk to Albert Pass?"

"I don't recall."

"On the day that you heard about the 'horrible' murders did you see Albert Pass?"

"No."

Sprague asked if Boyle was aware that Pass had testified under oath to a grand jury that the two of them were together in the Washington, D.C. office. But before he could answer, Rothman objected that during the prosecution case he wasn't allowed to question a witness about the grand jury testimony of a witness.

Carney sustained the objection, but the seed had been planted with the jury. Sprague then asked when Boyle next saw Pass. The witness answered that it was at IEB meeting on January 22, 1970.

Sprague had Boyle right where he wanted him. "And do you remember at that particular meeting of the IEB having the entire board get up and give Albert Pass a standing ovation?" he asked.

Rothman quickly objected that this question, too, was outside the scope of the direct examination. The judge again sustained the objection.

Without missing a beat, Sprague moved onto another IEB meeting—this one on June 23, 1969, shortly after Yablonski had announced his decision to challenge Boyle for presidency of the UMWA.

Rothman objected and asked for another bench conference at Judge Carney's dais.

"I intend to read, Your Honor," Sprague replied, "from a portion of what Albert Pass said on one point: 'Anybody who says they are going to destroy my dad's pension has got something else to think about.… We have got a great union and we are going to keep our union. President Boyle we are not going to leave you and the other officers sitting out in that field and these damned fellows behind the bushes shooting at you by yourself. By God, we will run them out from behind those bushes, we are going to back you!'"

Sprague wanted Pass's speech, which was tantamount to a threat, read to the jury. It seemed to only be tangentially tied to the defendant, which Rothman noted in an objection. The judge agreed with the defense attorney and didn't allow Sprague to read the speech.

Sprague returned to questioning Boyle. He asked Boyle if he was aware of the lawsuits filed by Yablonski and Rauh after the election.

Although aware that there had been some sort of legal action filed, Boyle said he didn't remember any details. Again, that would have been for the legal department to deal with, he said. The outcome of the election was so "conclusive" he wasn't worried.

Sprague pointed out that Boyle didn't need help remembering the conversation he had at the 1968 UMWA convention with Pass regarding the formation of the R&I Committee. Yet, the prosecutor noted, he seemed to have difficulty remembering something as important as a lawsuit questioning the legitimacy of the election.

Boyle shot back that "like most people" there were things his mind remembered, and things it did not.

The questioning was growing increasingly contentious as the witness grew agitated. But Sprague was relentless. He asked whether Boyle made any attempt to speak to Dave Brandenburg or Clifford Marcum, two of the pensioners on the R&I Committee who had been quoted in the newspapers in 1970 as saying they'd cashed the checks and kicked the money back.

Rothman asked for yet another meeting at the bench. He said he objected to the question as improper if the two pensioners weren't called to the stand during the prosecution's rebuttal so he could cross-examine.

"No, here are these men who now say that they cashed these checks," the judge pointed out.

"The question here is did he make any attempt," Rothman argued. "Is there going to be any testimony that he did?"

Judge Carney wasn't buying it. "Here is the president of the union, and it's public knowledge that these men kicked back or cashed the checks and gave them back to Prater and Pass. It is a proper question to ask him, as president of the union: 'Did you take any steps to find out if this is true?'"

The judge said Sprague could ask his question again. Boyle admitted that he had not.

Sprague then asked if he'd talked to William Turnblazer, the president of District 19, about the men on the committee saying they'd kicked the money back. This was the only time that the prosecutor said anything about Turnblazer, who was on the defense witness list, to the jurors.

"I did not." Boyle said he did not believe the money had been kicked back.

Sprague pointed out that as president of the union, when Pass and Prater were arrested, you could have easily found out what checks had been issued and to whom. "If you wanted."

Shrugging, Boyle replied that he could have. "But I was working eighteen-hour days…"

"But this wasn't important?" Sprague interrupted.

"It's only important now because of all the events that have happened," Boyle responded.

"But it wasn't important to you when it came out in the news that these men had kicked back the money," Sprague asked. "Why wasn't that important?"

"I didn't do it."

"I know you didn't do it, and is the reason because you knew what that money was used for?" Sprague's voice grew harder, more accusatory.

"I don't know what the money was used for, other than organizational purposes," Boyle retorted, adding that he didn't try to ask.

"What were you afraid that they would have told you?" Sprague demanded looking hard at the witness.

Boyle's face flushed angrily. Rothman objected and the judge sustained, but not before the witness shouted, "I am not afraid of anything!"

"Nothing, Mr. Boyle?" Sprague shot back.

Rothman tried to interject. "Now, Mr. Sprague, you are arguing now."

"I fear Almighty God if that's what you mean," Boyle snarled.

Having got under Boyle's skin and made his point, Sprague smiled and said, "I object to this."

The judge agreed. "We are getting off track."

Still, Boyle wasn't done. "I fear him!"

"Mr. Boyle, we will have no more arguing between you and Mr. Sprague," Judge Carney warned. "Answer his questions."

Delighted to have that reaction from Boyle, Sprague asked him now about being questioned by the FBI on January 8, 1970. "Do you remember telling the FBI that Yablonski caused resentment among the pensioners of the UMWA when he filed suit at the Department of Labor prior to the December 9, 1969 election to deny the pensioners the right to vote in the election?"

"It sounds like me," Boyle conceded.

"What suit did Mr. Yablonski file to deny the pensioners the right to vote?" Sprague asked.

Boyle said he wasn't sure because it had been referred to the legal department.

"Do you not know because Mr. Yablonski filed no such suit?" Sprague asked.

"I don't recall a suit."

"Then why did you say that to the FBI?"

"Because he campaigned on the basis that those pensioners shouldn't have the right to vote."

"That's not what you said," Sprague pointed out. "You said he caused resentment among the pensioners of the United Mine Workers when he filed suit."

Rothman objected saying that the agent may not have written Boyle's response accurately. The judge overruled him.

"But you were going around telling people that Mr. Yablonski was trying to deny pensioners the right to vote? Didn't you say that at the political meeting in Madisonville, Kentucky?"

"If it was during the campaign I did."

The line of questioning was intended to show that during the campaign, Boyle was setting Yablonski up as an enemy of the union and pensioners in particular. The prosecutor read from a transcript of the speech at the meeting in which Boyle accused Yablonski of associating himself "with outsiders" to try to take over the United Mine Workers.

"'He has dragged the good name of our union through the dust and filed expensive lawsuits,'" Sprague read. "'Lied about and defamed John L. Lewis.'"

"It sounds like me," Boyle said with a shrug. "I am satisfied I said it."

When Sprague at last wrapped up his cross-examination of Boyle, the former UMWA president looked like he'd been beat like a rented mule. He tried and only partly succeeded to muster a confident smile when Rothman rose for redirect.

Rothman started by asking if Boyle had made any attempt to remove the letters Pass wrote to him asking for money, or copies of the checks sent to the pensioners, from the UMWA files.

"Absolutely not."

The defense attorney then asked if he'd made any attempts to find out who killed the Yablonskis.

Nodding, Boyle said he'd done his best "to run this thing down." He noted that shortly after the murders were discovered he'd set up a committee made up of IEB board members who were authorized to hire attorneys, stenographers, "and whatever necessary to set up headquarters in Pittsburgh and invite anyone with leads or knew anything whatsoever."

However, he added, that the committee never got off the ground because Chip and Kenneth Yablonski "said I was trying to take over the duties of the FBI, so the committee folded and that was the end of that.... I was only trying to be helpful."

"You were very interested in getting to the bottom and catching the murderers of Jock Yablonski?" Rothman asked.

"Yes, sir," Boyle responded eagerly, "and I offered—I recommended to the board and the board approved a fifty-thousand-dollar reward."

Rothman ended his redirect and Sprague shot to his feet. "And in 1972, did you lose interest in catching the murderers and those behind the murders?"

"None whatsoever," Boyle replied.

With that Boyle's testimony ended almost five hours after it started. He wearily climbed down from the witness stand for all the world looking like a man who'd been unfairly set upon by the mean prosecutor.

In many ways, Sprague's questioning of Boyle wasn't as much about William Prater, as it was a precursor for when Boyle occupied the seat at the defendant's table. That was something Boyle alluded to in a press conference he'd arranged a few minutes after he walked out of the courthouse.

"You'd think it was me, not Prater, on trial today, wouldn't you, gentlemen?" he said to the assembled reporters and cameramen. He grinned, the tired old man no longer part of his act.

Asked who he thought murdered the Yablonskis, he raised his hands palms out. "I don't know," he said. "I wish I did. But I can tell you this; I'm sure it wasn't a member of the United Mine Workers of America. That's not how we operate."

"Like hell it wasn't," a loud voice boomed from the media crowd. It was Don Stillman, the new editor of the *UMW Journal*. "And you know it, Tony!"[51]

---

51   Lewis, *Murder by Contract.*

CHAPTER THIRTY-SEVEN

THE FAMILY MAN

MARCH 22, 1973

After three years in prison, Aubran Wayne "Buddy" Martin didn't look all that much worse for wear when called as a witness for the Prater defense. Clean cut and still looking like more of a choir boy than a killer, he'd been dressed in "civilian" clothes of a white shirt, red tie, and conservative blue suit so as not to negatively influence the jurors with his prison garb.

Before Martin could take the stand, however, Sprague requested a sidebar with the judge and Rothman. The baby-faced assassin had refused to appear as a prosecution witness, and instead sent a letter to the Philadelphia prosecutor saying that if he was subpoenaed by Sprague, he'd disrupt the courtroom.

Carney responded that he'd already been told by a state trooper that Martin threatened to cause a scene if called to the stand. The judge said he'd warned courtroom security to be ready to deal swiftly with any outbursts.

Apparently, Martin didn't have the same feelings about appearing for the defense. On the stand, he seemed to be enjoying his brief stint outside of prison walls. But he didn't provide any new information on the Yablonski murders. He stuck with his story that he thought he was going to commit a burglary when he left Cleveland with Paul

Gilly and Claude Vealey. The murder occurred when he was drunk and asleep in the getaway car.

It was possible that the jury might have believed the clean-cut young man with the soft Appalachia drawl. He seemed remorseful for what had happened. But Sprague made sure they saw the real Buddy Martin by asking him one victim at a time if he'd been convicted of first-degree murder for their deaths.

"I have," Martin responded, shaking his head sadly.

Then Sprague, after establishing for the jurors that the witness went by the nickname "Buddy," asked if Martin would read a letter to the jury that he'd written to Sprague.

Realizing that he was about to be exposed, Martin smiled as he accepted the letter from the prosecutor. "I would."

"Go ahead," Sprague urged.

"'Sprague, don't call me to Erie for that trial,'" Martin read. "'I have nothing to say, so if you force me to be present, I will disrupt the courtroom. You had better dig it. I used your subpoena to wipe my ass on. Buddy.'"

With that, Martin's air of innocence and remorse evaporated.

After Martin was escorted from the courtroom. Rothman moved on by calling Annette Gilly to the stand.

Sprague had avoided calling Annette during the prosecution case for strategic reasons. If he hadn't, Rothman would have been able to cross-examine her and imply that she was testifying against Prater to get a deal. But the defense attorney couldn't impugn the motives of his own witness. So, the only thing she added to the defense case was the discrepancy between the names Paul testified he told her to remember "when the time comes" and the names she remembered. Paul said he told her, "Prater, Pass, Titler, and Owens;" Annette told agent Curtis in her confession they were Prater, Pass, and Turnblazer. The implication from the defense point of view was that one, or both, of them were making up their story.

With that, court adjourned for the day. Neither Martin nor Annette had done much for the defense case. The best Rothman could hope for was that Boyle had at least one of the jurors convinced that the R&I Committee existed prior to the murders. He intended to try to bolster that with his last two witnesses the following day.

In the morning, he started by calling Albert Pass to the stand. Short, heavy-set, his thick, round face framed by dark tortoise shell-framed glasses, the former secretary-treasurer of District 19, member of the IEB, and reputed union enforcer, confidently took a seat like a prize-fighter waiting for the sound of the bell.

After waiving his right not to testify, Pass basically repeated the same story that Boyle had delivered with minor variations that contradicted his boss's testimony. One was that he said he'd talked to District 19 president Turnblazer several times about setting up the R&I Committee, and then approached Boyle for his approval at the 1968 UMWA convention in Denver. He also said that Turnblazer was with him when he met the then-UMWA president in the hallway to discuss forming the committee.

Despite having spent a year in jail awaiting his own trial scheduled for June 1973, Pass gave off the aura of a man used to being respected when he spoke. There was no doubt that the union was his religion as he repeatedly talked about "spreading the gospel of the United Mine Workers unionism."

Spreading the gospel to non-union miners in Harlan and Bell Counties was how he described the work of the R&I Committee from its alleged formation in 1968 and into 1969. He said that in September 1969, he was told that the committee members were angry because they had not been reimbursed for their expenses. He testified that after talking it over with Turnblazer, he decided to ask Boyle for the money to pay them.

Asked if he had anything to do with the murder of Yablonski and his family, Pass denied it. "Jock was very good to me. He got me my job on the Executive Board of the United Mine Workers."

When not repeating "the story," most of Pass's testimony was spent refuting the prosecution witnesses. The committee members, he said, never kicked back the expense money, and no one was asked to contribute part of their paycheck for Huddleston's defense. Nor had there been any discussions with Prater about killing Ted Q. Wilson or Jock Yablonski.

Pass said he hardly knew Silous Huddleston. They met in 1942, but Pass didn't see him again until 1968 when they both were at the Knoxville airport on the way to the 1968 UMWA convention in Denver. The old miner and field representative had never been to his house. Nor, Pass said, had he ever met Paul Gilly or any of his associates.

After Rothman turned him over to Sprague, the old enforcer could barely conceal his contempt for the prosecutor. He kept his voice modulated as he answered questions, but his voice dripped with disrespectfulness, treating his questions as nothing more than a nuisance.

Nor was he particularly understanding when Sprague asked Edith Roark, who was seated in the row behind the prosecution table, to stand. Pass, when asked if he recognized her, was obviously angry; he identified her as his bookkeeper since 1948, emphasizing that she no longer held the position: "[She] *was* my bookkeeper," he sneered.

Obviously, he expected loyalty to the union to extend to all employees no matter what. Even telling the truth was a sin if it damaged the union.

Sprague noted that Roark had testified that the records and expense reports that supposedly showed the work of the R&I Committee, and had been turned over to the U.S. Department of Labor in April 1970, didn't exist until January 1970. "Now, Mr. Pass, when these forms were made up as you directed Mrs. Roark to do, when was that?" Sprague asked.

"The latter part of September 1968."

Sprague smiled slightly. "You don't really mean '68 do you?"

Pass was getting irritated by Sprague's questioning and let it show in his response. "Yes, I really mean '68. Sure I do," he growled. Then he realized he'd made a mistake. The story was supposed to be that Roark recorded the expenses and wrote the checks to the pensioners in September and October of 1969.

"You see, Mr. Sprague," Pass explained, using "Mr." for one of the few times when responding to the prosecutor, "I am indicted for murder and have been in jail for nearly a year, and I can't remember as good as I ought to."

Judge Carney intervened. "Mr. Pass just answer the questions Mr. Sprague puts to you; no speeches, no quarreling."

Sprague kept pressing the point that the reports weren't created until after the murders. Pass insisted it was fall of 1969. He said that Boyle was furious that the payments to the pensioners were late. "It hurt the union's reputation."

During both his questioning by Rothman and Sprague, Pass dropped Turnblazer's name every chance he got. The reason was that Sprague had not indicted the District 19 president, which meant that when he testified for Prater as expected, he wouldn't be a "corrupt" witness who had to waive his right against self-incrimination.

As he had with Boyle, Sprague asked what Pass had done to ascertain that the committee members were "spreading the gospel" and actually incurred the expenses. And like Boyle, Pass said only that he trusted the old miners.

As the cross-examination went on, Sprague's tempo of asking questions increased, barely waiting for the witness to answer before shooting off the next. The pace flustered Pass who was caught in several discrepancies.

Pass testified that he initially told Boyle that he needed the two checks from the national office during their initial conversation. Boyle had testified that at first, he only knew of one and was surprised when the second request arrived.

Sprague caught him again when he asked Pass where he was and what he was doing when he heard about the Yablonski murders. Boyle had testified that he was alone and that Pass wasn't present.

Now Pass testified that he was "home" in Middlesboro, Kentucky and saw the news on the television. But Sprague pointed out that he'd told the grand jury that he'd been in Washington with Boyle.

Mopping the sweat from his wide face with a handkerchief, Pass said he was mistaken when he testified in front of the grand jury. He then said he'd also just misspoken; he'd actually seen the news at his Middlesboro office.

Here, Sprague demonstrated his legendary recall of details for every case he tried. "Do you have a television in your office?" he asked.

Pass again realized he'd tripped himself up. "No," he admitted, his face flushing.

When Sprague said he was done asking questions, Pass looked relieved. He was obviously shaken and grateful to be leaving the stand when Carney declared a fifteen-minute recess.

However, after the recess, Sprague asked Carney if he could ask a few more questions of Pass.

Pass exclaimed, "Oh my God! No, no not again!" He appeared to be on the verge of tears when the judge agreed.

Sprague didn't let up. He asked Pass if he'd ever personally written to Boyle before the two letters dated September 24 and September 30, 1969.

Defeated, Pass shook his head. "I don't believe I did," he said quietly. "I believe that was the only occasion."

Rothman's redirect was short and perfunctory. There wasn't much he could do to rehabilitate the witness, whose demeanor when he unsteadily stepped down from the witness stand was much different from the confident tough guy who'd taken a seat that morning.

William Prater did not fare much better when called to the stand in mid-afternoon to testify in his own defense. His attorney had advised against it, but the defendant insisted.

After the onslaught from the prosecution case, Prater thought it was his only chance to avoid conviction. He hoped that he would come off better to the jury than the overall-wearing, uneducated, and uncouth mountaineers who'd testified and the rough-edged Pass and Boyle.

Prater was tall and well-dressed, and though he had black lung, he still fared well. He'd served in the U.S. Navy and was better educated than most union members of his generation, having graduated high school and even briefly attended Purdue University in West Lafayette, Indiana.

As proof of his standing as a good family man, his loyal wife and adult children sat in the row directly behind the defense table. It was obvious they loved him.

All of this, Rothman made sure he emphasized with his client on the stand. Unlike other witnesses who had been kept out of the courtroom until called, Prater had heard all of the testimony and could conform his testimony to what had been said. As had Pass and Boyle before him, he dropped Turnblazer's name every chance he got. He claimed that he'd first heard of the R&I Committee from Turnblazer in 1968 after the Denver convention.

"As a consequence of this meeting you just told us about, what did you do, Mr. Prater?" Rothman asked.

"I made a study to think of who the people would be of the most benefit to us, and then I submitted their names to Bill Turnblazer," Prater replied. After getting the district president's approval, he'd then talked to the half dozen men he'd suggested about the proposed R&I Committee.

Asked if the men on the committee had submitted names of men who might be willing to join the UMWA, Prater nodded. He estimated the number to be "several hundred people." He claimed to have signed most of those up for union membership though he could provide no proof.

Throughout the rest of direct questioning that afternoon, Prater remained calm and seemingly open about his activities. He came off as honest and the devoted family man as he smiled at his wife and children during breaks in the questioning.

However, Sprague intended to dispel those impressions the next morning when he began his cross-examination. "Mr. Prater, didn't you help Lucille Williams and Grace Bailey raise money for Silous Huddleston?"

Prater froze and looked physically ill. Williams was Huddleston's daughter and Bailey was Huddleston's adult granddaughter. As Prater stammered and tried to wiggle out of what he knew was coming, Rothman attempted to protect his client with several objections to the line of questioning. The objections were summarily dismissed by the judge.

Sprague produced records of eighteen meetings Prater had had with the women at Lexington area motels between 1970 and 1971. He noted that after these meetings, the women had turned over thousands of dollars for Huddleston's defense to someone he did not yet name. He asked if they got the money from Prater.

"No, sir," Prater said shaking his head. "I don't know how they got that money."

The prosecutor ticked off date after date and motel after motel assignations before contending that the women eventually handed over a total of $23,068. "Is that amount correct, Mr. Prater?"

"Sir, I don't know anything about that." He looked at his attorney, his family and the jurors as the walls closed in around him.

"And the reason you were meeting them at these motels was not for the purpose of arranging to give them money to make sure Huddleston kept his mouth shut?" Sprague asked.

Trap sprung, Sprague had Agents Estill and Quinn to thank for looking through two years' worth of registration cards at dozens of motels. It took hundreds of hours, but making it somewhat easier on the agents, Prater had signed the registration cards using his real name.

Now the defendant was faced with a dilemma. He either had to admit that he'd given the women money to silence a witness in a murder case, which was a felony and indicated knowledge of guilt. Or, in front of his wife and sons, he had to admit that he wasn't the loyal husband and good family man he portrayed on the witness stand. He chose the latter.

After dodging the initial question and glancing nervously towards his wife, who had her eyes down as a son put his arm around her shoulders,[52] Prater finally replied to Sprague's insistence that the defendant explain why he met the women at the motels. "I met them there for one thing," Prater said. "I like to have a good time, and we had a good time. They wanted to talk to me and bring a couple of fellas. We will have a little party, or something along that line."

Sprague arched his eyebrows and gave the jurors a telling look. "In other words, Mr. Prater, you left LaFollette, Tennessee after you

---

52 Lewis, *Murder by Contract.*

testified before a grand jury, and there has been talk of Huddleston being involved in the murder of Jock Yablonski, to go down to Lexington with relatives of Huddleston to have a 'good time.' Is that what you are saying?"

"That's exactly what I am saying, yes, sir," Prater replied red-faced and stammering.

Prater tried to explain that the women just wanted to talk about what was going on with their father, and that he brought whiskey and cigarettes to help everybody relax. He denied having sex with them.

Without knowing it, Prater had walked into another trap. But the prosecutor didn't spring it quite yet. "Right, but you don't know at all about twenty-three thousand dollars put up to pay for Huddleston's defense?"

"No, sir," Prater replied. "I know they was always telling me they needed more money to pay for the attorney and stuff like that, but I kept telling them I didn't have money, other than my own personal funds."

Prater said he'd given the women a hundred dollars every time he met with them. But, he said, it was out of his own pocket.

For the moment Sprague left that trap open and moved to another, this one also made possible by Agent Estill's detective work.

Innocently, Sprague asked about records supposedly submitted by R&I Committee member Harvey Huddleston, no relation to Silous Huddleston. "That card is dated September 29, 1968, correct?"

Prater agreed. Then Sprague asked if that meant Harvey Huddleston gave it to him on or about that date.

"Yes, sir. I am positive of that," Prater said. "I would say within a week of September 29."

Sprague next handed Prater a receipt Harvey Huddleston had allegedly signed for his expenses. "Now, sir, you have his expenses there totaled up for September and October of '68?"

Prater again agreed and the prosecutor had him. Shaking his head as if he couldn't believe the perfidy of the witness, Sprague asked, "Isn't it a fact that from September 18 on, Harvey Huddleston was in the hospital for brain surgery in 1968?"

The defendant looked stunned. Then, though he had to have known that Sprague wouldn't have asked the question without supporting documentation, said that he was "absolutely positive" Harvey Huddleston wasn't in the hospital at that time.

In the course of less than an hour, Sprague had reduced the once-confident union official and family man to a partying philanderer, a liar, and probably a conduit for money to silence a prosecution witness, as well as a conspirator in a murder plot. Prater looked like a beaten man, but the prosecutor kept him on the stand for another hour, most of it denying that the R&I Committee was a sham set up to funnel "blood money" to the killers.

Drawing to the end of his questioning and after accusing Prater of taking the kickback money from the R&I members he recruited, Sprague asked, "Did you ever do anything to harm these men?"

"Never!" Prater said, almost shouting.

"But, Mr. Prater, you say each one of them is lying, is that not correct?"

Finally, Prater could no longer keep his temper under control. "I am saying, Mr. Sprague," he snarled through clenched teeth, "that they are under pressure, tremendous pressure. If they hadn't said what they said, they would be in jail like me for the past twelve months."

Sprague wasn't fazed by the accusation. "Who do you think is pressuring them to lie?"

"The Department of Labor and the Department of Justice."

"You think there is a big conspiracy to get them like they got you?" Sprague scoffed.

Prater, his eyes hard and angry as he looked down at his antagonist, nodded. "Sir, after twelve months in jail, yes."

A few minutes later, after a weary defendant stepped down from the stand, Rothman rested the defense case. The line had been drawn in the sand. Boyle, Pass, Prater...they'd stuck to their story, and hopefully at least one juror would buy it.

All there was left was to get through Sprague's rebuttal case, which the defense attorney thought would not likely be much more damaging. Then they'd give closing statements before the jurors were sent to deliberate the fate of his client.

If he'd known what was coming, Rothman might have thrown in the towel. But when he rested the defense case, he set in motion a series of events that even Sprague did not expect. Once again, the cause of justice would be swayed by a man's conscience, and perhaps a healthy dose of fear and self-preservation.

CHAPTER THIRTY-EIGHT

"STAND UP AND
BE STRONG"

MARCH 24, 1973

"The People call William J. Turnblazer."

As a man in his fifties entered the courtroom, Sprague stole a glance at the defense table and was satisfied with the stunned expressions on the faces of defense attorney Rothman and the defendant, William Prater. *Didn't see this one coming,* he thought with grim satisfaction. *Well, to be honest, neither did I.*

Sprague had wrapped up the court session the day before by calling four rebuttal witnesses: Edith Roark, the bookkeeper for District 19, two of the field representatives, and Suzanne Richards, an attorney who had worked for the UMWA for twenty-five years including as Boyle's executive assistant.

During a rebuttal case, a witness can be called to present evidence or testimony that disputes what a previous witness for the other side stated regarding a relevant fact. The rebuttal witness cannot testify without good cause about new issues. The witness can only rebut facts already placed into evidence.

Roark again told the jury that Pass had ordered her to make up vouchers and receipts for the twenty-three pensioners on the R&I Committee in January 1970. Pass had testified it was September 1969.

The bookkeeper also disputed Pass's testimony that he had hand-delivered the letter for the first request for money to Boyle. She said she mailed the letter. "In all the years I worked for Mr. Pass and the United Mine Workers, I have never written to Mr. Boyle for a transfer of funds," she replied when Sprague asked why she recalled this so clearly.

The two field reps, Noah Doss and G.W. Hall, followed her to the stand. They repeated their testimony that the twenty-three pensioners had cashed the checks and given the money back, which had then been passed on to Prater and Pass.

Richards was the last witness, and it was clear that she wasn't happy to be there. Still, she answered honestly when Sprague asked her if Boyle had asked her to call Pass and tell him to meet with him at the airport before the late November 1969 speech in Madisonville, Kentucky.

Boyle had denied he ever made such a request. The call was important to Sprague because he believed that was when Boyle told Pass to call off the Yablonski murder until after the election.

"Did Mr. Pass say he would be there?" Sprague asked.

"Yes," Richards, who'd been fired when Boyle got kicked out of office, answered tersely. She said she remembered the telephone call because it occurred on Thanksgiving, and she'd been alone in the UMWA building.

After Richards stepped down, Judge Carney announced that the trial would continue the next day even though it would be Saturday. He then adjourned the court.

Back in his office for the usual session to prep for the next day's witnesses, Sprague seemed preoccupied, and FBI Agent Curtis noticed. "What's up, boss?" he'd asked.

Sprague said he was wondering why Rothman had not called District 19 president William J. Turnblazer to the stand. He was on the witness list and had presumably been subpoenaed to appear.

An attorney, Turnblazer presumably would have made a favorable impression on the jurors, especially as he had not been indicted so far as one of the conspirators. It was perplexing, especially because the other union officials—Boyle, Pass, and Prater—had all gone out of their way to repeatedly refer to him during their testimony. They obviously expected him to corroborate what they said.

"Something's up, Bill," he said. "Let's get someone to go talk to him, see what he has to say."[53]

So, Curtis called Agent Estill in Knoxville and let him know what was going on. Wasting no time, Estill and Agent Starns drove to the FBI office in Middlesboro, which happened to be across the street from the District 19 office. They called Turnblazer, who was in his office, and suggested it might be a good idea to talk. He agreed and walked across the street.

Sitting down with the two agents, it didn't take long for Turnblazer to tell them why he didn't testify. He was done lying. So, he'd called Rothman and told him that he didn't want to appear on Prater's behalf. And that if he was forced to respond to the subpoena and take the stand, he'd recant what he'd told the grand juries.

Turnblazer admitted to the feds that there was no legitimate R&I Committee until January 1970, at least not one that had done anything more than cash "expense" checks and hand the money back to the field reps to be passed on to Prater or Pass. He said he'd never met with Boyle and Pass in the hallway at the 1968 convention to discuss forming the committee.

The admissions were stunning. But it took several hours of gentle persuasion before Turnblazer agreed to testify as a rebuttal witness for the prosecution.

Kept in the loop with the development, Sprague asked Estill to put Turnblazer on the first plane from Middlesboro to Erie before he changed his mind.

The turnabout wasn't completely unexpected, even if the timing and reason behind the switch was out of the blue. When sizing up the conspirators after Huddleston's confession and determining which one was most likely to crack under pressure, Sprague thought it would be Turnblazer. He wore a different coat of arms. He had

---

53 As told by Richard A. Sprague to Robert K. Tanenbaum, 2020.

COAL COUNTRY KILLING

never worked in a mine, never manned a picket line, or physically butted heads with antiunion thugs and corrupt law enforcement. He didn't have that feeling of a brotherhood that came from shared hardships and spilled blood.

Turnblazer was an attorney. He knew how the game was played and that it was only a matter of time before he was indicted.

The admission was a game-changer for the prosecution. Up to that point, Sprague was by no means confident that the jury would convict Prater; in fact, he thought there was a good chance they would acquit.

The evidence against the defendant was mostly based on the testimony of "corrupt" witnesses. The defense attorney had certainly worked to make a case that the witnesses who connected Prater to the murder conspiracy had been under pressure from the FBI and had reason to believe that failure to cooperate would result in charges being filed, especially the R&I Committee pensioners.

It wouldn't be a stretch for at least one juror to give credence to the testimony given by Boyle, Pass, and Prater. At least to the point of not believing that Sprague had proved the People's case beyond a reasonable doubt.

Now it would be difficult for the defense to discount Turnblazer's testimony. The other union conspirators had essentially talked about him like he would be their star witness.

Turnblazer was also voluntarily exposing himself to a great deal of legal liability, and Sprague wasn't offering a deal. He would be admitting that he'd committed perjury in front of the grand juries; that alone could cost him not just prison time but get him disbarred. More importantly, he was also confessing to being part of a murder plot that killed three people.

The District 19 president arrived at the Erie airport at 10:30 p.m., where he was met by Curtis and taken to the motel where Sprague was staying during the trial. Sprague didn't want anybody to know Turnblazer was in town, much less going to testify for the prosecution, so Agents Quinn and Curtis snuck him in a side door while the media were in the bar and none the wiser.

Sprague could hardly believe the good fortune that dropped another unexpected witness in his lap at such an opportune time. Phillips, Huddleston, and Annette Gilly didn't count; they were all trying to save themselves. But Paul Gilly? What did he have to gain except a place in heaven with his family? Same for the field reps and pensioners of the R&I Committee. They'd stuck to the story until some old-time minister and his gentle pressure on their consciences prompted them to come clean, too.

And now Turnblazer? A Hollywood film writer couldn't make this stuff up.

The sudden turn of events put the defense at a severe disadvantage. If Turnblazer had started the trial as a prosecution witness, counsel could have prepared to counter his testimony and impugn his credibility through cross-examination.

In all likelihood, he would have also had his other union witnesses downplay the District 19 president's role during their testimony, and even made him out to be a liar.

After Turnblazer was sworn in and seated in the witness stand, Sprague asked Judge Carney for a sidebar. Once counsel joined him, the prosecutor said he wanted to give an offer of proof for the record. "I propose to prove by this witness, Your Honor, that in fact there was no conversation in 1968 between him and Mr. Boyle concerning a Research and Information Committee and the fact that Mr. Boyle has never spoken to him about a Research and Information Committee, specifically not at the Denver convention or at any other time.

"Secondly, I also propose to prove by this witness that at no time in 1968 or 1969 did Albert Pass discuss with him the Research and Information Committee. This witness will further testify that prior to the issuance of the checks in question, Albert Pass told him that he had arranged to get twenty thousand dollars from Tony Boyle to be used for election purposes, and then just prior to the issuance of these checks this witness was present when Albert Pass called field representatives, who have been named, into his office and told them that they were to pick out these groups of men and Pass would then distribute checks and have them in that group—by the way, including Prater—and have these men, their men, cash the checks and return the money to the field representatives, who in turn would turn them back to Pass.

"This witness will further testify that in fact there was no Research and Information Committee in the years 1968 and 1969. The people to whom these checks had been given were to go subsequently in 1970, and recruit people and submit names.

"This witness will further testify that the Commonwealth Exhibit as testified to by Edith Roark was not prepared or made up until January 1970.

"This witness will further testify that he had lied to the grand jury in Cleveland and Pittsburgh and the reason he did so was he was told to do so by Mr. Pass."

Sprague also noted the conversation between Rothman and Turnblazer when the latter said he would not willingly appear on behalf of the defendant. He was testifying now for the People, the prosecutor told the judge, "because his conscience told him to."

Rothman objected to the relevancy of his conversation with Turnblazer being included in the direct examination, so Sprague voluntarily withdrew it. The defense attorney then said he would state for the record that Sprague's statement about the conversation was accurate.

With that out of the way, Rothman returned to his seat and Sprague waited while Judge Carney warned Turnblazer that he had constitutional rights against self-incrimination and to have an attorney present. Turnblazer waived his rights. Sprague began his questioning.

"Do you know this defendant?" Sprague asked.

Turnblazer, who'd worn a sad, resigned expression since entering the courtroom, didn't take his eyes off Sprague but nodded and replied, "Yes, sir."

"Will you look at him?" Sprague said.

Turnblazer looked over at Prater whose face was ashen. "Who is he?" Sprague asked.

"William Prater."

Sprague's direct examination lasted only about fifteen minutes and closely followed the points he'd outlined for the judge at the sidebar. He ended by asking Turnblazer about his testimony before the grand juries in Cleveland and Pittsburgh. "Did you lie before both those grand juries?"

"I did."

"Did anyone tell you to lie?"

"Mr. Pass said that we ought to keep our stories together, and he was very persistent and very persuasive. And I did."

When he finished, Sprague knew he'd dealt the defense a major blow. He didn't think Turnblazer had told the FBI agents everything he knew, especially when it came to Boyle's involvement. He'd also testified that he thought the money was being raised for political campaigns, which Sprague knew was questionable. But it was enough for now.

There wasn't much Rothman could do as he rose from his seat while his client sat quietly with his head down, staring at the defense table. He tried to attack Turnblazer's credibility by portraying him as someone who knew he was breaking the law and could also be disbarred.

The intention was to portray the District 19 president as someone who lied, even risked his standing as a lawyer, for his own ends. But as he'd already admitted as much, it didn't carry much weight.

Although the fight had been taken out of the defense, Sprague was making sure he'd hammered all the nails into the coffin. He called three more rebuttal witnesses between Turnblazer leaving the witness stand Saturday and the Monday morning session.

First, he asked the University of Tennessee hospital administrator to produce records that Harvey Huddleston had entered the facility in early September 1968, undergone brain surgery, and was discharged on October 2, 1968. Prater's response that he was "absolutely positive" the old miner had not been in the hospital was proven to be a lie.

The next witness was Lucille Williams, the daughter of Silous Huddleston, who Prater admitted meeting at several different motels along with her daughter. She said there was no "partying" at the motels. The only reason for the meetings was to receive money from Prater totaling more than $23,000 for her father's defense fund. The money, she said, was turned over to her dad's lawyer.

With Sprague's devastating rebuttal case in the books, Judge Carney informed the jury that the attorneys would next present their closing statements. Rothman went first. He attacked the credibility and motivations of the prosecution's "corrupt" witnesses, as well as Turnblazer, who he noted had not been indicted and was trying to avoid prosecution by testifying.

The defense attorney's argument was expected; it was basically his only choice. But what Rothman did next incensed Sprague. The defense attorney accused the prosecution, the federal attorneys, and law enforcement of engaging in a massive conspiracy to unjustly bring down the United Mine Workers of America with the ultimate aim of prosecuting Tony Boyle. He labeled it "a railroad job" and "a national scandal."

Perhaps sensing the mood, Judge Carney called a short recess. When court was back in session, Sprague faced the jurors and said the recess had come at the right time, giving him a chance to cool off.

"You would think at this stage in my own life that I would get used to that kind of speech," he said, letting the anger out in his voice. "You hear it over and over, but my blood continues to boil each time I hear that type of false narrative, always making everybody else the culprit."

Sprague said that as Rothman talked about a "railroad job," he thought about the FBI agents who'd worked countless hours over three years, the extraordinary efforts of the divers who recovered the weapons from an icy river, the FBI agents and police officers who'd carefully combed through the snow at the vantage point above the Yablonski home to recover beer cans and whiskey bottles, the auditors who'd sifted through thousands of UMWA documents, and the meticulous care all of those involved had used to preserve the evidence. All of it for the purpose of bringing justice for Jock, Margaret, and Charlotte Yablonski.

"And then I hear in this courtroom someone glibly getting up and making the statement that it is a railroad job…." Sprague let his disgust hang in the air. Then, having made his point, he moved on to the crux of his statement.

"Defense counsel said everybody in this courtroom is sorry for what happened," he said before turning towards the defense table and pointing at Prater. "Everybody but one person, who sits right in front of you, who sat on that witness stand and so insincerely testified, thinking what a job he can do in front of you, how he will in his cunning, kind way, talk his way out of this."

Sprague derided how the defense suddenly switched from portraying Turnblazer as the corroborating witness who would back up what Boyle, Pass, and Prater said, to being part of the government conspiracy. Pointing now to Rothman, he said, "Imagine if, all of a sudden, he was the lawyer defending Turnblazer, he'd be telling you why Prater is guilty.

"I kept waiting. I thought that maybe he would include the dog in this conspiracy and end up trying to suggest that it was the dog, perhaps, that took the weapon from the hands of Vealey, Martin, and Gilly, and because he can't talk, he did it."

Piece by piece, Sprague laid out the puzzle of the prosecution case and demonstrated how each fit with the others, corroborating what the witnesses said and deconstructing the defense contentions. Much of that had to do with the testimony of the R&I Committee members on which the defense case, and future defense cases, rested.

When he was ready to end, he concluded, "There can't still be the slightest doubt in your mind that there was no Research and Information Committee set up in 1968. The committee members didn't do any real work until after January 1970. And only then to cover the conspirators' tracks."

Sprague knew he needed to counter the defense attack on the credibility of his "corrupt" witnesses. "When people hire thugs and murderers to commit crimes for them, they don't hire rabbis and parish priests. And it would be a sad day if we catch a murderer, but we don't talk about the person who hired him."

He made no excuses for the shooters. "I am not fooled by them, they're a pack of killers, but who set this pack of killers loose?"

Noting the presence of Chip and Kenneth Yablonski in the courtroom, he reminded the jurors that they were waiting for justice to be done. "Not just with the three gunmen...but back to the people who initiated this dastardly crime."

As for the defense calling the prosecution of William Prater, and by implication Pass and Boyle, a national scandal, Sprague said, "This is not a scandal, it's a nightmarish tragedy." He pointed out that to remain in control the union, its leadership was willing to resort to murder and "use the despairing pensioners, getting them to lie."

He said it wasn't possible to fully convey to the jury the power the union leadership had over its members. "When Albert Pass speaks, when a William Prater barks, what do you think happens?" he asked. "The pensioners didn't ask why. When they were told to jump, the only thing they obsequiously needed to know was 'How high?'"

After testifying at Prater's trial, Boyle had joked to the media that based on the questioning, he thought he was the one on trial, not the defendant. Sprague now indicated the former union president wasn't far off the mark.

"So why is Tony Boyle lying about it?" he asked the jurors. "Because there you have the beginning; you have the person that set this chain of events in motion."

Boyle's mistake, he said, was that he believed that all he had to do was get on the stand and tell the jurors not to believe the government's case. "And that you would follow his dictates," like everyone in the UMWA."

Sprague then explained why he believed that the former union hierarchy had showed up to testify at Prater's trial. "Why is Boyle coming in here at the trial of Prater? Why is Pass coming in here at the trial of Prater?" He let the questions sink in before answering. "Because they are on the line, and here's where they have decided that they have to put up their fight. Because of the efforts of law enforcement, the administration of justice is on the move in this entire case—from the people at the back end to the beginning. And we are going there.

"Defense counsel tried to say that this is a railroad job. Let me assure this jury, other juries have not flinched from their task in the administration of justice. Don't you," he said, "because this case is going on. As I said to you in the beginning, we are starting at the end, but we are going back to the beginning, and right here today we are at one point along that road from the end to the beginning."

As he finished Sprague made one last appeal to the jury's sense of duty to their community. "If ever there is a time that each one of you is going to stand up and speak for this community, it is now," he said, taking his time to look from face to face. "Don't flinch. Stand up and be strong. Return a verdict of guilty of murder in the first degree for each charge. Thank you."

It was almost 5 p.m., March 26, 1973, when the jury was sent off to begin their deliberations. Seven hours later, as Prater sat emotionless and his family wept, the jurors returned their verdict: guilty of three counts of murder in the first degree.

CHAPTER THIRTY-NINE

"THEY WERE REALLY TELLING THE TRUTH"

JUNE 11, 1973

Like a long-running Broadway play, the trial of Albert Pass followed the same script as those that preceded it. After a week of jury selection, the same actors took the stage and essentially repeated the same lines.

There were a few significant differences. Tony Boyle did not testify for his erstwhile enforcer. Neither did William Turnblazer. Sprague now had more time to question him and was certain that Turnblazer was still covering for Boyle. So Sprague didn't call Turnblazer, sending him a not so subtle message to start telling the truth. And the biggest difference of all, William Prater joined the list of prosecution witnesses.

It all started shortly after Prater's conviction when his wife, Maxine, was allowed to visit with him in his cell. She'd been convinced of his innocence before the trial began, she told him, but not after she heard the evidence.

"If I'd been on the jury, I would have convicted you, too," she said.

"Then you would have convicted an innocent man," he retorted angrily.[54]

Prater continued to maintain his innocence the next day when his attorney, Rothman, came to see him, partly to explain how the appeals process worked, and in part at the urging of Prater's family. The defense attorney, who would later admit that he would have voted to convict his client, too,[55] told Prater that if he was guilty, he should confess not only for his own conscience but the sake of his family.

If he didn't, Rothman said, they'd spend the rest of their lives in bitterness, believing that the government had railroaded him. "You owe it to your family to tell the truth."[56]

A few days later, Prater requested a pencil and paper and began to write out his confession. The federal prosecutors, as well as Sprague, were told what was happening but made no effort to talk to him, not wanting to pressure him.

On April 6, 1973, Prater contacted Sprague's office and asked for a meeting. The convicted man was brought to the FBI office in Pittsburgh where he turned in the twenty-three-page confession. For the next three days, he was questioned by FBI agents Curtis and Quinn, as well as Bob Dugan from the Pennsylvania State Police.

Prater confessed to everything he'd been accused of during his trial. He also implicated Pass. But like Turnblazer before him, he didn't yet fully bring Boyle into the picture.

Once again, Sprague was surprised that without any prodding or promises from the prosecution side, one of the conspirators had come forward voluntarily to admit to lying and willing to testify for the Commonwealth. He'd never experienced or even heard of such a thing before.

True, Prater had waited until he was convicted before finding his conscience. But he knew that Sprague wasn't making deals, nor had the convicted man asked for one. In fact, after writing out his statement, he'd pleaded guilty to the federal charge of violating Jock Yablonski's civil rights and was sentenced to life in prison. Then

55 Lewis, *Murder by Contrac.t*
56 Richard A. Sprague to Robert K. Tanenbaum in relating a post-trial conversation with Rothman.

the day before his testimony in the Pass trial, he'd appeared before the judge and withdrawn his appeals for his convictions on the state charges.

After Sprague heard from Curtis how the confession came about, he wasn't overwhelmingly surprised. Granted, the convicted conspirator had willingly gone along with the plot to kill Yablonski. Also, he had a reputation as a close associate of the notorious union head-buster Albert Pass. And there were character questions about his philandering. But he seemed to have been a good father who had raised his children, who clearly loved him and had been devastated by his conviction—as good, productive citizens would naturally be.

In Sprague's view, Prater got caught up in the culture of absolute loyalty to the union and its autocratic leadership. Like Huddleston, Turnblazer, and tens of thousands of UMWA members who voted for Boyle in both the 1969 and 1972 elections, he'd believed that Yablonski was a traitor and out to bring down the UMWA. It wasn't an excuse for what he'd done but confessing and testifying for the prosecution was a step towards making amends, and he'd done it for his family.

As for Rothman's role in Prater's about-face, Sprague's opinion of the man had also changed. He'd been incensed by the defense attorney's depiction of the investigation team and accusations of a "railroad job." But Rothman had been a standup guy when he talked to his client about coming clean.

On the witness stand at the Pass trial, Prater began by admitting that he'd lied to the grand juries and at his own trial. Asked by Sprague why he'd changed his mind and decided to tell the truth, he said he did it for his wife and seven children.

"I knew that I was guilty, but I still maintained my innocence. I was going to fight the case," he said. "I was subsequently informed by attorney Mr. Rothman of the procedures for appeals, and I told him I wasn't interested in going to court anymore for any reason— that I had been lying and wanted to do what I could to straighten out the situation. Mr. Rothman recommended that I write out a full and complete statement."

Prater also told the jurors that he also wanted to come forward on behalf of the twenty-three pensioners he'd defamed. "I wanted to correct the record regarding witnesses I said were lying. They were really telling the truth."

Responding to Sprague's questions, Prater corroborated the other prosecution witnesses, explained the role he'd played, and condemned his longtime friend, the fifty-four-year-old Pass who he described as "the real boss" of District 19. "Officially, the president of District 19 was William Turnblazer, but Pass was in charge."

When Huddleston, who he also described as a close friend, told Prater that the hitmen were having a difficult time finding Yablonski, Pass met with his two friends in his house in Middlesboro. There he produced the map that showed the location of the UMWA building in Washington, D.C. to give to Paul Gilly. He also gave Prater a photograph of Yablonski standing with two other union officials and drew an arrow to indicate which was the target to give to Gilly.

In November 1969, Prater testified that Pass met with him and Huddleston at the Knoxville airport where he told them to call off the murder plan "because the election was drawing too near, and if anything happened to Yablonski, the public would get the idea that he was killed to prevent him from being elected president of the UMWA."

Then several days after the election, Pass called him to say the assassination plan was back on and that the price would be raised to $15,000 if done before January 1, 1970. Prater said he heard news of the murders on the television news and called Pass during the broadcast.

Asked by Sprague why he participated in the murder conspiracy, Prater gave an answer that would have made sense to many in the UMWA. "My father and grandfather were coalminers," he said. "I went to work in the mines in '37. In '42, I joined the union and worked in the mines for almost twenty years. I've been with the UMWA for thirty-four years. I was loyal to the union."

Prater paused to look over at the defendant whose face bore no emotion but whose eyes glittered with anger. "After speaking to Pass, I thought I was protecting the union."

Perhaps not willing to face Sprague again, Pass, who sat impassively listening to his former colleagues and friends drive nails into his coffin, didn't take the stand in his own defense. Defense attorney Harold Gondelman, a respected Pittsburgh trial lawyer, could only fall back on the same strategy of attacking the credibility and motivations of the prosecution witnesses as they took the stand.

In his closing statement, Gondelman did try one new tact. Instead of denying that there was a plot to kill Yablonski, he cast the blame on Huddleston.

Sprague addressed that in his closing statement. "Did he forget that behind Huddleston was Prater? And that behind Prater was Pass?"

As for the pensioner and field reps, whom the defense attorney accused of giving into pressure from investigators, Sprague asked the jurors to understand the hold the union leadership had over their lives. "Did you see some of those people?" he asked. "You ask yourselves, those people that had worked thirty or forty years in the mines, here they all of the sudden have no other means of income… what happens to them? Do you think they can just get themselves another job?"

Sprague told the jurors that early in the investigation he'd wondered why Pass had written directly to Boyle asking for the money, something he'd never done before. Then it dawned on him, he said if Pass had instead written to Bill Owens, the secretary-treasurer of the national office, then he, Owens, would have asked to see the records indicating the work they'd done and the expenses.

At the end of his summation, Sprague again asked the jurors to not "flinch from your duty.… Who is it that literally marked Jock Yablonski for death? Who is it that drew on that photograph to identify which one was Jock Yablonski?"

Sprague turned to point at Pass. "The person who marked them for extinction, assassination, sits right there," he said. "You have a duty to do. The only proper verdict in this case on all three charges is guilty of murder in the first degree."

On June 19, 1973, it took the jury six hours to return the verdict that Sprague asked for: guilty on all three counts as charged.

Ever the tough guy, the man who preached "the gospel of unionism" smiled as he was led from the courtroom.

Once again, the curtain closed. Before it would open again, a lot of the scenery would change.

CHAPTER FORTY

"ASSASSINATION IS HIS BIG CRIME"

APRIL 3, 1974

The courtroom of Judge Francis J. Catania in Media, Pennsylvania held 210 spectators and was packed with state and national press, court watchers, investigators who worked for either side, and family members of the deceaseds and the defendant. They'd gathered for what everyone believed would be the final curtain call of the Yablonski tragedy.

Looking frail, pale, and grandfatherly in an ill-fitting dark blue suit, Boyle was seated between two lawyers from his part of the West, Charles F. "Timer" Moses, a tall former basketball player with a reputation in Montana as a great trial lawyer, and D. Frank Kampfe, a younger man but already the winner of several well-publicized trials in Montana, Idaho, and Wyoming.

Boyle's wife of forty-six years, Ethel, and his daughter, Antoinette, a lawyer who had worked for the UMWA, sat directly behind the defense table. When he turned around to smile and give them a thumb's up, his daughter cried out, "Good luck, Daddy!"

Sitting at the prosecution table were Sprague's assistants, Bill Wolf and Pamela Higgins, and, quietly concentrating on notes as he

absently rubbed the balding spot on top of his head, the man himself: Richard A. Sprague, unexceptional law student, chess master,
legendary prosecutor, and avenging angel of murder victims.

In the row behind the prosecution table were a half dozen FBI
agents, including Sprague's right-hand man Bill Curtis, the "gentle
pressure" team of Wally Estill, Hank Quinn, and other law enforcement officers such as Pennsylvania State Trooper Elmer Schifko.

Four years after the Hillbilly Hitmen began hunting Jock
Yablonski, Sprague was ready to bring to justice the man who set
them on the trail. It began the night of September 5, 1973 when
Schifko of the Pennsylvania State Police appeared before Judge
Thomas Gladden of the Washington County Court of Common
Pleas to file a complaint to procure murder warrants.

After naming all the other conspirators involved in the murders,
Schifko got to the heart of the complaint. "On June 23, 1969, W.A.
'Tony' Boyle, the president of the United Mine Workers of America,
sought out and spoke privately with Albert Edward Pass and William
Jenkins Turnblazer inside the national headquarters of the United
Mine Workers in Washington, D.C.

"At this private meeting, W.A. Tony Boyle initiated and instigated
a plan to assassinate and murder Joseph Albert 'Jock' Yablonski.
W.A. Tony Boyle told Albert Edward Pass and William Jenkins
Turnblazer that Yablonski had to be done away with.

"In response to W.A. Tony Boyle's statement, Albert Edward
Pass offered to accept the assignment and stated that District 19
would take care of it. The private meeting ended with W.A. Tony
Boyle stating he was in agreement."

Judge Gladden signed the state murder warrants and Sprague,
who was waiting in Philadelphia, was notified at 3 a.m. Assistant
U.S. attorney general Henderson was also informed and immediately
obtained a federal indictment against Boyle. He then told the FBI to
arrest Boyle, who was in Washington, D.C.

As fate would have it, a little after 11 a.m., Boyle was being
deposed by Chip Yablonski, who was now general counsel for
the UMWA. They were in the office of an attorney representing
Edward Carey, who had held Chip's job until his friend Boyle was

ousted. The new administration of the UMWA had filed a civil suit regarding Carey's questionable practices during his tenure as general counsel.

The deposition came to an abrupt end when three FBI agents entered the hearing room and announced to Boyle that he was under arrest on a federal charge of violating Jock Yablonski's rights. "Specifically, that you conspired with others to cause the murder of Jock Yablonski."

Boyle was stunned. The agents informed him that the press had already gathered in front of the building "and we are just going to gently lay our hands on your arms and push you right through as quickly as we can."

"When will that happen?" asked Boyle, who couldn't seem to comprehend what was happening.

"Our car is right out front."

As promised, the agents gently laid their hands on the former union boss and ushered him through the throng of press who shouted questions at him. "I don't know what this is about," Boyle answered. As he was being assisted into the backseat of the car, he called the charges "ridiculous" and added, "I never expected this to come through. I had no forewarning."

In Philadelphia, Sprague met with the press and informed them of the arrest and that Boyle would be extradited to Pennsylvania on September 25 to face state murder charges. "Ladies and gentlemen," he said, "this is the end of the line for Tony Boyle."

Boyle had other ideas. Just hours before he was to be extradited, he attempted to commit suicide by ingesting a large number of sodium amytal "sleeping" pills while at home on bail. He was rushed to the hospital where he was listed as critical. The prognosis was that even if he survived, he would suffer so much brain damage, he'd never be able to stand trial.

Sprague was disappointed. While he would have gladly sent Boyle to the electric chair if the death penalty was still in place for the murder of the Yablonskis, he wanted "Tough Tony" exposed for what he was and what he had done in a public courtroom.

Dying from an overdose of pills would deprive the Yablonski brothers of seeing the man responsible for the slaughter of their family exposed as the evil man he was. It would also leave unanswered questions about his guilt, especially for those union members who still believed in him.

Instead, the old man tried to cheat justice and those it served. But Boyle turned out to be tougher than even he counted on. He not only survived, but on October 23, he was declared fit to stand trial. Like it or not, he was going to have his day in court.

However, there was a question whether Sprague would be there with him. In November, his boss, Arlen Specter, lost his bid for a third term as the district attorney of Philadelphia. There was speculation that his replacement, Emmet Fitzpatrick, would fire Sprague and replace him with his own man as first assistant district attorney. If so, there was a question of whether Sprague would be allowed to try Boyle on the state charges.

However, the initial concern was alleviated when high-ranking U.S. Department of Justice attorneys like Henderson, who'd come to respect the firebrand prosecutor for the way he'd handled the Yablonski case, stepped in. They saw to it that he was sworn in as a special prosecutor to try Boyle on federal murder charges if he couldn't go forward with the state case.

In the end, the federal move wasn't necessary. Fitzpatrick reappointed Sprague as his first assistant and allowed him to continue to prosecute Boyle.

On December 18, a federal judge ordered that Boyle be transferred from the hospital to a federal prison in Springfield, Missouri to begin serving a three-year sentence for his federal convictions. He'd lost his appeal to overturn the convictions, but his sentence was reduced from the original five-year term.

However, the drama soon ratcheted up when Sprague asked the federal judge to allow Boyle to first be brought to Pennsylvania for arraignment and to set a trial date. On December 20, when U.S. marshals arrived at the hospital and informed Boyle, who was still lying in a hospital bed, what was about to happen, he flew into a rage. He wouldn't get dressed, and when they tried to get him out of the bed, he fought with them until collapsing to the floor.

They gave up. The next day, Boyle gave a repeat performance when the marshals returned to transport him to Pennsylvania. But as he raged in his pajamas, they tossed a raincoat over him and half-carried him out to the car and from there to the airport.

Boyle arrived at the Allegheny County airport in a snowstorm. At the courthouse, he was placed in a wheelchair and pushed through a side door still wearing his bright green pajamas beneath a blanket. His thin hair was disheveled, his face pale, and eyes darted wildly as he was wheeled through the waiting press.

At the hearing a trial date was set for January 1974, but when the defense later requested a change of venue, Sprague did not contest it. As a result, a new trial was set to begin March 25, 1974 in Media, a bedroom community just twenty miles from Philadelphia.

It had been quite a journey since that bitterly cold day on the banks above the Monongahela River when Curtis wondered what sort of leader it would take to mold local, state, and federal law enforcement officers into a single-minded team. It had been a Herculean task to take an incredibly complex and wide-ranging investigation and build cases against nearly a dozen conspirators, bringing five of them to trial while wrenching guilty pleas and testimony from others.

Granted, the investigation and prosecution had been aided by an extraordinary run of luck—to the point that more than one of the investigators believed that divine providence was at work. But Thomas Jefferson once said, "The harder I work, the more luck I seem to have," and no one worked harder than Richard Sprague.

The investigation was one of the largest and most expensive in U.S. history, rivaling even those associated with the political assassinations that had epitomized the 1960s, costing millions of man-hours and millions of taxpayer dollars.

Still, none of it would have mattered if not for the intense man with the bulbous eyes, prominent nose, and thinning pate sitting at the prosecution table waiting to give his opening statement in the *Commonwealth of Pennsylvania vs. W.A. Tony Boyle*. Armed with the voice of a Baptist minister and a chess master's mind, he'd let everybody know who was boss from the beginning and then walked the walk.

There were a thousand ways the case could have derailed. But he'd anticipated the pitfalls, like knowing that giving deals to the likes of Claude Vealey and Paul Gilly would have played into the hands of defense attorneys whose only real chance was to attack the credibility and motivations of the "corrupt" witnesses. He'd shut that down—to the surprise of investigators and consternation of federal prosecutors and District Attorney Costa—and played hardball, willing to live with the consequences.

Otherwise, he'd used every tool at his disposal, including the death penalty when it was still in effect, holding it over the conspirators' heads to strike fear into their black hearts. Then after the U.S. Supreme Court took that away, he made sure that the guilty understood that he would be arguing for three life sentences, even for those convicted who later came forward.

Like assistant U.S Attorney Henderson said when Sprague rejected Vealey's demand for a deal, the prosecutor could be a "hard man." Yet, he was also capable of tempering justice with mercy, as was the case of the twenty-three pensioners of the faux R&I Committee and the field reps who recruited them. Although they'd pleaded guilty to a federal charge of perjury for lying to the grand juries, they'd received no jail time, as Sprague had declined to press state charges against them.

Their crime had been blind loyalty to a union that they'd venerated all of their lives, and to the legendary John L. Lewis, and then his anointed successor. They'd been lied to—about the reason for the kickback scheme, and about Jock Yablonski's efforts to destroy the UMWA. Then when it became increasingly clear what the money had really been used for, they were afraid of losing their meager pensions and health benefits.

So rather than threaten and frighten them, Sprague patiently waited for Agents Estill and Quinn to work their "gentle pressure," with kitchen Bible meetings, respect, and even friendship. Given time and space, the tight-lipped mountaineers had eventually listened to their consciences and atoned by testifying with no promises of leniency.

What would have been the point of sending them to prison anyway? They were old, most of them sick and beat up from lifetimes spent in the mines. The fierce prosecutor from the big city of Philadelphia decided to let them live out what remained of their days smoking on their corncob pipes and praying for forgiveness, surrounded by family and the green hills of their homes.

As wonderful as his mind was, Sprague often went on what his gut told him. He intuited that Vealey would be the first of the Hillbilly Hitmen to crack and that Silous Huddleston and Annette Gilly would see the writing on the wall if left to stew in jail as material witnesses.

Studying the conspirators, he'd correctly guessed that William Turnblazer would be the weak link among the union leadership and left him unindicted and dreading the moment when FBI agents would show up at his door with an arrest warrant. He might not have foreseen how Turnblazer's change of heart would come about, but he'd been savvy enough to realize something was up when the District 19 president wasn't called by the defense at Prater's trial.

As the complaint filed by Trooper Schifko to obtain the arrest warrants for Boyle indicated, Sprague had been right that William Turnblazer had more to say about Tony Boyle's part in the conspiracy. The former District 19 president had finally linked Boyle directly to the murder plot by confessing that he and Pass had met Boyle in the hallway at the June 23, 1969 IEB meeting where he told them Yablonski needed to be "done away with." It was that command that set in motion the gears that ground to a brutal, horrific end.

After four years on the case, Sprague's work ethic was renowned among those investigators, as well as the Yablonski brothers, who attended his strategy meetings and prep sessions after court recessed each day. Often working eighteen-hour days, seven days a week, over four years, he'd lived and breathed the case. His total recall of every least detail—such as Vealey's off-hand statement about Martin asking him for help firebombing a house—had become the stuff of legend.

Like the chess master he was in what used to be his free time, he excelled at leading defense attorneys, hostile witnesses, and defendants into traps—sometimes of their own making that he exploited, others that he set by thinking many moves ahead, anticipating how his opponents would react.

Now, all these years after that frigid day above the Monongahela, Curtis and others on the team eagerly anticipated watching Sprague ensnare this defendant and his defense attorneys.

With the jury seated and the attorneys and the defendant present, Judge Catania gave Sprague the go ahead to address the jury. So began the prosecutor's opening gambit in the final chess match of a series that had begun on November 9, 1971 with the trial of Aubran Wayne "Buddy" Martin.

Rising from his seat to enter the well of the court to face the jury, Sprague made sure all eyes of the jurors were on him as he turned to walk slowly towards the defense table. Pointing a condemning finger at the defendant, who seemed to shrink into his seat, he said, "Here at the end of the murder line sits W.A. Tony Boyle, 'Tough Tony,' the man who ordered Jock Yablonski's assassination."

Sprague continued until he loomed over Boyle, who was looking anything but tough. "What's this man guilty of, ladies and gentlemen of the jury?" he asked as he turned his back on Boyle to face them fully. "Murder in the first degree!"

When he finished, he promised that through witness testimony, documents, and physical evidence he would show them how the trail would lead from the killers to the defendant. That testimony, he said, would include District 19 president William Turnblazer's account of "how 'Tough Tony' Boyle said, 'Jock Yablonski's got to be done away with'...and how he provided the money for those executions."

Having laid out his case-in-chief, he sat back down. His traps were set and waiting for the defense attorneys to walk into.

Defense attorney Moses rose and began by asserting that Boyle and Yablonski were close, personal friends and that his client had no motive to kill. However, he said, those who did have reasons to want Yablonski dead were the prosecution's witnesses William Jackson Prater and Silous Huddleston.

They were afraid, he said, that Yablonski would expose corruption in District 19 that Boyle knew nothing about. And they were aided in their scheme by Turnblazer, "a self-confessed embezzler, a thief, and a perjurer," Moses sneered. "Are you going to believe this man?"

When Moses finished and took his seat, Sprague began moving his pieces on the board. The pawns. The rooks. The knights and bishops. Kenneth Yablonski. Claude Vealey. Paul Gilly. Silous Huddleston. The FBI agents, cops, and forensic experts.

The most dramatic moment arrived when Buddy Martin was dragged into the courtroom by a pair of burly state police officers during Gilly's testimony. Protesting loudly and struggling, Martin was stood up in front of the witness stand.

"Do you know this man, Mr. Gilly?" Sprague asked as he stood within a few feet of the killer who cold-bloodedly shot Charlotte Yablonski twice in the top of her skull and then emptied his gun into her parents.

When Gilly, looking down and not at his snarling accomplice, only nodded, Sprague loudly demanded that he speak up. "Is this the man you're talking about?"

"Yes, sir, that's him."

"You goddamned hillbilly redneck!" Martin shouted before turning quickly to lunge at Sprague while screaming. "You dirty mother-fucker..." He punctuated his tirade by spitting on the prosecutor.

With no more reaction than swatting at a fly, Sprague took a handkerchief from his pocket and wiped the spittle from his face. "Take him away," he quietly told the troopers.

Martin was dragged from the court shouting that he'd been kidnapped and brought to the courtroom against his will. When he was gone, Sprague continued his assault.

The old men of the R&I Committee in their clean overalls shuffled to the stand and to a man acknowledged that they'd lied to the grand jury because they'd been told to by Prater, Pass, and the field reps. Then they explained their role in the kickback scheme.

Prater, too, admitted his lies to the grand jury "and at my own trial." He didn't have much to say that directly implicated Boyle; his part was to reveal the kickback scheme, as well as engage Silous Huddleston to find men willing to kill Yablonski for money.

However, Prater did have one seemingly unimportant anecdote to relate to the jury. He testified that the night before he was going to testify at Prater's trial, Boyle requested a meeting through Prater's attorney, Rothman.

They spoke for about twenty minutes outside the hearing of anyone, Prater said. Before Boyle left, he warned him to "stick to the story" no matter what. Even if you're convicted, "stick to the story."

As Sprague had indicated in his opening, Turnblazer testified about the June 23, 1969, conversation in the hallway of the UMWA building when Boyle said he wanted Yablonski "done away with." Albert Pass, he said, told Boyle that District 19 "would take care of it."

Turnblazer made two more statements in his testimony that at first glance didn't seem to mean much. One was that he sat next to Boyle on a plane from Washington, D.C. to Pittsburgh to testify before a grand jury. During the flight, he said, Boyle told him that he'd heard that some of the R&I pensioners were meeting with FBI agents and that they needed to be reminded to "stick to the story."

The former president of District 19 also testified that Pass had given him an excerpted portion of the transcript of the minutes from the January 22, 1970 meeting of the IEB that recounted the secretary-treasurer's description of how the R&I Committee got started in 1968. Pass told him that Boyle wanted him to read the excerpted transcript so that he got the story straight in case he was ever questioned by law enforcement.

After Sprague presented the prosecution case, defense counsel began by calling Boyle to the stand. Although he seemed to have had difficulty climbing into the witness stand, Boyle's voice was loud and clear as he pronounced that he was innocent of the charges.

"Jock was my friend," he swore adamantly. "He and I were very close. When I heard of his death, I was sick to my stomach."

Boyle was so distraught by the murders, he said, that he instructed his assistant Suzanne Richards to offer a $50,000 reward for the arrest and conviction of the Yablonski killers. He said he was "only trying to help" when he formed a committee to gather tips for law enforcement until the Yablonski brothers complained.

It was Pass who first talked to him about the R&I Committee, and only later in the day did he mention it to Turnblazer. He said his only involvement was to "green light" the project.

Turnblazer lied to them on the witness stand, Boyle told the jurors. He denied sitting next to the former District 19 president on the flight to Pittsburgh. And he never talked to him at all on the flight, much less told him to warn the R&I Committee members to "stick to the story."

Boyle said he never saw a transcript of the minutes from the January 22, 1970 meeting of the IEB, or any other meeting transcripts for that matter. He didn't consider it part of his job responsibilities. Therefore, he did not hand Pass the transcript and tell him to give it to Turnblazer.

Under further questioning by defense counsel, the former union boss said he met with Prater the night before he testified at his trial at Prater's request. He said the meeting only lasted six to eight minutes and was conducted in front of Rothman and his own attorney Cacheris.

"And I said, 'Well you are looking good. I hope you stand up; you are going to be proven innocent.'"

During cross-examination, Sprague's questioning of Boyle was mostly a repeat of their back and forth at Prater's trial. By the time he was done with his cross-examination, Boyle had been on the stand for three hours. He looked exhausted but also that he'd prevailed in his battle with the prosecutor.

Sprague, however, knew better. Like setting up an opponent in a chess game, he'd lured his opponent into guessing he was after one thing when he had something else entirely in mind. The prosecutor was almost disappointed that he'd have to wait until morning.

In the morning, Sprague began by calling Suzanne Richards to the stand. Although Boyle's longtime executive assistant was clearly unhappy to appear at Boyle's trial, she seemed to have accepted the task now, and in any event wasn't going to perjure herself for her old boss.

Asked by Sprague if Boyle suggested the fifty-thousand-dollar reward for the apprehension and conviction of the Yablonskis' killers she shook her head. "No, sir, he did not."

"Whose idea was it then?"

"The idea was mine, sir," Richards said as Boyle was seen to wince at what he had to view as a betrayal.[57] "I told Mr. Boyle we should offer a one hundred-thousand-dollar reward. He said he'd have to think about it, and I should come back later. I did and he then said it was okay, but he cut the amount to fifty thousand dollars."

Sprague then asked her if she was on the airplane from Washington, D.C. to Pittsburgh when Boyle was scheduled to appear before the grand jury.

"Yes, sir, I was."

"Was Mr. Boyle on that flight?"

"Yes, sir, he was."

"And who did he sit with?"

"He sat with Mr. Turnblazer."

"The entire trip, Mrs. Richards?"

"Yes, sir, the entire trip."

With just a few questions, Sprague had exposed Boyle as a liar. His former executive assistant had exposed his effort to portray himself as seeking to avenge his friend's murder by offering a reward to find the killer or killers.

And whatever the jury thought of Turnblazer, there was no reason to doubt her account about who Boyle sat with on the plane to Pittsburgh. She wasn't facing any charges and had nothing to gain. Her old boss had lied, which gave more credibility to Turnblazer's account.

Richards's testimony was so incontrovertible that the defense didn't bother to cross-examine her.

Sprague continued to play out his strategy. He surprised everyone but his team when he called Prater's defense attorney, Rothman, to

---

57 Lewis, *Murder by Contract.*

the stand. Once again, Rothman proved to be a standup guy as he contradicted Boyle's account of his meeting with Prater the night before he testified.

Boyle had testified that Prater had requested the meeting through Rothman. That, the defense attorney said, was a lie. It was the former UMWA president who called and asked to meet with his client.

Prater had also testified that he and Boyle were left alone in a room and outside the hearing of Rothman and Boyle's attorney for about twenty minutes. During that time, he'd told the jury, Boyle told him to "stick to the story. Even if you're convicted, stick to the story."

However, Boyle claimed he said no such thing. He testified that the two of them met with the lawyers present and talked for only six to eight minutes, most of it a pep talk.

As a rebuttal witness, Rothman now backed up his client's account. He said the two men met alone in a room for about twenty minutes, and that neither he nor Boyle's attorney could hear what was being said. However, he added, the room had a window through which he could see them talking.

With Rothman's testimony, another witness had shown Boyle to be a liar, and one desperate for a co-conspirator to "stick to the story." It could be argued that Rothman was parroting his client, but it was unclear why, as an officer of the court, he would do that under oath.

Sprague moved on inexorably towards the king, who sat at the defense table looking far more like a defeated old man than the one-time arrogant demagogue of the most powerful union in the United States. But the wily prosecutor had saved the coup de grâce for last.

Sprague called Turnblazer back to the stand where he repeated his testimony that Pass handed him a portion of transcript of the minutes from the January 22, 1970 IEB meeting.

Now Sprague added a twist. "And did you turn over that copy of the minutes to Agent Quinn of the FBI?"

"Yes, sir, I did."

With those few words, Turnblazer was again dismissed to be followed to the stand by Quinn. The federal lawman testified that he'd indeed received the minutes from Turnblazer.

Sprague retrieved an envelope from the prosecution table, the contents of which, the agent testified, were the transcript.

"And did you have Mr. Turnblazer sign each and every page?" Sprague asked.

"I had Mr. Turnblazer sign the bottom page and initial every other page," the agent replied.

"And did you also mark each and every page yourself?"

"I placed my initials on the last page and sealed it in this envelope and placed my initials and the date on the envelope."

After sealing the envelope, Quinn said he sent it by registered mail to the Identification Division of the Federal Bureau of Investigation.

"To Mr. Groenthal?" Sprague asked.

"Yes, sir."

Sprague then recalled FBI fingerprint expert Charles Groenthal to the stand. Handing him the envelope with the transcripts, Sprague turned to the judge. "I offer that into evidence at this time as Commonwealth's Exhibit number sixty-five—the excerpted transcript minutes of the January 22, 1970 IEB meeting."

"It may be admitted," Judge Catania ruled.

"Thank you, Your Honor," Sprague replied.

After once again ascertaining Groenthal's extensive resume as the FBI's foremost fingerprint examiner, as well as "in charge of the training in the Identification Division," Sprague asked, "Now did you have a fingerprint of this defendant W.A. Tony Boyle to compare with fingerprints on that document?"

"Yes."

"Mr. Groenthal, did you find a fingerprint of this defendant W.A. Tony Boyle on Commonwealth's Exhibit sixty-five?"

"Yes."

"Where was that fingerprint?"

"The latent fingerprint was developed on page sixty-nine."

"That is the very first page there, is that correct?"

"That is correct."

At that moment, the brilliance of Sprague's strategy became apparent.

Boyle had testified that he never looked at and never so much as ever touched any transcripts of board meetings.

Sprague had taken a big risk waiting for the rebuttal case to catch Boyle in his lie. If he'd introduced the transcript during his direct examination of Turnblazer and then called Quinn and Groenthal to the stand, Boyle would have known what was up. He then would have testified that, yes, he'd looked over the minutes as part of his duties as union president.

Once again fate had smiled on Sprague. The transcript fingerprint evidence had come about when Turnblazer finally came clean about the items he'd left out of his confession for the Prater trial. The main point had, of course, been providing the direct link from Boyle to the murder plot by testifying about the meeting in the UMWA hallway on June 23 between himself, Pass, and Boyle.

"Yablonski needs to be done away with" had—if Turnblazer was to be believed—set everything in motion. And Turnblazer's believability was why the transcripts with the damning fingerprint was so important. Boyle's credibility had just been annihilated by a single fingerprint on the front page of the excerpted January 22, 1970 transcript. And Turnblazer's truthfulness was secured.

Once again, it was hard to believe that something more than luck was not involved. What were the chances that Turnblazer, who at the time was an unrepentant co-conspirator desperate to avoid prosecution, would not destroy the transcripts after reading them, and had instead kept them so pristine for four years that a single fingerprint had been preserved?

If Boyle's trial had been a chess match, this would have been the time for the defense attorneys to tip the king over on the board to concede defeat. Still, after Sprague rested his rebuttal case and the judge called for closing arguments, defense counsel tried to save his client.

While he replayed the usual tactic of labeling the Commonwealth's witnesses liars, defense counsel took it a step further. He blamed the murders entirely on District 19 from Huddleston to Prater to

Turnblazer and, by implication, the ever-loyal Albert Pass, who several witnesses had identified as the real power in the district.

They were afraid that Yablonski knew about their corruption and hired the hitmen to kill him, counsel claimed. They'd murdered Tony's good friend Jock, he said, shaking his head theatrically, and then conspired to have the innocent union leader to take the blame. It was all but over, and the defense attorney and his client seemed to know it when he sat down.

In summation, Sprague argued the prosecution case one witness, one piece of evidence, at a time. He finished with the fingerprint evidence that along with the testimony of other rebuttal witnesses proved that Boyle was a liar. However, he argued, "Lying under oath isn't Boyle's biggest crime. Murder, assassination is his biggest crime."

With that the jury was sent off to deliberate shortly after noon. They returned six hours later with their verdict: guilty of three counts of first-degree murder.

As the verdict was read, Boyle, who'd been standing, slumped towards the floor and had to be held up by U.S. marshals who then carried him out of the courtroom. As he passed by, his daughter, Antoinette, told him not to worry, you'll get a new trial.

Later that evening, Kenneth and Chip Yablonski threw a victory party in honor of Sprague and his team. The prosecutor stayed for only one drink before leaving. He was exhausted and just glad it was over.

Only this time, Richard A. Sprague was wrong.

CHAPTER FORTY-ONE

FATALLY FLAWED

On January 28, 1977, the Supreme Court of Pennsylvania (SCOPA) reversed the murder convictions after jury trial of the defendant, W.A. "Tough Tony" Boyle, and ordered a new trial. SCOPA ruled that "Boyle was prejudiced when he was not permitted to offer testimony of a witness who would establish that others allegedly involved in the slayings acted with motives and methods without Boyle's knowledge."

The witness the court referred to was Thomas Kane, a federal auditor, who, pursuant to the directions of the prosecution team leader, Richard A. Sprague, audited the finances of District 19 of the UMWA located in Middlesboro, Kentucky. The purpose of the audit was to confirm and corroborate that individuals in UMWA's District 19 were acting in furtherance of the Boyle-created conspiracy to assassinate UMWA reformer Jock Yablonski. *The defense never spoke to the witness, Thomas Kane, nor had it ever read the contents of the audit!*

Simply, in response to the trial court's request that the defense render an offer of proof as to the witness, Kane, and the underlying audit report, defense counsel opined that he believed that there was probably evidence of motive in the audit report that would incriminate other individuals acting with motives to murder Yablonski for reasons and methods unknown to Boyle. Since defense counsel never spoke to the witness and never read the audit report, he offered no factual basis to satisfy the basic rudiments required to permit a witness to testify at trial. Defense counsel speculated what the witness would likely testify to and that such speculative testimony would be helpful to the defense. Sprague was also required to engage in offers of proof regarding each of the substantive Commonwealth witnesses throughout the trial and was always factually precise, specific, and comprehensive.

A trial is a search for truth under the rules of evidence. Trials are not public psychological encounter sessions. Neither venting nor basing opinions on rank speculation and drawing inferences therefrom are permissible. Facts and evidence are stubborn things. They are not always consistent with one's hopes, inclinations, or theories. Witnesses qualify to testify at trial when the testimony to be elicited seeks to clarify the trial issues in dispute regarding innocence or guilt.

SCOPA shamelessly based its opinion not only on defense counsel's wrongful, wishful, speculative proffer but took it a step further by embellishing upon it, giving the rank speculation a façade of evidentiary certitude. Yet, the true and accurate trial record refutes the entire underlying basis of the opinion's faux so-called speculative beliefs.

Not one individual union person ever committed any overt act to engage in the murder of Yablonski without direction and approval from Boyle. Not one fact can be found to suggest that anyone other than Boyle was the sole mastermind of all the plans to murder Yablonski and that no evidence exists that anyone else acted to kill Yablonski outside the confines of the Boyle conspiracy.

SCOPA was legally required to adhere to the evidence adduced in the trial record. For a fair and reasonable court to reverse the Boyle 1974 conviction, it would have had to be forced to swim upstream against a tide of evidence too strong to resist.

Lest one forgets or disregards the evidence, "Tough Tony" Boyle was not convicted for stealing a loaf of bread to save his sister's son. The overwhelming evidence condemns him as a psychopathic assassin bent on the destruction of innocent human life all for his own benefit. His acts were evil incarnate.

SCOPA's opinion incomprehensibly granted a lifeline to Boyle. It violated honored jurisprudence and accepted criminal procedure. Could it not be more morally repugnant and legally incongruous to have Boyle's case reversed on profoundly unsound, whimsical, and vacuous analyses while so many lives were savaged with their families still suffering unbearable sorrow? Undaunted and committed to justice, Sprague retried "Tough Tony" Boyle in February 1978. At no time during that trial did the defense ever mention Thomas Kane or his audit report!

CHAPTER FORTY-TWO

THE FINAL ACT

In August 1974, Judge Sweet found Silous Huddleston, sixty-five, and his daughter, Annette Gilly, thirty-four, guilty of second-degree murder for their roles in the Yablonski murders. The judge sentenced them to four-and-a-half years for murder and two more years for obstruction then waived the sentence for time served. After adding ten years of probation for the murders of Margaret and Charlotte, the pair were given new identities, released from custody, and sent outside of Pennsylvania.

The three Hillbilly Hitmen, as well as James Charles Phillips and William Prater, were all in prison. Martin remained unrepentant.

The court sentenced William Turnblazer to fifteen years in prison primarily for his testimony at the Prater trial, which Sprague believed was pivotal.

The R&I Committee members, the pensioners, had been placed on probation for perjury; their sentences were suspended.

Sprague remarked the second Boyle trial was consistent with something New York Yankee legendary catcher and famed philosopher Yogi Berra once said, "It's déjà vu all over again." Sprague began preparing for the second Boyle trial calendared for late January 1978.

However, almost like it was a requirement in the Yablonski trials, Sprague called a witness he never expected to see testifying for the prosecution. Albert Pass, who was serving three life sentences, contacted Sprague. He wanted to tell the truth.

After Sprague let it be known that he still wasn't making deals, the old union head-buster said he wanted only one concession: a single life sentence instead of three. It was a long shot given his health and age, but he hoped to be able to see his family—especially his bed-ridden daughter—one last time outside of prison walls. The prosecutor agreed.

So, on the fourth day of the second Boyle trial, Albert Pass climbed up onto the witness stand, exchanging malevolent glares with his former friend and leader. His testimony began with him pointing out that all of the District 19 officers, including himself, as well as the field reps, were appointed by Boyle. They owed their jobs to him and had been loyal to him.

Pass said he had known Jock Yablonski since 1942. In spite of everything that happened, he said, he had no personal animosity towards him during all those years "up to and including the murders."

"Why did you participate in the arrangement that led to the murder of Jock Yablonski?" Sprague asked.

"I was ordered to do it by Tony Boyle."

"Why did you comply?"

Pass paused to look at Boyle before answering. "Because of my fierce loyalty to him and my belief in the union. And the fact that Boyle advised me that Jock and the oil companies were going to destroy the union."

Corroborating Turnblazer's account, he said he was with the District 19 president and Boyle when the latter first gave the order to do away with Yablonski on June 23, 1969. "We were in the hallway just outside the boardroom of the UMWA building in D.C."

If there was any doubt as to Boyle's intentions towards his rival, he made it clear, Pass said, when they met in Boyle's office on July 15, 1969. "Boyle said: 'That goddamned Yablonski. That damned dumb Polack son of a bitch. He isn't satisfied with what I have tried to do for him. The oil companies are trying to take control of the union and if Yablonski is elected president of the union, it will be destroyed.'"

Boyle went on to say that the oil companies would use Yablonski to show that money was illegally sent from Labor's Non-Partisan League to the '68 presidential campaign of Hubert Humphrey, as well as other congressmen and senators who were considered friends of the union. This was what led in part to Boyle's conviction on federal charges in 1972.

"He said that Yablonski is the cause of the trouble and we would all go to jail. 'He is going to have to be taken care of.' I then said, 'Do you mean for Yablonski to be killed?' And Boyle said, 'That's just what I mean.'"

On the witness stand, the old union enforcer testified matter-of-factly and with no more emotion than he might have had talking about the weather when describing the plot to murder Yablonski and the scheme to get money to pay the killers. As Sprague carefully had him corroborate testimony of other witnesses, he made no excuses. He'd just done what he believed necessary to protect the union and deal with a threat. His brutal honesty made his testimony all the more believable.

When at last Sprague reached the end of his questioning, he asked Pass why only now he'd decided to testify against his former friend and idol. Waiting for his answer, it seemed like everyone in the courtroom, especially those who knew Pass's brutal background, held their breath and leaned forward to hear, including Boyle.

"After seven years of silence," Pass began, "I decided to tell the truth and confess to relieve my conscience of the guilt I felt caused by the sin I committed.

"I also fully realized that Boyle has tried to make it appear that I was the originator of these murders. I just want to get the record straight."

In a nutshell, Sprague thought the jury would understand what had motivated Pass to break the code of silence that protected his former friend. Boyle's fatal flaw was that he had not shown the same sort of fierce loyalty to his followers as he'd been shown. In fact, he, the originator of the plan to murder Yablonski, tried to incriminate the one man who'd stuck with him through it all to save himself, and in the culture of coal country, that was unforgiveable.

However, Pass had one more reason. For the first time, the tough-as-nails secretary-treasurer of District 19, choked up and wiped at the tears that formed in his eyes. "And I hope to have just one life sentence to see my family again."

Closing arguments followed. Then after six hours of deliberation, a jury once again found W.A. "Tough Tony" Boyle guilty for the first-degree murders of Jock, Margaret, and Charlotte Yablonski. This time when Sprague walked out of the courthouse, it truly was over.

POSTSCRIPT

In my judgment, Richard A. Sprague will be welcomed into the Pantheon of the Just. No matter the burdens, frustrations, or length of time, he relentlessly sought justice righteously. He thrived in the courtroom where rules of evidence and court-imposed discipline provided the perfect arena in which to pursue the search for truth. No one more than Sprague was able to rationally, reasonably, and persuasively present his case seeking justice.

In the spring of 2021, Dick Sprague died at age ninety-five. During his long illness, he remained extremely sharp. He expected us to speak to one another at least once a week. We tried to accomplish just that.

We chatted about many varied matters. Certainly, he regaled me with his ideas and thoughts regarding this book. Also, he spoke about how we developed our personal value system, defining who we truly are.

Often, we discussed the values of historical figures and how their actions reflected who they truly were. Dick knew of my respect for Winston Churchill who believed that "courage" was the most important defining characteristic because, he argued, without it none of the others would be possible. Dick agreed, but also hoped he'd be remembered for his honor, integrity, and loyalty. I assured him that would be the case.

Dick's knowledge was broad. He ended this conversation by referring to one of Churchill's favorite value-oriented statements from Macaulay's *Lays of Ancient Rome*. In its entirety, it reads as follows:

"Then out spake brave Horatius,
The captain of the gate:
'To every man upon this earth
Death cometh soon or late.
And how can man die better
Than facing fearful odds,
For the ashes of his fathers,
And the temples of his gods....'"

I can assure you that Dick and I shared those sentiments. A week later, Dick died. I will always miss him.

ACKNOWLEDGMENTS

FROM STEVE JACKSON

First, I would like to thank my co-author Robert K. Tanenbaum, without whose peerless research, guidance, hard work, and dedication to the truth, this book could not have been written. Through many years of collaboration on this and other projects, his friendship and mentoring has meant so much more than even our outstanding working relationship. I hope there are many other projects in the years ahead.

I would also like to thank my family and friends for their love and support through the years, especially these last few as I faced serious health challenges. In particular, I want to thank my children—Mackenzie, Hannah, and Lillia—my ex-wife and still best friend Carla Torrisi Jackson, and brothers from other mothers— Doug, Roger, and Dana as well as Jim and Kathy Duke, who have always been there for me. And my gratitude to my agent and friend Chip MacGregor of MacGregor Literary. He's the best in the business, and proved it once again.

FROM ROBERT K. TANENBAUM

To my colleague, co-author, and special friend, Steve Jackson. Beyond doubt, Steve is an extraordinarily gifted and talented scrivener whose genius flows throughout the manuscript and whose contribution to it cannot be overstated. Thanks also to my literary agent on this project, Chip MacGregor.

To my legendary mentors, District Attorney Frank S. Hogan and Henry Robbins, both of whom were larger in life than in their well-deserved and hard-earned legends—everlasting gratitude and respect. To my special friends and brilliant tutors at the Manhattan DAO, Bob Lehner, Mel Glass, and John Keenan, three of the best who ever served and whose passion for justice was unequaled and uncompromising—my heartfelt appreciation, respect, and gratitude.

FROM THE CO-AUTHORS

In the research and writing of this book, the authors used many sources to both ensure the accuracy of the various accounts, as well as provide contemporaneous descriptions of events and people. These sources included the complete transcripts of the numerous trials and hearings, provided by Dick Sprague to Robert Tanenbaum, as well as hundreds of newspaper, magazine, and television reports. The authors have endeavored to footnote and credit the use of these accounts where appropriate.

The authors also would like to acknowledge the exemplary journalism by the authors of two previous books written during or soon after these events: *Act of Vengeance* by Trevor Armbrister, Saturday Review Press, January 1975; and *Murder by Contract* by Arthur H. Lewis, Macmillan, January 1975.

—Fall 2022